Finding
Hildasay

25/05
£1

WITHDRAWN

C017213893

Finding Hildasay

How one man walked the UK's coastline
and found hope and happiness

CHRISTIAN LEWIS

MACMILLAN

First published 2023 by Macmillan
an imprint of Pan Macmillan
The Smithson, 6 Briset Street, London EC1M 5NR
EU representative: Macmillan Publishers Ireland Ltd, 1st Floor,
The Liffey Trust Centre, 117–126 Sheriff Street Upper,
Dublin 1, D01 YC43
Associated companies throughout the world
www.panmacmillan.com

ISBN 978-1-0350-0679-3

1 3 5 7 9 8 6 4 2

A CIP catalogue record for this book is available from the British Library.

Map artwork on pp. *viii–ix* by ML Design Ltd
Typeset in Fairfield LT Std by Palimpsest Book Production Ltd, Falkirk, Stirlingshire
Printed and bound by CPI Group (UK) Ltd, Croydon, CR0 4YY

Visit **www.panmacmillan.com** to read more about all our books
and to buy them. You will also find features, author interviews and
news of any author events, and you can sign up for e-newsletters
so that you're always first to hear about our new releases.

To my two beautiful children, Caitlin and Magnus,
my greatest achievements.

Contents

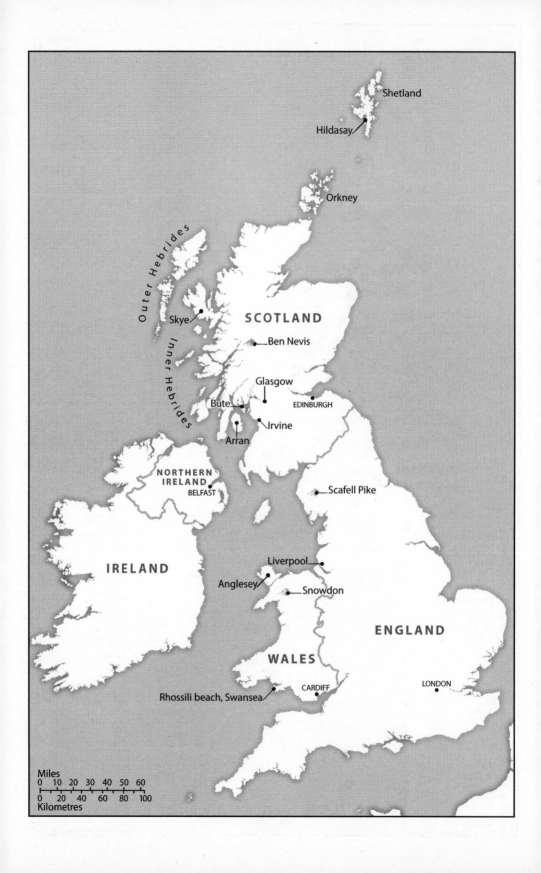

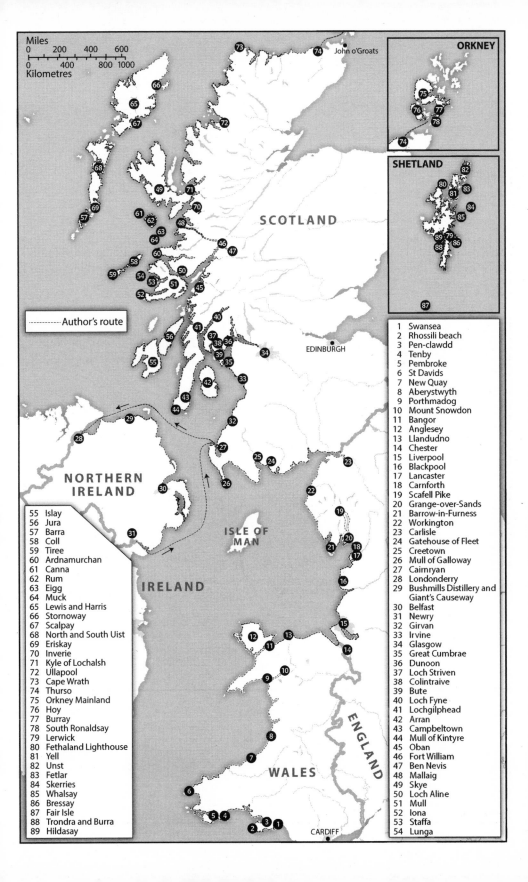

Miles
0   200   400   600
0   400   800 1000
Kilometres

ORKNEY

SHETLAND

SCOTLAND

John o'Groats

EDINBURGH

---------- Author's route

NORTHERN
IRELAND

ISLE OF
MAN

IRELAND

ENGLAND

WALES

CARDIFF

1	Swansea
2	Rhossili beach
3	Pen-clawdd
4	Tenby
5	Pembroke
6	St Davids
7	New Quay
8	Aberystwyth
9	Porthmadog
10	Mount Snowdon
11	Bangor
12	Anglesey
13	Llandudno
14	Chester
15	Liverpool
16	Blackpool
17	Lancaster
18	Carnforth
19	Scafell Pike
20	Grange-over-Sands
21	Barrow-in-Furness
22	Workington
23	Carlisle
24	Gatehouse of Fleet
25	Creetown
26	Mull of Galloway
27	Cairnryan
28	Londonderry
29	Bushmills Distillery and Giant's Causeway
30	Belfast
31	Newry
32	Girvan
33	Irvine
34	Glasgow
35	Great Cumbrae
36	Dunoon
37	Loch Striven
38	Colintraive
39	Bute
40	Loch Fyne
41	Lochgilphead
42	Arran
43	Campbeltown
44	Mull of Kintyre
45	Oban
46	Fort William
47	Ben Nevis
48	Mallaig
49	Skye
50	Loch Aline
51	Mull
52	Iona
53	Staffa
54	Lunga

55	Islay
56	Jura
57	Barra
58	Coll
59	Tiree
60	Ardnamurchan
61	Canna
62	Rum
63	Eigg
64	Muck
65	Lewis and Harris
66	Stornoway
67	Scalpay
68	North and South Uist
69	Eriskay
70	Inverie
71	Kyle of Lochalsh
72	Ullapool
73	Cape Wrath
74	Thurso
75	Orkney Mainland
76	Hoy
77	Burray
78	South Ronaldsay
79	Lerwick
80	Fethaland Lighthouse
81	Yell
82	Unst
83	Fetlar
84	Skerries
85	Whalsay
86	Bressay
87	Fair Isle
88	Trondra and Burra
89	Hildasay

Foreword

The first time I heard about Chris was a newspaper story during lockdown about a former soldier and his dog, 'cast away' on an island in Shetland. I was transfixed.

Having spent a year marooned on a Scottish island myself (with my dog Inca) for the BBC series *Castaway* back in 2000, I remember it clearly because part of me was incredibly jealous.

A man and a dog on a Scottish island was meant to be me, but instead I was in lockdown with my own family (and dog, Storm) in landlocked Oxfordshire.

A year later, I found myself on a small boat in the Shetland isles. 'That's where Chris and Jet lived throughout the pandemic,' explained the skipper with pride.

I looked him up online and started following his journey on social media, and like thousands of others I was soon obsessed. The simplicity of his nomadic life walking the entire coastline of the UK.

It wasn't long after that when I found myself at a pub with Chris, Jet and Kate.

I have been fortunate to meet some inspiring people over the years. Every so often a bright, blazing star of humanity appears, and for me it was Chris.

I don't need to tell you why or how – this book will do that – but Chris and his story really moved me. I found myself wanting to be his friend.

Honest and humble, kind and generous, Chris really is my hero.

A man who began a life-changing journey with a tenner and a tent.

A man trying to overcome his demons and change his life for the better.

Full of charm and compassion, I hope this book will change you, as Chris has changed me. He has helped me look at the world from another perspective. He has given me hope and humility.

Perhaps our friendship was over our mutual love of dogs; maybe it was our shared love of Scottish islands, or walking, or the coastline, or the fact we have both supported SSAFA; or maybe it's because we have both embarked on journeys in search of something.

Bursting with positivity and hope, Chris, Kate, Jet and little Magnus remind us that in a world of uncertainty, love conquers all.

Ben Fogle

1

Into the storm

Saying goodbye to my daughter Caitlin at Swansea train station was the most soul-destroying experience of my entire life. Never have I felt such a failure. The walk back to my flat was a complete blur. I cried all of the six miles home only to walk into an empty shell of a flat knowing she had gone. I looked at her bed, the covers still pulled back just as she had left them a few hours before. Part of her presence was still here. My whole body went numb. Broken, I collapsed to the floor sobbing like an inconsolable baby, wishing that I'd never existed.

To make matters worse, it was only a few weeks before I'd be evicted. My anxiety and depression had taken hold of me with such force by this point that even the simple task of going down to the Civic Centre to try and sort out my deteriorating financial situation seemed impossible. I could barely step out the front door; ironic, really, given how much I hated the place. As I looked around the flat I realized what a dark and confined space it had become. It was like a prison, and every day spent within its drab walls seemed like part of a long sentence. On a basic, primal level I knew I had to get out of there before its black energy sucked me further into dark despair. After a good old sob, guided by an inner wisdom, I finally found the energy to pick myself up and get changed into my wetsuit. I was so desperate to feel *some kind of normal* and escape from my own mind and I knew the only place I had even a remote chance of doing this was the surf.

After ten years of raising Caitlin on my own, the depths of my depression had become apparent to both of us, and was, I believe, one of the reasons Caitlin left in the first place. It took an enormous amount of willpower to get out of the house; I grabbed my surfboard, a few Welsh cakes and two litres of water and left the flat, but not before punching a hole in the wall out of pure anger at myself. Then I headed out to start the walk to Llangennith beach on the Gower Peninsula.

I'll never be entirely sure what was going on in my mind on that ten-mile stretch. All I can remember is the feeling of having let down someone that I loved so much. It was unbearable. The outdoors have and always will be my happy place. I remember as a boy when my parents were going through a divorce, I'd run to the woods and sit in a tree for hours. Being outside was embedded in me, and that has held true my entire life.

However, this time my walk to the beach had a different purpose. The only therapy that might help that hollow day was the ocean, and I found myself walking incredibly slowly and short of breath, my body racked with anxiety, constantly on the cusp of a panic attack. I was often stopping, sitting down somewhere out of sight of any other walkers and bursting into tears. Up until this day, I can honestly say I hadn't cried for all of my adult years. It was like someone had turned on the tap after decades of it being switched off. I felt completely numb; consumed by the recurring thought that I had failed at what to me was the single most important thing I couldn't afford *not* to succeed at: being a good father to my daughter. My mind adrift, my heart broken, after this I had absolutely no idea where I was heading; I was lost. The word 'failure' stuck in my throat like a leech, and the constant question rattling around my brain was: 'What the hell do I do now?' I had no money, and eviction and homelessness were on the cards. At thirty-seven years old, I was a prime example of somebody suffering severe depression.

It was about three hours before I reached Llangennith beach. Together with Rhossili, they make up one long beach stretching about three miles long – a beautiful place and an incredibly popular surf spot in the right conditions. This beach had become a home from home, as I spent every waking minute here that I could, whether it be surfing for my own pleasure or taking people out coasteering. I'd spent so much time here over the years that I knew it extremely well – enough to know that a strong onshore wind made it inevitable that the swell was going to be big, the surf choppy and all over the place.

As I arrived, I looked down from the hundred-foot cliffs of Rhossili at the ocean and thought to myself, *Shit, look at the size of that surf!* It was much bigger than anything

I had ever ridden before. I can definitely surf, but I'm no professional, and looking back, my state of mind had clearly overpowered my normal sense of fear. Any other time, I would have walked away immediately. Today, however, I just didn't seem to care.

The paddle out through the rough white water to reach where the clean build can be surfed behind was just too much for a mortal to handle. Llangennith and Rhossili are renowned throughout Europe for having one of the biggest paddle-outs going. My only option, I decided – and it was lunacy to do so – was to climb down the cliffs to reach a ledge from which I could jump into the water; rather than paddle out to face this monster head on, I would sneak up behind it.

I stood for a while on the ledge, staring aimlessly out at sea, the spray hitting off the rocks pluming thirty feet into the air. Despite the danger of the situation I was about to put myself in, I felt an immense sense of calm – or was it abandon? I attached the leash cord from the surfboard onto my ankle and realized that once I'd taken the five-foot plunge into the water, there was no returning to the ledge. The next time I would feel land would be 400 yards away on the beach. This brought me to my senses. I had a choice whether or not to cast myself into the maelstrom. I wasn't suicidal. That's just not me; I am too much of a coward and I simply hate the thought of dying, especially drowning. There is a huge difference between not wanting to exist any more and the thought of committing suicide. I loved Caitlin and I would never want to leave her with that burden, and was still emotionally aware enough to know that if I did something like this, I would destroy her even more. Killing myself wasn't on the cards.

I looked up at the dark, brooding sky and shouted 'FUUUCK!', then jumped into the turbulent water. Suddenly finding myself at the mercy of nature in this way, I realized how vulnerable and insignificant a human being can be. Paddling as fast as I could to get away from the ledge and the rocks, I headed towards the break. Then, behind me, thundering out of nowhere, came a killer wave. I turned myself and my board to face the oncoming slaughter, to give myself half a chance to dive underneath it. As it hurtled towards me, however, I realized I would never be able to duck-dive this – it was a muscular wall of white water, a speeding avalanche that could leave nothing but broken bones in its wake.

I grabbed my board as hard as I possibly could, squeezing it so tightly that I was almost welded to it. It was my flotation, without which I might not come back up to the surface again.

It's incredible how many different thoughts the human brain can have in such a short space of time in a panic-stricken situation, but immediately I knew I had to regain control of them and focus on the only thing that was important: getting my feet back onto the sandy shores of Rhossili beach.

The white water hit me so hard my board was immediately ripped from my body. My arms and legs were being dragged every which way and felt as if they were being pulled from their sockets. One second it was light, the next minute it was dark; I had no idea if I was upside down or facing upright. After what felt like an eternity, but was in reality only about fifteen seconds, I returned to the surface, gasping desperately for breath. Somehow, my leash was still attached to my leg, and I pulled my board towards me and managed to scramble back on, giving myself a second to compose myself.

I was still shaking like a leaf with adrenalin and fear when, soon enough, I saw another angry set of waves coming in. I'm not a religious man, but as I saw the first wave heading my way, I figured that it was *just* about rideable, and I was sure the gods were on my side. *I must catch this!* I thought to myself. You can't fight the sea for long; she always has more power than you in the end. Had I not committed every fibre in my body to riding this giant, I'm sure I would have taken my last breath there.

Once again, I turned and paddled towards the distant beach as hard and as fast as my arms would take me. The wave started to pick me up and then, incredibly, there I was, standing up on my board looking down the face of the biggest wave I would catch in my lifetime. It was nothing like I'd ever seen before. I dropped into the wave and hung a left, somehow managing to catch it perfectly. It was fast and ferocious and how I stayed on it, I will never know. Every muscle in my body was working perfectly in sync; never had my concentration been so intense. It would be the longest and most beautiful ride of my life.

Breathless and feeling like I'd just done five rounds with Mike Tyson, my trusty stick and I were gracelessly dumped on the beach, where I collapsed, kissing the sandy solidity of terra firma like it was a long-lost family member. It was surreal – the contrast of sudden safety after feeling so frightened a few seconds earlier. The two extremes of emotion were too much to process. I was both disappointed and angry at myself for doing something so stupid and selfish, and pumping with adrenalin.

I left the board on the beach and climbed back up the cliffs to Rhossili, to the exact same spot I'd been standing on before jumping into the water. But this time, I felt different. Out at sea, I'd felt like nature was fighting me, but now I had fought back and won. It was the first battle in a long time where I had triumphed. I felt an incredible sense of calm, and as I stared down miles of beach, for the first time in much too long, I felt happy and grateful to be alive.

2

A sea change

In the moments that followed my safe delivery to the beach from the monster wave, something in me changed – I had an epiphany. I realized that if I didn't make a massive life change now, things would not turn out well. No – they would be bloody awful. The way things had been going had resulted in my daughter leaving. Depression had wound around me so tight that I'd lost all sense of self-respect, and through a combination of self-loathing and poor fathering, which had seen us on the brink of homelessness, I had now driven the most important person in my life away: my sixteen-year-old daughter, Caitlin. I had to accept where I was, who I was, and have faith in myself to change things. Not so much a mental makeover – more like knocking down the ruins that my life had become and starting all over again.

Each one of us has the potential to be happy, and I

knew that if I stayed here where I was, doing what I'd been doing, I was on the spiral in the opposite direction: to nowhere and worse. As I looked at the grassy sand dunes and driftwood-strewn beach disappearing into the horizon as if it went on for ever, I heard a voice in my head.

'Walk the UK coastline,' it said.

'What?'

'*Walk the UK coastline.*'

The voice came from deep within me, and it wasn't my ego. Rather, it came directly from the soul; the one place within us that knows exactly what we need and when we need it. I felt an immediate sense of excitement – a feeling that had been missing from my life for far too long. I needed to escape my life and get moving; things could only get better.

Not for one second did the enormity of the task cross my mind. Neither did the question, 'How the hell am I going to do this with absolutely no funds, no kit or even the vaguest notion of a plan?' In my mind, I knew somehow I'd make it work. It was 29 July 2017, and my life was about to change for ever.

I'd been camping on the odd occasion in the past but, more often than not, just sleeping out on the beach after a surf without a tent. I was by no means a guru in the art of camping or clued up on the sort of things I would require. It was something I would have to learn along the way. First up, though, I knew I would need a tent, a sleeping bag, some boots, a knife and something to cook on.

On my way back to the flat, I stopped in at the local shop and used £10 of the last £40 left in my bank account to put some credit on my phone. Still topping up a basic phone with credit in 2017 was pretty behind the times, but that was the reality for me as a single parent; I was always skint.

I immediately got to work phoning friends, asking if they could help me with any of the kit that I needed, as I had absolutely nothing. I was loath to ask the Soldiers, Sailors, Airmen and Families Association (SSAFA), the Armed Forces charity that had already supported me through hard times as a single parent. In fact, as soon as I thought of SSAFA, I decided that, rather than them helping me, I wanted to be the one to help them this time, and I would raise money for them on this walk.

In only a couple of days, I'd managed to acquire a tent from an ex 1 Para fella called Dom, who was a good friend of my brother, Mark (who in turn lent me a pair of boots); a sleeping bag from my good friend Alan Pugh; a camping stove from another close mate, Luke McCord; and a knife donated by my friend Chris Carree. As much as I was stupidly grateful for all of these items, it soon became apparent that the boots were too big, the Crocodile Dundee-style knife oversized and not great to be caught with, and the tent had a hole in the top (not terribly suited to a typical wet Welsh summer). But, on the bright side, the gas stove worked perfectly. I was so excited to get on with the walk, I just needed to leave; the further away I got from the flat, the calmer I felt inside.

Before I started, I told only a handful of people, all of whom knew I'd been going through a hard time lately. I'd always been a dreamer, often coming up with big ideas which had nearly always been met with the response of,

'Dream on' or 'Come back to the real world', and so it came as no surprise that the vast majority of those I told looked at me as if I'd now totally lost the plot. And why not? If they'd told me they were going to walk the UK coastline with no money and very shabby kit, I probably would have laughed too. But I'm stubborn, and I've always lived my life with a 'Go big or go home' mentality.

The penultimate night before I left Swansea, I slept down on the beach. Although I knew I couldn't put it off for ever – I had possessions in there and would have to face up to it soon enough – I just didn't want to go back to my flat. On 31 July, I returned to Number 15 Coed Lan for the last time. Despite my excitement and finally having this new focus and the freedom to be able to go, the second I walked into the flat, I burst into tears just thinking about Caitlin. After a decade of me parenting her as a single father, she'd decided life with me was too diffi-cult and, at just sixteen years old, she'd left. I felt like the biggest failure.

I never drank. Other than a few at New Year, I could probably call myself teetotal; it just didn't interest me at all. I had a bottle of whisky in the flat that had been stashed away in the cupboard for years, and I remember thinking to myself, *Fuck it. I have a real job on my hands here going through all of my stuff and I don't want to spend the entire evening crying like a baby, wallowing in self-pity.* So I opened the Jack Daniels, took a humongous swig, and got to work, grabbing anything that I thought might be able to help me on the walk, including the most manky, horrendously hole-ridden socks you'll ever see. All of my clothes, anything I owned, I'd leave behind in the flat for the landlord to throw out. All I could think to do was walk. Little did I know that this journey would be my way to process a lifetime's worth of pain and running away.

It was apparent, not being a drinker, that I was feeling the effects of the alcohol pretty quickly, and was getting more and more pissed as the evening went on.

Someone I knew in the area saw me outside the flat, and it was obvious that I'd been crying and was drunk. He told me to wait there and that he had something for me that would definitely cheer me up. To be honest, I would have eaten a cactus if it had made me feel better. Soon enough, he came back with a huge mug of coffee and told me to drink it.

It definitely tasted a tad strange, that's for sure, but I didn't care; I necked half of it in blissful ignorance. I had nothing to lose. Around ten minutes later, I felt like I wanted to clean up the entire fucking world! It turned out that I'd just swigged half a cup of coffee heavily laced with amphetamine – i.e. speed! The only way I can describe it is feeling like the old lady hoovering frantically in *Something About Mary* after the speed pill flies through the window and lands in her Martini glass while she's asleep. I was so focused and yet so drunk at the same time, it was incredible. My work ethic had picked up tenfold!

The flat in Swansea had two small bedrooms, and the carpets were mostly gone as there had been a leak, so it was more like a cell than a home. It was in a building with a series of apartments, and had a communal back garden which was lovely; flowerbeds all around the sides and a table and chairs in the middle where the neighbours would often gather together and sit and have lunch or the occasional party. We also had a metal bin that we would use for a fire out there. In my current amphetamine-fuelled state, washed down with caffeine and a load of JD, it suddenly occurred to me that if I was going to leave for this walk then I may as well erase all traces of myself. So, I built a fire and started burning all of my paperwork, including my passport, driving licence, birth certificate and any other document one needs to prove their rightful existence. As far as I was concerned, I just wanted to go off-grid.

Looking back, it's quite obvious that I was trying to give myself a fresh start. My life had always been about fitness and being outside, so I had never been into drink or drugs. Necking that well-meaning but diabolical cocktail clearly wasn't the smartest move, however, as I had no idea that the after-effects meant I wouldn't be sleeping at all that night. Around 3 a.m., it finally became clear to me that sleep was not on the cards. I sat down and stared deeply into the fire. I made a pact with myself that I would return to Swansea a complete and happy man again, and that I would prove to Caitlin that you can do anything you put your mind to.

Excited and proud of this prospect, I stood up too fast, fell forward and, light-headed and dizzy, knocked the metal fire pit towards the floor. Unthinking, I grabbed it with my left arm, forgetting it was boiling hot. I picked it back up and a few seconds later felt the most excruciating, searing pain in my left wrist. I had melted the skin on my arm. I ran inside and held the burn under a cold tap, after which I used the remainder of the whisky and poured it around the wound. I pulled out a washed sock from the washing machine and cut off its end to turn it into a bandage. Then I wrapped masking tape around it and was good to go. Nothing was stopping me from leaving!

Just three days after I first decided to walk the entire coastline of the United Kingdom, I was ready to go.

My mother and stepdad, Sam and Dave, had arranged to meet me at my flat at 9.30 in the morning. It was 6 a.m. and already the sun was up. I kept going through my bag, checking everything, and to my relief I started to feel the effects of the booze and drugs wearing off. I felt like total shit, as if I were heading into a really nasty comedown. It was something I promised I would never in my life do again. Half past nine came and, like clockwork, Mum and Dave turned up, beeping the horn to let me know they were here to take me down to the start of the walk on Rhossili beach in the Gower. I don't think they took me seriously at this point. In the past I'd wanted to be an actor, a musician and an adventurer – none of which had come to fruition.

I ran to the bathroom and looked in the mirror, only to discover that the previous night's antics had left me looking like Smeagol from *Lord of the Rings*. Cursing myself, I flung on my shades to hide my face before leaving the flat with my incredibly overpacked bag. On the journey down, they chatted away to me, excited at the thought of my adventure to come, while I sat in the back of the car sweating and muttering 'Oh my God' to myself, over and over again. I felt horrendous. Thank God for the shades; they were the perfect disguise.

My thoughts turned to other adventurers' expeditions, the likes of Sir Ranulph Fiennes, and how meticulously planned they must have been: the precision of their packing, the great equipment, the funding . . . and here's me – sprawled in the back of my mum's car feeling more like I should be going to hospital than embarking on a walk around the UK. It was just me and a bag full of things I'd packed while incredibly high. A recipe for disaster if ever there was one.

We arrived at Hill End car park, the spot where I surfed all the time, and there had a small send-off with my mum, stepdad, my friend Chris and his parents. I focused on not stumbling over my words and did my best to act normal. I said my goodbyes and picked up my bag. I overheard Chris turn to my mum and say, 'Sam, I really think this is going to be the making of him.' I silently agreed and those words of his I'll never forget. I knew deep down that all my mum and family wanted was to see me happy again. It wasn't the first time I'd run away from everything, and they knew this adventure was something I needed to do.

Chris said he wanted to walk me down to the end of the beach, so we set off up the wooden planked pathway, sand dunes either side, following it down onto the main beach. I remember him getting his camera out, filming me and asking how I felt. I just felt sick and hot and needed food in my system. I didn't even know whether I was going to go left or right when I got to the beach. Left would mean heading towards Bristol and down to the south of England. Right would take me to the west of England and then north up to Scotland. It was so absurdly unplanned it was almost funny. *But how on earth can I plan for something when I have no idea what needs planning?* I thought to myself. The only plan I had was to keep moving forward.

As we arrived on the beach, the question of 'Left or right?' desperately needed an answer. About half a mile to my right, I noticed some surfers at a place we call Peaks (because of the shape of the waves). I headed in that direction with my best impression of conviction. North it was, then! As we reached the bottom of the beach, Chris said goodbye, wished me luck and walked back up to Hill End car park. As soon as he was out of sight, I walked around the corner over some rocks, dropped my bag onto the floor, and threw up. I was so thirsty I drank nearly all my water, forced some food down me, and immediately fell asleep for an hour.

When I woke, my brain was fuzzy and confused. I decided to eat a bit more, drank the last of my water and watched the surfers for a while. Having just eaten most of my two days' worth of rations, I looked at the map to find the next shop on my route to stop for supplies with my £10 fortune. Unbeknown to me, edging around the coast trying to locate the next shop would become the system I would use throughout my journey. Often, my only aim each day was to get from one shop to the next in one piece.

Still feeling awful, but having now fully sobered up, I picked up my gear and looked back down Llangennith beach over to Rhossili and The Worm's Head – a huge slab of rock that gets cut off on a high tide and is very famous in these parts. It was given the name by the Vikings when they landed on this beach, noticing when doing so that the rock formation looked like a dragon. Worm's Head means 'dragon' in Norse and that name has stuck to this day. I nodded my head, a solemn goodbye to a place that

I felt had been my home, my surf spot and my safe place for many years. I wondered about some of the things I might have experienced by the next time I saw it.

This was the official start; the point where I took the first steps on my journey around the UK coastline. Little did I know, these would mark the beginning of the most incredible five-and-a-half-year adventure.

3

Getting my teeth
into Wales

My first few days walking would take me through places I was already familiar with: the Gower, Llanelli and Burry Port. I knew once I'd passed Burry Port, about fifteen miles from where I'd first started, that my journey was really beginning. Already I could feel that every footstep that took me further from Swansea was distancing me from the centre of a mental health storm. From here on, it would be the start of ground that I'd never walked before, and I'd be out of the comfort zone of anyone near that would be able to help.

I felt nervous, knowing that the safety blanket of friends and family was going to be behind me, especially as I had no money or clue where my next meal was coming from, or where I would be sleeping. Leaving with only a tenner would bring a whole different dimension to this challenge. The walk itself would be tough enough, carrying my house on my back, but the energy I was already burning, especially given that I'd always been such a big eater, was a daunting thought – making the journey without funds ten times more difficult. Obviously, being out of work now, if I'd wanted I could have claimed benefits, but deep down I thought it would be unfair to do this when I'd chosen to embark on this journey of self-discovery. Hand in hand with my desire to go completely off-grid, it was an easy choice to make. It made the journey far purer and the adventure bigger and more challenging. I suppose crossing the line would feel like a greater achievement for me if I knew I'd done it in the most nomadic way.

Before leaving, I'd asked my sister, Molly, to make me up a Facebook page. I think she was glad to see me enthusiastic about something for a change and was happy to help. I was completely useless with technology and social media; the only time I'd ever use it would be to check the wind direction and the swell of the sea if it was a good day for surfing. My mother had got me an iPhone 5 on eBay so that I could take some photos and download them onto the page that Molly had made for me, titled, 'Chris Walks the UK'. It wasn't until Day Three before I would work out how to upload photos and videos.

My first night was in Pen-clawdd, a coastal village by the Gower Estuary. To be honest, my first evening was just one big blur as I was so exhausted from my antics the night before. I pitched up on the marsh overlooking the estuary and didn't even eat anything as I'd consumed all my rations earlier that day. But I do remember I just kept thinking about logistics and practical matters. I also started my journal, and the ritual of concluding each entry with 'Goodnight Caitlin'. And I just wanted to wake up the next day feeling fresh and determined. I promised myself I would never feel this bad again. Most of all, I thought about the great escape I was making from the mess my life had become.

After seven days of walking, I'd already made it to Tenby, west Wales, and I'd hardly eaten at all, apart from the odd instant pasta dish, heated up on my little gas stove. But, two days before arriving in Tenby, I'd rocked up at a place called Pendine. I pitched the tent in the bay near some folks who had vans equipped for camping – or should we say 'glamping'? We got talking and I was soon invited to come and join them for a burger and a beer. I would never have asked for food, but, being so hungry, I was elated by the prospect. They asked me what I was up to, so I told them. They thought it was epic that I was walking around the UK – it was something they said they all wished they could do.

After a few hours, I was full of food and had gained four followers on Facebook. I remember going back to my tent feeling really pleased by how interested they were and how impressed they had been by the scale of what I was attempting. It was a lightbulb moment.

Chris, I said to myself, *you're doing this for charity. The more effort you make to speak to people as you move forward, the more people will follow and donate.*

I made a pact with myself that from now on I would call in to as many places as I could, regardless of how tired I was, to talk about my walk. It was time to say goodbye to the recluse who would avoid people at all costs. Little did I know, this marked a real turning point and was the beginning of my road to recovery.

I got out my journal and wrote down ideas of places I could best meet people. Pubs were an obvious choice, given their ubiquity. I had one battery pack to charge my phone, so if I could make it to a pub and at the very least afford a cordial, then I could do my best to eke out the drink for hours, charge my phone and also make conversation with locals to promote the walk; in my eyes, it was a win-win situation.

After my phone had charged, I would retreat to my tent, aware that, since wild camping is against the law in Wales, England and Northern Ireland, I was doing so illegally. I hated this, as the last thing I wanted to do was upset people, and I was keen to avoid confrontation at all costs. At night, I'd keep all my stuff in my bag ready to go apart from my sleeping bag and my diary. This was in case I had to pack up and move on if asked to. The evenings consisted of no more than a brief journal entry and then sleep, which came easily, as I would be shattered from the day's walking. I would turn the phone off to save battery at night and also preserve the little data that I had.

Back in my old life, my nightly routine would be to put on the TV and watch some *Family Guy*, *American Dad* or anything that was easy to watch; something to force a smile and fall asleep to. I found it really hard at first being subjected to absolute silence and darkness in the tent. Obviously, I had a head torch, but I could only give myself ten minutes of light each night as I couldn't afford new batteries. Having no light while camping is a disaster.

After seven days' slog, I arrived in Tenby absolutely

exhausted, without a single penny to my name. I knew this was going to be a tough day. I'd had to give myself enough time to get out the other side of town before it got dark, so I could camp up in a place where I wouldn't potentially be found, which is nigh on impossible in built-up areas.

So early in the walk, I was still yet to find my feet, and was clueless but hopeful that I could make this endeavour work. I was learning by the day, but measuring my limits as a person was something I was still far from discovering. I always knew this would take time.

I'd been wearing a thick pair of beige trousers and a grey wetsuit top up until this point. Already filthy and with a huge bag on my back, it was obvious by the way I looked that I was up to something. I did get some funny looks from passers-by, but shrugged it off, assuming that they just thought I was homeless. Then it struck me: I *was* homeless. It also occurred to me that I should really be advertising what I was doing, so I popped into a cafe to ask for some water and to borrow a pen to write 'Walking the UK coastline for SSAFA' on the front of my neoprene top.

A young waitress who worked there offered to write it for me. When I told her what to put on it, she gasped and said, 'Are you kidding me?! I find it hard to even walk to the shop, never mind the UK coast!' She went to go and get the manager, who came out of the kitchen, shook my hand and gave me a menu. 'Order whatever you like,' she said. 'This is on us.'

It was the first time this had happened. I found it hard to say yes as I wasn't in this for handouts, but, desperate for food, I ordered the cheapest meal on the menu – beans on toast – so as not to take the piss. I sat down and ate it like a caveman, and as I did so I could feel my body regenerating. The staff at the cafe sent me on my way with a full belly of food as well as a packed lunch and a can of Coke. They also made a donation to the charity. If only for that day, I didn't have to worry about the basic necessities; it was a great feeling for that continual nag about food to be removed. I was ready to take on the day very differently now compared with how I had woken up that morning.

Up until this point, the weather had been hot and kind. Over the next few days, however, I would have my first taste of what would be a very wet Welsh summer. But for the occasional half-day off, the coming weeks brought nothing but rain.

I wouldn't have minded walking in the wet if I knew I'd at least be dry and warm come night time, but unfortunately there was a hole in the top of my tent that had become a complete disaster. No matter what I stuffed in the hole to block it, water trickled into my tent at a rate of knots, soaking me, my sleeping bag and everything else inside it. It was an unbearable nightly torture and meant my kit was constantly wet.

After days of this, my morale was low. I just wished I had something like a tarp to cover the tent, but, having no money, this was out of the question. At night, I would put my bag in the centre of the tent and sit on top of it, shivering uncontrollably, moving my arms around and tapping my feet to try to warm myself up. Being awake the entire night and waiting what seemed like an eternity for the morning light so I could get the hell out of the tent and start moving again was no easy feat, exacerbated by the fact that I had to conserve the batteries in my head torch. I remember asking myself whenever things got hard, *What would you rather be doing – sitting back in the flat, living a life you were so desperate to escape from, or doing this walk?* The freedom of the walk won every time.

Over the next few days, running on fumes from the lack of a good, warm meal, I would grow increasingly more tired and cold at night. Effectively, I was in a shit state, and just wished the rain would stop. My fortunes were about to change, however.

I came across a caravan park called Lydstep. The morning was wet but, by lunchtime, nature decided to give me a break and turn off the taps. Desperate to dry out my gear while I had the chance, I walked into the caravan park and approached a member of staff and asked if I could fill up my water bottles and hang my stuff up to dry on the railings for the afternoon. I remember the young lad looking at me as if to say, 'What the fuck have you been doing?' As he walked off to go and ask his manager, every fibre in my body was wishing that he would come back with a yes; I really needed this. About ten minutes later, the manager, a lady called Sue, walked towards me with a big smile on her face.

'Chris, we'd heard about you and have been messaging you on your Facebook page. Mate,' she said as she got closer to me, 'you look like shit.'

I chuckled and said, 'Trust me, I feel it!'

'My colleague said you wanted to dry out your kit.'

'I'd be so grateful if I could.'

'We can do one better. We'll take all of your gear, wash and dry it, and you can stay here free of charge in one of our caravans. We would also like to feed you up. You can eat and drink as much as you like.'

There was an awkward silence as I tried to get over my shock.

'You can say yes if you want!' she said, laughing.

'It would mean the world to me,' I replied.

In no time, my gear was gone, and I was standing in a beautiful caravan with a shower and everything. I set it as hot as it would go and sat down with my head in my hands. It felt like heaven! I'm not sure if it was from exhaustion or sheer relief, but I had a cry and remember thinking that what I had just endured was fucking awful – and that I *had* to get my tent sorted. After an hour's sleep, my kit was returned and I sat outside under a tree and wrote in my journal. It was the first time in a long time I had felt amazing.

That night I went into the complex where they had entertainment and food and ordered a huge pizza. To my surprise, the entertainer kindly put out over the Tannoy, 'We would like to welcome Chris who is with us tonight. He's walking the entire UK coastline.' The whole place stood up and clapped. I had a tear in my eye given the effort I had made to get here. A little bit of recognition was just the ticket.

One by one, people came up to say hello and would ask me questions. Some of them even handed me a tenner. 'Chris, mate, this is not for the charity,' they whispered in my ear, 'it's for you to eat and see you through the next few days.' I couldn't believe the kindness. I ended up with

£60 to live off as I moved on from Lydstep. I genuinely felt rich. At the end of the night, I got a photo with all the staff and headed to bed tipsy from the couple of drinks I'd had. I walked back to the caravan smiling the entire way.

As I started getting my teeth into Wales, heading in the direction of Pembroke, my understanding of what this walk required – both physically and mentally – was growing by the day. I focused on keeping my kit clean and dry, and popping into cafes to charge my phone. I was becoming a better camper and getting a grasp of the safer places to stay. After my unexpected windfall in Lydstep, I stocked up on some batteries for the head torch so I could have more light in the evening. This would mean I could camp up just after dark and set my alarm for an hour before sunlight so I could be gone before anybody knew I'd been there. It was a great system and it worked well. I also started to realize that, on occasion, if I was stealthy enough, I could find other accommodation – the odd bus stop, and once I even sneaked into an estate where I noticed a beautiful garden with a treehouse in it. It was amazing not to have to pitch the tent and I got a wonderful night's sleep. I was gone before anybody noticed.

I slowly moved north through Pembrokeshire, passing through sleepy places like Angle, Rhoscrowther and Dale. Once I arrived at each destination, I'd stock up on a bag of rice and more tuna to see me through the next few weeks. It would mean only one meal a day, but it was food. I'd been losing a considerable amount of weight, easily noticeable after a month into the walk. I felt weak pretty much most of the time, but as I moved further away, my confidence and belief in the fact that I might actually be able to do this grew. Because it was tourist season, I was really working my nuts off, making every effort to stop and talk with anyone I could. Truthfully, it was the last thing I wanted to do, feeling as weary as I did after a day's hard walking, but I was beginning to understand the impact this had on my Facebook page and the amount of donations I was receiving.

Wales is the only place in the UK where, apart from the power stations, there's a coast path running all the way along it. There were some stunning little villages that reminded me of Dylan Thomas's *Under Milk Wood*. In fact, the film version was filmed in Fishguard, which was another place I passed through. The water in Pembrokeshire is a lovely bottle green and there are some of the best beaches in the world, including that at Stackpole.

I loved sitting on the shore in the evenings watching old men returning from the sea in their little lobster boats, doing what they and their forefathers had done for centuries.

By now, I just about had Snowdonia National Park in my sights. It was a big landmark and a huge boost for me, giving me the sense that real progress was being made. Sadly, that night, I hardly slept at all. The sleeping bag I had was far too thin, and because of the constant walking, I'd lost practically all the body fat I had. At night, even in your sleep, if the body is cold then it burns a stupid amount of calories to try and keep warm. Even though I was lying still, I may as well have still been walking. I couldn't afford the amount of food that I'd need to sustain adequate body warmth, but at 5 a.m. the next morning, tired of being cold, I set off after a bowl of porridge.

I walked along the cliffs on the coast to my first view of New Quay. From up high, it looked like such a pretty little town with a lovely beach that today was absolutely heaving with tourists. I went down the steep steps that took me into New Quay and although I'd always wanted to visit here, I marched straight across the beach towards my next destination. Later, I felt really annoyed with myself that I'd just missed a wonderful PR opportunity with all those people.

That night, I pitched the tent on the edge of a farmer's field just outside some woodlands I'd passed through. I looked at my phone once I had settled, only to see a message from a pub in New Quay offering me a meal and a place to pitch the tent in their back garden. I was so gutted to have missed the chance of fresh food – the sight of more rice and tuna was becoming less and less appealing. I was going too fast to take in any of the beautiful Welsh coastline that had inspired me to set off in the first place. What was my hurry, anyway? During my walk through Wales, there was never an average daily mileage, as everywhere was different. I covered as much as I could, anywhere from eight to twenty miles per day. Hunger dictated where I stopped for the night.

How I'd get a better sleeping bag and more warm kit, as well as a new journal, I had no idea. Until that miracle happened, I'd just have to cope. I'd covered Pembroke, sleeping at night under its huge bridge, St Davids (the UK's smallest city), Fishguard and Cardigan, but it was always the small, quaint little fishing villages that caught my eye. Wales has a seriously beautiful coastline. It really was the perfect place to start and set the tone for the rest of my journey. I loved the stretches where I was miles from any towns or villages. Although they were more demanding, with all the hilly ups and downs, the scenery was stunning.

Often at night, when I was in a place where I knew I couldn't be seen, I'd get a fire on with driftwood I'd foraged and use it to cook my rice to save my stove gas. At the time, I thought I was good at making fires, and don't get me wrong, I wasn't bad at all. Looking back, after half a decade of making them all the time, I definitely had a lot to learn. Once the fire was strong, I would strip off stark-bollock naked and go for a paddle in the sea to wash.

Rather than absorbing the stunning countryside around me, I found that so many of my daily thoughts were governed by my anxiety to have somewhere to sleep that coming night. I needed my sleep to be able to do the walk, and even if it involved an extra two-hour yomp inland to woods, or sleeping on the island of a roundabout, I was happy to do either to guarantee six hours' shut-eye.

It was embedded in my head to stick to the coast as rigidly as I could. As I had said I was walking the UK coastline, to me, that meant sticking as close to the sea as possible. Often the coast path would go inland a few miles, and when that happened, I would come off the coast path to stick to the *actual* coastline, dragging my arse through thick gorse bushes, nettles and everything and anything that could cut, scratch or sting you. A saltwater bath kept infection away from cuts and scrapes and made me feel fresh before I went to bed.

At night, when I was still, I'd often find myself thinking about Caitlin. I really missed her and found it incredibly difficult being away from her, but this time on my own, without any interruptions, advice or opinions, would prove vital in helping me claw my way back to being a happy man again and the father I wanted to be, without my personal issues affecting mine and Caitlin's relationship.

I'd had a big few days and was now firmly into the Welsh coast path. The stretches I'd covered were peaceful and spectacular. It was now September. I'd been walking for around five and a half weeks, and holiday season was well and truly over. I immediately noticed the difference in terms of how few people were now on the coast path, and this worried me. The kindness I'd received from holiday-makers had been incredible. Some days, after chatting with people, I'd been given the odd chocolate or protein bar that they'd had going spare. It wasn't a lot, but it made a big difference.

Only a week before, I had sunk to a new low while in Newport town. My rice and tuna rations had run out and I sat in Newport town, my vision blurring as I started to shake and feel sick. I needed food. My body was going into hypoglycaemic shock (a lack of sugar in the system and very dangerous if not sorted quickly). In my desperation, I made my way to McDonald's and sat outside on a wall next to the bin, waiting for anyone who had finished their food to throw it in. As soon as they left, I would pull out the packaging looking for any leftovers. Surprisingly, this worked a treat. On my first attempt, I had half a cup of chips and a few bites of a burger. After an hour of repeating this process, I'd probably eaten the equivalent of three Happy Meals. I immediately felt better and the shaking stopped; it felt wonderful to be full. Not one of my proudest moments, but unless you've ever been that hungry, you will simply never know. Desperate people do desperate things. It was the only way that I could move forward, so it had to be done and I don't regret it.

4

The kindness of strangers

Before I left and started the walk, I had lost my faith in humanity. Television, papers and social media always seemed to be so negative. I'd often think to myself that I'd love to just disappear and go and live in a cave and get away from all the whingers. More than anything, it's probably just because I cared. The chances of us being alive here on this earth are so miniscule it's almost incomprehensible. To watch what human beings are capable of doing to our planet and each other genuinely destroys my soul. However, slowly but surely, as I made an effort to slow down and take stock of the communities I walked through, I was beginning to see a different side to people. Small acts of kindness from those I would never have normally spoken to would be a key turning point in helping me discover the inner happiness I was desperate to find.

I was about eighteen miles south of Aberystwyth, the

next major town on my journey, when I came across a set of head-high standing stones in a small hamlet at the bottom of the hills. There were three upright stones with a further horizontal slab. I took five and sat down against the standing stones, completely aware, once again, that food and a place to camp was a massive problem. I was contemplating pitching the tent here for the evening as I was physically done by this point and low on energy. Subconsciously, I knew I had eighteen miles to do the next day to reach Aberystwyth, and was wondering how this was going to be possible having just had a big day and nothing to eat that evening. I was anxious about my recent hypoglycaemic episode and knew that if that were to happen to me on the coastal path when nobody was about, it would not be good news. After five minutes of arguing with myself as to what to do, I started to get really cold and wet from the rain that we'd had throughout the day. I decided to get up and push on a little further towards the hamlet.

On the beach I saw two men, one middle-aged and one an elderly gentleman, walking back from the sea holding a lobster. Another lightbulb moment struck me: the answer to my lack of food problem was simple: I needed to learn to forage. At the time, I knew a little about foraging, but nowhere near enough to sustain myself throughout the journey. If I put some work into this, this would be something I could learn about as I progressed. Fishing was off the menu as it would take too long, and besides, I lacked the rod and experience to make it work. Although not resolving my immediate situation, it forced a much-needed smile.

I approached the two men – the young one was called Steve, the older was Mike – and asked if they knew anywhere safe in the area where I could camp without upsetting the locals. They pointed me in the direction of a campsite around two miles inland up a B-road. I complimented their lobster, shook their hands and headed up towards the campsite that I had absolutely no money to pay for. About ten minutes into my walk up the hill, I heard a voice shout my name. It was one of the gentlemen that I'd just been talking to. I reluctantly made my way back down, knowing that I'd have to walk all the way back up this same hill again.

'Chris, we've hired a holiday cottage near where we were talking to you. As soon as we got back, we told the family about you and without hesitation they told me to come back and get you. We have a fresh lobster and plenty of food we'll be having shortly. We would love for you to come and join us.'

I wanted to throw off my bag, jump up and wrap my legs around him out of sheer joy, but managed to restrain myself and reply: 'That would be wonderful, so long as I'm not imposing on your holiday time.'

'Not at all,' he said. 'We would be delighted to host you. If we can't help each other, then what's the point?'

I immediately liked him.

I walked into the holiday home, greeted by a family of around eight people. They welcomed me with open arms. Never in a million years would I have agreed to sit and have a free dinner with a table of strangers before I left for the walk. Meeting and talking to so many kind and selfless people was clearly beginning to have an impact on me. I felt welcome and relieved at the thought of some home-cooked food. They immediately sent me in the direction of the shower and said food would be ready in about an hour. After getting out of the shower, I caught my reflection in the mirror; I looked like a skeleton wrapped in skin. I was so thin that it made me tear up. I'd always been in good shape and kept myself healthy, and perhaps seeing myself in such an emaciated state was the catalyst I needed to put more time and energy into my diet and personal health, and make sure I consumed more so I could put some weight back on.

Their house was a cosy cottage with a games room upstairs. I'd already logged into the Wi-Fi, and as I had half an hour before food would be served, I put my clothes on, sat on the toilet and started to screenshot as much information about coastal foraging as I could so I could read up on it as and when. I was soon called down for dinner and we all sat around a perfectly laid table with jugs of water and full wine glasses.

They were a close-knit family who had moved all over the country but still found time to get together, and it was a happy atmosphere to be a part of. I had to remind myself that only two hours ago, I was sat by the standing stones clueless as to what I was going to do. *God, I nearly camped there*, I thought. *That would have made this a very different evening.*

Over dinner, I was asked lots of questions and we had plenty of laughs over what seemed like an endless supply of good wine. After only an hour, I felt like I had known these people for years.

Near the end of the meal, Steve, who I'd initially met

in the bay, said, 'Chris, have you done much travelling on the west coast of Scotland and its islands?'

'No, mate. I've never been there before in my life.'

'You've told us how rigidly you are sticking to the coast and, boy, I admire that so much, but how on earth are you going to do that in the Highlands? I've seen it for myself. There are some incredibly wild sections, and if you stick to the coast the way you say you want to, I can't help but feel genuinely concerned for you.'

He stood up and proceeded to show me a map of mainland Britain on the wall, pointing out some of the sections he was worried about. 'If I were you, I would start to plan this now if you're going to have any chance of completing this,' he said. 'Maybe you could ask for a sponsor, as, even with all the kit you could possibly want, this would still be no mean feat. As admirable as it is that you're doing this with no funds, Scotland is a different ball game and would be impossible this way.'

The man had a very valid point. 'Steve,' I said, 'the reason, and I say this with inverted commas, I don't fit into "normal" life is because I find the whole idea of planning so far in advance annoying and unnecessary. I'm a very shoot-from-the-hip kind of guy and have always taken each day as it comes.

'This didn't work for me before in anything that I've done, but this journey ties in so well with my mentality and the way that I am because it's literally just a case of one foot in front of the other and problem-solving as I go. As difficult as this is, my system has got me this far. I fear if I start seeing the enormity of the challenge that lies ahead, it may have a negative impact on me.

'I figure that if I channel all of my thoughts into how the hell I'll get through the next day and spend my energy on that, one day at a time, so long as I'm heading north, then I'm making progress. That's the aim. As I walk, I'll become better and better at this.'

The elderly father lifted his glass. 'Chris, that's a great attitude. People have become a bit bloody serious these days!' We all laughed and made a toast to good health and my onward journey. Steve looked at me, nodded with a wink and a smile, and softly said, 'Fair play, mate.'

After the most delicious meal of freshly caught lobster in a creamy tagliatelle sauce, I stood up in a total food coma and announced it was time for me to leave and go and find a spot to camp.

'Chris,' Steve said, 'you will do no such thing. You may have noticed a games room upstairs with a sofa? Well, it's got your name on it. We would be delighted to have you stay with us.' I smiled and sat back down as a glass of wine was already being poured for me. I had the most wonderful evening with the most beautiful people.

The coming days would take me through a stunning Welsh coastline of cliffs, gorges, tiny coves with freshwater streams running into the sea, and deep forests to keep me cool in their shade. My journey took me up through Aberystwyth (where I did my first ever local radio inter-view), Borth, Porthmadog and Pwllheli, taking me alongside Snowdonia National Park. Slowly but surely, I was beginning to find a rhythm and gain an insight into how and what I needed to do daily to get through each one safely. Sometimes, when I had food for the day, I'd find myself in a really good place in my head, feeling much happier. At these times I'd often break into a jog from sheer joy, training myself up for the more physically demanding sections of the walk as I progressed north towards Scotland.

If I had a few quid spare, I'd walk into a launderette to freshen up my clothes. By putting an army poncho over my filthy clothes and removing them one by one before putting them in the washing machine, I'd devised an effective way to get all my clothes clean without having to sit totally naked and potentially getting arrested.

Without doubt the elephant in the room, I'd sit silently while the old ladies chatted away, though I know they were secretly itching to ask what I was doing. After all, it was probably not every day they saw a bearded bloke sitting beside them covering his modesty with a poncho! As for me, I loved nothing more than watching my clothes spin in the machine as the water browned with weeks of dirt and sweat.

Once every few weeks, someone would approach me having recognized me from social media. The effort I'd been putting into my Facebook page, and the amount of people I'd stop and talk to along the way, very slowly meant my following and the charity donations were creeping up. I think at this point I had around 800 followers and £1,000 in the charity kitty. It wasn't much, but it was still right at the beginning of the walk, and having started with about fifteen followers and £100 donated by family and friends, it was a good morale boost and a sign that things were heading in the right direction.

Practically anyone I met on the path who had either stopped me or been approached by me asked if I was eating enough as I looked so gaunt and thin. I'd always reply with a yes and that it was just the way that I was built, although this was absolutely not the case, mainly because I didn't want to sound like I was hinting at something. Either way, as I'd put my heart and soul into getting this far, having someone tell you, 'Keep going, pal – you're doing amazing!' was always a great morale-booster.

Making it to Snowdonia National Park was a massive landmark for me. A few days before in Porthmadog, I'd received a message, to my delight, from an old friend I'd served with in the Parachute Regiment. Mark and I had gone through basic training together. He drove from the Midlands to come and visit me, and I was delighted to see him again for the first time in eighteen years. Nothing had changed – well, apart from the fact we both looked much older, he was much fatter and I was much thinner! It was my first link to the Paras again, which seemed like a lifetime ago.

That evening as we camped up, Mark told me about a few of our good friends who had been killed in action while serving in Afghanistan and Iraq. It broke my heart. After I left the Paras, life had become incredibly busy for me and, like many who leave the Forces, I'd lost touch with many of my old friends. I'd often thought of them, though, so to hear this news was devastating.

Before bed, I sat and shed a little man tear in their memory and felt so grateful that I'd left the Forces when I did. It really got me thinking that, aside from my personal reasons for doing this walk, I was really proud to be raising money for SSAFA. Hearing this tragic news only added fuel to the fire inside me to do everything in my power to raise as much money and awareness as I could for our veterans and their families. It also put my own situation into perspective.

5

The Three Peaks Challenge

Snowdonia was also a sure sign that the west coast of England was ever encroaching and I'd soon be entering my first new country. Once I reached Bangor, I was only around fifty miles from the border. It was an exciting prospect, and I was eager to give myself a little pat on the back for making it this far (little wins!). Under different circumstances I know I would have thoroughly enjoyed walking the beautiful coastline of Snowdonia National Park, with its sudden appearance of mountains and abundant freshwater streams, which gave me a welcome respite from the muggy September weather. However, I was still extremely inexperienced at foraging so my constant hunger and anxiety about where my next meal would come from were always at the forefront of my mind. I simply couldn't appreciate the scenery with much more pressing issues to worry about. At this point, I was in sheer survival mode.

The nights were the worst. With hunger pangs keeping me awake, I spent hours staring at the inside of my tent wondering if I'd be able to summon the energy to walk again come morning.

I'd made it along the coast adjacent to the tallest mountain in Wales, Mount Snowdon. To my joy, my good friends Al, Paul and Gareth, from Killay in Swansea, drove up to come and spend two days and two nights with me. When they arrived, I was so happy to see some friendly, familiar faces. After we pitched up in the safety of a campsite and sorted the admin, the lads unloaded a barbecue and a box of food, full to the brim with burgers, sausages, chicken . . . the works! Obviously, I didn't want to tell them that I'd been starving for as long as I had or even show the slightest inkling that I could have easily dived into the box and eaten the whole lot raw. That night, we sat and ate like kings with a couple of beers, compliments of my buddies. It was an amazing evening and so satisfying to go to bed with a belly full of food. I will never forget that feeling.

The next morning, on 30 September, we packed up our gear, jumped into the van and headed to climb Snowdon. If I'm honest it was the last thing I wanted to do, since I'd prefer to use little visits like this as rest days, but they had made the effort to come all the way up so a cheeky mountain was the least I could do. The climb up Snowdon is manageable as it's pathed all the way up. We eventually made it to the top where the visibility was zero and there was a cold wind. To our despair, the cafe near the summit was shut. We huddled out of the wind for a short break before we made our descent to the bottom. 'Chris,' Al said, 'you know the three highest mountains in Wales, England

and Scotland are all practically on the coast? Have you heard of the Three Peaks Challenge?'

'Of course,' I replied. It involved climbing those three highest mountains: Snowdon, Scafell Pike in the Lake District, and Ben Nevis in Scotland.

'Mate, I heard of a guy who'd walked from one mountain to another but on the roads. You could be the first person to have ever climbed all three mountains, walking between each by sticking to the coastline.'

'I'm not really fussed if I'm the first person, but it's a bloody good idea!' It would be a really cool thing to do given how much I love climbing. However, I kind of shrugged it off because at the time it just seemed a million miles away. I was more concerned about what on earth I was going to eat after they left. After a great few days with Al, Gareth and Paul, they dropped me back on the coast where I'd left off. Before we said our goodbyes, they kindly gave me the leftover food from the barbecue and then drove off. I picked up my bag, shrugged my shoulders and said aloud to myself, 'Right, boy, here we go again!'

Although a lovely gesture, I knew that meats are a big problem in the summer as they go off quickly, and so I'd have to eat as much of it as I could that day to avoid food poisoning. I must have eaten three plates' worth of burgers and sausages – I could hardly walk afterwards. Food is food though, and in this game, you have to take it where you can get it.

By now, I was on completely unknown territory walking the coastline alongside Snowdonia National Park, and it was here I felt my health beginning to deteriorate. With exhaustion setting in, I started making stupid decisions, keeping going when I knew I should have stopped and rested. This led to me going the wrong way, choosing the wrong path, and tripping over tree roots and hurting myself. What's more, I was getting frustrated with myself so easily. I'd look down at the coast and whisper 'Fuck!' to myself, deflated at the thought of how much more I had to do that day. My mind and my body were both starting to pack up. I often felt that if I wasn't continually troubled by the urgent need for money and food, walking the beautiful coastline of Wales would have been a dream.

I felt so hopeless and yet was still unable to ask anyone for help, even though I knew full well that if I just reached out, someone would have come to my aid in no time. I was just who I was and had always been. It was my biggest fault. The one thing I will say is that at no point did it cross my mind to quit the walk. I'd promised myself this the night before I left, and I was not going to break that vow.

Over the next week, I walked a beautiful peninsula with huge long sandy beaches bookended by cliffs, forestry and freshwater streams running down the coast from the hills. It took me through Aberdaron, turning the corner heading north once again, finishing off the thirty miles that took me into the busy student town of Bangor. I was excited at the prospect of getting closer to my first island on this walk: Anglesey. On my way up, I passed through some beautiful little bays, coves and fishing villages.

As much as I didn't realize it then, in hindsight I wouldn't have done the adventure any other way. It made the walk so much more difficult, but I always knew that when I did eventually cross the finish line, I'd feel a great sense of satisfaction and achievement knowing that I'd done it in the purest way possible. I'd like to think one day that I'll come back and do the Welsh coastline again, but this time without having to worry about the basic human necessities of food, good shelter and water.

As well as my tent, I stayed in some random places at night during my stretch to Bangor. Little gems like barns and sheds offer amazing comfort and protection from the rain and winds, and one night I sneakily nestled into another tiny treehouse (in this one I was unable to fully stretch my legs). I enjoyed the challenge of finding inventive spots to sleep. It felt like useful practice for the more diverse environments I was likely to encounter further north and as I swung around the busier, more populated areas of the south of England.

After a long haul, I arrived in Bangor, and from there I would cross over to Anglesey, the largest of the Welsh islands and the last known settlement of the Druids. The coast path stretches roughly 125 miles, hugging the coast all the way around. For the first time since I started, I was genuinely excited. As per usual, I was skint and a bit worried about heading onto the island with absolutely no money, but I kept reminding myself that I'd come this far, so another 125 miles was completely possible. I'd moved along the coast incredibly fast until now, and it was like I was running from something or someone. Maybe I was, but strangely this had kept me going. Adopting the same attitude for Anglesey, I crossed the Menai Suspension Bridge feeling optimistic. I kept the sea to my left, heading north along the west coast, and started my Anglesey adventure.

Summer season was well and truly over, and so I hardly saw anyone on the coast path. About two days into a beautiful coastline, filled with little crags, lovely beaches and yet more quaint little fishing villages, I stopped for the evening and pitched the tent. Once again, I'd been without any food and was beginning to feel the effects. This would be the first time on my journey so far that I would forage for my meals. While I knew foraging was key to being self-sufficient on my journey, anyone who knows me knows I hate any kind of shellfish. This wasn't going to be easy. I walked to the shoreline with my cooking pot, armed with a table knife – not the best of tools – and clambered onto the rocks, unenthusiastic about what lay in store for dinner.

I put my hand into the water and used the knife to pry off a limpet from the rock. I was surprised how difficult it was – though no doubt a strong steel blade would have made my life a hell of a lot easier! I collected around ten before heading back to the tent, my knife bent in all directions. I boiled the limpets for about fifteen minutes in seawater to get as much salt into my body as possible (when you're exercising in heat and you sweat, the body loses an incredible amount of its salt, which can cause serious cramp). One by one, I swallowed the limpets whole, desperate to avoid any flavour, constantly reminding myself I was fuelling my body with vital carbohydrates, proteins and that all-important sodium. Far from full, but in the knowledge that I'd done myself a huge favour, I settled for the night and went to sleep.

I ended up moving very fast around the island of Anglesey, knowing that when I finished it and was back on the mainland, I'd been promised a slap-up meal by an old friend who lived a few miles out of Bangor. By the third day, I had covered an amazing amount of ground – around eighty-six miles. That evening, I searched for a place to camp and came across a pub. I was practically out of battery at this point, and aside from not being able to post, I was gutted because I couldn't use it to take photos; proof that I'd been to the places I said I had. I'd never really thought about photography before, but I was really starting to enjoy it and was slowly developing a good eye for a decent photo.

I wandered into the pub and asked the bartender if it wasn't too cheeky to order a pint of ice-cold water and put my phone on charge. Although I'd done a lot of PR for the charity, never once did I walk into a pub and say, 'Look what I'm doing!' I'd always adopted the attitude that if someone had read my T-shirt and wanted to approach me, they would. This didn't always work but, often, given the way I was dressed along with my bag and general demeanour, it didn't take long before someone did.

Sure enough, the manager of the pub popped over to ask me what I was up to. He was a lovely fella and a veteran himself. I told him what I was up to and who I was doing it for, at which point he sat back in his seat sharply and said, 'Fuck off!' Then he stood up, grabbed my icy water, walked to the barman and told him to pour me a pint of ale.

After that, he disappeared into the kitchen and came back with a menu, even though food wasn't being served.

'Chris,' he said, 'it's obvious you have no money. I really admire that you said nothing. We get charity walkers, cyclists and sometimes runners in here often. They have amazing posh bikes worth thousands, dressed from head to toe in all the best gear, and still ask if they can have a free meal because what they're doing is for charity.

'We always do it because it's for charity, but the cheek of some of these people boils my blood. Then there's people like you who genuinely need it and ask for absolutely nothing apart from a glass of water. Please eat as much as you can, including a pudding, and I'd be honoured if I could sit and join you for dinner.'

What he said really touched me, and I immediately felt less guilty taking him up on his offer. We spent a lovely few hours chatting, having a laugh at our own expense with a huge sprinkle of military banter. He sent me on my way with a litre carton of ale, a full belly of food and a huge smile on my face. *There really are some amazing people out there*, I thought. Little did I know that this would be my last meal until I crossed the bridge back into Bangor.

The next day, feeling more energized, I put in a huge shift, taking me about thirteen miles from crossing the bridge, but I was really struggling to find a place to camp that was out of sight. Frustrated, after searching for over an hour, I stumbled across Henley's Golf Club at around 7 p.m. It was empty and, desperate to rest my legs ready for the final push to Bangor tomorrow, I noticed a beautiful big oak tree in the middle of the course. It had been a warm day and was set to be a rain-free evening, so I got my sleeping bag and bivvy bag out, leaving my tent inside my bag to avoid being seen, and, with nothing for dinner, slept under the tree for the night.

I had all good intentions of bailing in the early hours to

avoid any confrontation with golfers or the owners of the club, but this didn't go quite as planned . . . Instead, I awoke to the sound of a golf buggy hurtling towards me at full speed, and a very vocal worker driving it, clearly very pissed off. Never have I exited my sleeping bag so fast! I glanced towards the road. I had just enough time to make it off the golf course if I legged it now, but nowhere near enough time to pack my stuff before he reached me.

Without a second thought, I threw my bergen over one shoulder, my sleeping and bivvy bags over the other, and, holding my incredibly worn out, almost unusable trainers, ran like Forrest Gump! Annoyed as he was, if this man chasing me in the golf buggy didn't laugh at the ridiculousness of me sprinting off with all my gear flapping around behind me, he must have been dead inside!

Even in my desperation, running with only my hole-ridden socks on, I still found time to have a little chuckle to myself. I made it to the fence, threw all of my gear over, half of which spilled onto the road, and then followed suit. I continued my escape, sprinting for at least another mile down the road to get well clear. I passed one or two people who were on their driveways, and as I ran past them like the wind, I wished them good morning. They stared on in disbelief watching a fleeing shoeless man who looked like he had just escaped from prison. Either way, I made it to safety, repacked my gear into my bag and carried on, eventually crossing the Menai Bridge that afternoon.

Anglesey was where the very last settlement of Druids once was, and I'd heard a brilliant story about them from a historian called Sally. To fend off the Vikings, the Druids had built a path of logs across the river, onto which they scattered magic mushrooms in abundance. As the Vikings made their way down the Menai Strait, the Druids set fire to the logs, which released their potent vapour and clouded the ships in hallucinogenic smoke. In what must have been a very confused altered mental state, the Vikings turned tail.

Bangor would mark the final five days walking the Welsh coast path, during which time I would be passing through Llandudno. I stopped off for the evening to visit the charity Blind Veterans, Wales, who had contacted me on Facebook and invited me for dinner and to stay the night. The charity cares for veterans, young or old, who are partially or completely blind. I loved spending time there and had the most wonderful day gaining an insight into the amazing work the charity does and was equally amazed by the veterans I met. I found their resilience and strength of character inspiring and it put life into perspective for me. It served as a reminder that no matter what it was I went through, there would always be someone out there who had it harder.

My last night in Wales was on 2 October 2017. By now I was posting on my Facebook page twice a day, and that morning I received a message from the Powell family to ask if I would like to come over for some dinner. Always happy for another feed and to meet some new people, I accepted. I took to them all immediately. Melanie, Ray and Jackie were such a kind, caring, warm-natured family and simply couldn't do enough for me. They had followed my journey for a while and over dinner I told them of my adventures and also some of the hardships involved. My tiny yellow tent had definitely seen its day; the seams let water in any time it rained, letting it seep through and soak the bottom of my sleeping bag and anything that was touching the sides – always guaranteed to ruin my day. They kindly offered me a two-man tent they had for the grandkids to play in. Obviously, this tent was in no way, shape or form up for the challenge but, as ever, I was incredibly grateful for the offer and the idea of at least one dry night in the tent when it rained (we'd had so much of it that summer) was a huge relief. It was a great evening. The next morning, after the most superb fry-up made by Ray, I set off to cross the border into my first new country.

6

Leaving home

Crossing the Welsh border into England was a great feeling. I stood by the 'Welcome to England' sign and asked a passer-by to take a photo of me. After he'd left, I had a quick scope around to see if anybody was there; the coast was clear, so I dropped my bag from my shoulders, thrust my arms into the air and shouted 'Yes!' as loud as I possibly could. I felt an immense sense of personal achievement. Only I knew what it had taken and what I'd endured to get to this point. It was a slightly lonely feeling, but I wasn't in this to prove anything to anyone apart from myself, and Caitlin, of course.

I checked in with Caitlin once or twice a week. I remember calling her when I reached England to share the news. She was so happy for me, and it was the only voice I needed to tell me, 'Well done, Dad. I'm proud of you.' I hung up the phone with tears rolling down my face:

one, because I'd just finished Wales, and two, because of what she'd said. That phone call will stay with me for ever.

After Bangor, I had made my way through Conwy, Llandudno, Prestatyn and eventually over the border to Chester. It soon became apparent how good I'd had it in Wales and just how much I was going to miss its rugged coast path. I was now walking in far more built-up industrial areas, all the time realizing that camping was going to be an absolute nightmare. *Fuck*, I thought, *my next big stop is Liverpool.* It would take me a few days to get there and an overnight stay in a small bus stop, as it was impossible to camp and not be seen. My main concern was attracting pissheads or people who were just out to cause trouble. I feared I'd lost so much weight and strength that I'd not even be able to defend myself if someone came after me. It was clear I'd have to up my game when it came to finding places to spend the night.

In two days, I made it around to the port on the opposite side of the Mersey estuary to Liverpool, from where you can catch the Woodside Ferry that plays the iconic song, 'Ferry Cross the Mersey' by Gerry and the Pacemakers. I sat outside the terminal and took an hour's break to check the maps of possible places to sleep as I worked my way around the estuary. Soon after, a middle-aged lady approached me and asked if I was the guy walking around the UK coastline. 'I am indeed,' I replied. She had been following me since close to the start and, after a brief conversation, she told me to sit tight while she walked into the ferry terminal. About five minutes later, she appeared holding a ticket to get me over.

'Wow!' I said. 'How kind. I've always wanted to do this,

but the problem is I refuse to miss any of the estuaries or coastline, so if I did, I'd feel like I was cheating.' She chuckled and said, 'I thought you were going to say that! I got you another ticket that's open for a week so you can walk around the estuary and get the boat back over, so you won't miss anything.'

'That's so sweet,' I said, 'but I have no money to be able to pay you back.'

'Just keep going and keep raising more for SSAFA,' she said. 'That means far more than paying me any money. I have a close family member who was helped by them. Consider it me giving them something back.' I gave her a big hug and thanked her for her kindness. As she walked off, I called her to ask what her name was; I definitely recognized her from somewhere. She turned around and said with a smile, 'Who cares? No doubt we will never see each other again. Just keep going.' She gave me another smile and walked away.

Beaming, I crossed over on the iconic Liverpudlian ferry singing along with the Tannoy, even though I had no money, food or an inkling of a place to pitch the tent. As soon as we touched ground, I walked off the tiny harbour and in front of me was the city of Liverpool. It looked absolutely amazing, and massive too! I immediately checked the maps for any signs of parks or woodland for sleeping spots, but it was clear there was nowhere safe and secluded. Just to get anywhere beyond this concrete jungle was going to take me a few days, and so, for the first time on this walk, I was totally clueless as to what to do.

As I looked around at a city I'd never been to before, to my right I noticed the Hilton hotel. I remember thinking,

My God, what I'd do to stay in there tonight! I'm not sure what came over me at that moment, as I really can't stand asking for anything, but I was desperate. This was a first for me, actually reaching out for help. I headed over to the plush hotel and passed through the spinning doors into the lobby reception. I took my turn at the back of the queue and, as I waited, I did some people watching; I couldn't help but notice how nicely everyone was dressed. It was late afternoon, so I could only assume they'd dressed up for dinner. I got some funny looks in return; the night before, I'd been sleeping in a small bus stop and my beige trousers were now blackened from lying on . . . well, what-ever was on the floor. (If I'm honest, I prefer not to think about it!) Either way, I looked like a scruffy mess.

My turn came and I was almost shaking with nerves. In the politest, most well-spoken voice I could conjure up, I said, 'This may be the cheekiest thing I have ever asked, and I hope you don't think bad of me . . . but I'm walking the UK coastline for the veterans' charity, SSAFA. I arrived in Liverpool only half an hour ago and I have no money. I camp along the way and have just left Wales. Now that I'm in a big city, I'm finding it really hard to find a safe place to camp and was wondering if you had a cupboard or if I could sleep in the car park or even on the roof?' I chuckled at the ridiculousness of what I was asking. 'I have a Facebook page called "Chris Walks the UK" that you can look up so you can check I'm not lying to you. I have around a thousand followers.'

The lady was really friendly and replied, 'Bless you, Chris – give me ten minutes and I'll go and speak to the manager.' I stood back from the queue and marvelled with disbelief that I'd had the audacity to do this. I was fully expecting a massive 'Piss off!' and to be sent packing, doomed to spend the night walking around the city. Instead, the receptionist returned and called me over.

'Chris, I'm sorry, we can't let you stay in the car park – or a cupboard for that matter!' she chuckled. 'We looked at your page and my manager totally admires what you're doing and has a brother in the army. We'd like to offer you a room for the night and some vouchers to dine in our restaurant.'

I couldn't believe it. I leaned over the counter and gave her a massive hug. 'You have no idea what this means to me,' I said.

'Go have a shower and get some rest – you deserve it.'

I grabbed my bag and the key, smiling from ear to ear as I walked through the lobby looking like a total misfit compared with everyone else. I felt like the richest man alive, even if only for an evening.

After some food and a shower, I locked the door to my room and stayed in it the entire night. A real bed felt incredible and I sat totally starkers on it. I turned the TV off and began to read through my latest journal, taking time to reflect on the walk so far – through Wales to England. I could see a clear pattern to the times when I'd been distressed or worried: it was either when I was fretting about food or when I was piss wet through in the tent. I knew it took a certain kind of person to endure this night after night, I just hoped that was me.

I started to think of how my life had panned out up until now, and all the things that had led me to start such a journey and have the minerals to cope with constant uncertainty from day to day. I think for me it all started in my teens, when I was around fourteen years old. That's when, like so many do, my parents split up. I think it would be safe to say that it wasn't the most pleasant of splits, but what I do know is that our parents loved me, my older brother Keith, three years my senior, and my younger brother Mark, five years my junior, and we loved them too. Up until this point, we were a great, solid family unit. Over the next year, we would live with my mother, Sam. It wasn't easy for her, that much I do know: two teenagers and a nine-year-old were enough to test anyone.

When I was sixteen, my mum moved out to live with her new partner, Dave, in Reading and my dad moved back into what was our family home with his partner Jane, along with our one-year-old half-sister, Molly. My brothers and I were now to be looked after by my dad and Jane. I was gutted; I loved my mum – as I did my dad, and I knew they were just trying to do the right thing for us – but watching my mum go was so incredibly sad and I felt a little let down. I'd always been the cheeky child and knew she had a bit of a soft spot for me. Us boys would miss having her around terribly.

My dad, Jane and Molly soon settled in with us and they tried their very best to make us gel as a new family. Sadly, it didn't take long before some cracks started to appear for me. The new family routine was so different to everything we had been used to and I didn't take well to it. I was a fully-fledged teenager; I'd taken the split really hard and started to resent the changes that were being made. I found it really difficult to have another woman in my house telling me what to do. As a result of this, there would be a lot of arguments, and I started getting in more trouble at school as well as in fights.

I had a horrible knack of bottling up my feelings; I was extremely reserved and would never speak to anyone about how I felt. I paid no attention in class, which would often get me into trouble and, naturally, I'd then go home to be sat down for what felt like a three-hour lecture. I hated it so much; I was getting angrier and less tolerant. Every given chance, I'd run to the woods and cry, sitting at the top of the biggest tree that I could climb. It was my safe place, and I knew nobody would find me there.

Not surprisingly, my exams crashed and burned. Don't get me wrong, I was never going to be an academic genius, but I ended up walking out of two exams simply because the lad sat next to me was chewing gum so loud that I genuinely wanted to punch him. It was a complete disaster, and I knew it, confirming how much the last five years at school had felt like nothing more than a prison sentence. My teachers, however, really liked me and I was always told that I would do well in life just because of my outgoing personality. Mrs Howells, my form tutor, never once told me off for any of my outbursts. Instead, she would take me outside the classroom and give me a big hug. She could clearly see that I'd been bottling things up and pleaded with me to open up and talk to her, but I would just stare with glazed eyes and say nothing. I wish one day I could see her again and thank her.

I was sent to college nine miles away and put on a foundation course, which would only make me feel more stupid than I already did. I was only there to see my mates; it was that simple. For about three weeks, I was getting a lift from my elder brother's mate, Vicky, but soon burned that bridge as I had no money to pay her for fuel. I'd pretend to my dad and Jane that I was going to college but would spend most of my days in the woods collecting bugs, climbing trees and making up my own little adventures.

Only a few months into college, and things at home were not good. Unbeknown to them, I think I'd already decided I wanted to leave but didn't have the guts just yet to do so; it was just a question of waiting for the right time. I'd always been strong-willed and once my mind was firmly set, that was that.

The moment came when, one day, we all piled into the car to go out and get a family photo. Having done nothing but argue the night before, I resented the idea. I can't remember exactly what it was I said as we were driving to the photographer's studio (something cheeky, no doubt!), but my brothers and I couldn't stop laughing. Whatever I had said had triggered something. The idea was totally scrapped, and the car was turned around to go home while we boys were still in fits of laughter. This obviously turned the situation from bad to worse, and when we arrived back home, we all got out of the car and Jane, my dad and I had another bust-up.

During the argument, I turned to my brother Keith and said, 'Sorry, mate, this is it. I'm leaving,' and I sprinted away as fast as I could in no particular direction. It wasn't long before my dad caught up with me, asked me to stop and tried to persuade me to come back home. I was crying in anger and told him that I wouldn't be coming back. Seeing the state that I was in and sensing that perhaps I just needed some time, he respected my wish and I continued running. But I had meant what I said. That day I left home for good with only the clothes on my back. I did not return.

That evening, however, I went back to the house in the dark, making my way through the hedges in the back garden, and saw them all sitting in the living room. I knew there was a tent in the garage that belonged to my uncle Ian, so I leopard-crawled through the back garden, grabbed the tent out of the garage and stealthily made my escape.

Now I just needed somewhere to sleep, so I went up to my favourite spot – Caversham Park Woods near the bomb crater – and pitched my tent. I had no sleeping bag, no money, and mobile phones didn't exist then. It was a cold night and I'd spent most of it sitting up a tree. In a strange way, without knowing it, this would be my first training session for a walk that I would do some twenty-six years later.

Despite the fact that I valued my freedom more than security, it came at a cost. The next few months would be a rollercoaster of sleeping in the woods, in my friend Adrian's garage and the occasional sleepover at a mate's. I really didn't want to tell my mum, who was now living in Reading with her partner, Dave, in a tiny flat. I didn't want to worry her or put any unnecessary stress on her, so I said nothing. It was the same with my friends and their parents; whenever anyone asked how I was, I would always tell them that everything was fine. It was a lie, but I was embarrassed by the truth. I was also never one for sympathy; I hated it. Before long, I was starting to feel a real sense of guilt going to my friends' houses and asking if I could have dinner with them. Obviously they were always happy to oblige, but after a while and judging by my general appearance, I could see in their eyes they were beginning to twig that something was up. While most of my mates were zooming off on mopeds, playing computers and just being teenagers, I was already in full survival mode, always wondering where I would be sleeping that night and how on earth I was going to eat.

The day after Bonfire Night in 1996, my desperation got me caught out. It was a particularly cold evening, and there was a big bonfire in the middle of the village where loads of mates and their families came out to have some fun. It was really lovely seeing everyone, but disheartening to watch all my friends having fun with their families. It made me sad that I wasn't with mine. I knew my dad had been out looking for me, as he'd knocked on some of my friends' doors, but I'd made my decision and avoided him at all costs.

As the evening drew to a close, the families began to disappear one by one. Soon enough, I found myself lying next to the dying fire, lapping up as much of the remaining heat as I could. It was bitterly cold, and I remember my hands hurting so much that it felt like they had been stabbed with a thousand needles. It got so bad that I even went back to my old home, my fists clenched and ready to bang on the door. But I just couldn't bring myself to do it. I checked the car, our black Golf, and to my surprise it was open, so I decided to sit in it for a few hours. Still freezing cold, my instincts told me to get walking, as at least it kept me warm. I walked about a mile up to the local shops and, exhausted, lay down on a bench. The next thing I remember was my elder brother's mate, Steve Bradbury, giving me a shake to wake me up and asking if I was okay. I simply replied, 'Yes, mate, I must've fallen asleep. All is fine.'

Hungry and desperate to warm myself up, I decided to walk the five miles into Reading near the Royal Berkshire Hospital where my mum and Dave's flat was. But, to my total disappointment, nobody was in. I'd walked this far and needed food desperately, and I noticed the tiny bathroom window was open. To this day I will never know quite how I managed this, but, pushing every ounce of air out of my body, I slithered my way through the bathroom window and came crashing down head-first on top of the toilet, smashing the plant pot that was next to it, sending soil all over the place. I made my way to the fridge and was delighted to find half a cooked chicken. Like a Neanderthal, I devoured all of it with my hands there and then. I necked a can of Coke, let out the most almighty burp, did my best to clean up the soil on the bathroom floor and made my escape through the latch-locking front door. There was one tiny bedroom in the flat and no space for me to stay there, and anyway, I would never have asked.

My burgling skills were clearly not up to scratch, however, as the second my mum and Dave got home it was obvious someone had been in there. What burglar on this planet would break into a flat, leave every valuable but devour half a chicken? I remember doing a reverse charge call to my mother, feeling so guilty, to let her know what I'd done. She was so upset, now knowing the position that I was in.

She took me to a friend's house (Tim Buckley) to have

a chat with his parents to see if I could stay there for a few months while I found my feet. They agreed that I would pay £100 every two weeks as rent. My mum put me on a lifeguard course in Reading; I passed it and in no time landed myself a job nine miles away at the Henley Leisure Centre as a lifeguard. This was all good and well, but I had no transport to get there, so I had to get up stupidly early each day and walk or run the nine-mile backroad stretch into work, do my shift, then – in the dark – run or walk the nine miles back home. That's eighteen miles a day, five days a week, with a nine-hour shift each day in between. Food was included in my rent but, sadly, it was nowhere near the amount I needed to sustain my incredibly healthy appetite, given how much exercise I was doing. I was spending more money on food than I could afford – so much so that I started falling behind on the rent, causing massive tension between Tim, myself and his family. It was time for me to leave.

I couldn't keep up with the journey to work in Henley; I was physically shattered all the time and hated running the treacherous backroads at night, where I'd often been close to getting wiped out by a car. I was done. My mum came over to Tim's house to thank the family for helping me. It was an awful moment as Tim's mother was such a lovely woman and I could see her crying as I left. My mother had made a call to her parents, my grandparents, Grampy and Lyn, who lived just outside Watlington in a small place called Nettlebed, some thirty miles away from Reading, to ask if they could have me. When we arrived, I remember my mum crying so hard before she left, giving me a big hug as she said goodbye. On the one hand, I was very sad that things had ended up this way, but at the same time, I was grateful to have a permanent roof over my head and an inkling of stability at last.

7

Joining up

After a few months of sofa surfing and sleeping rough, and before I went to stay at my grandparents', my friend Alan Hunter had taken me to the army careers office in Reading to sign up for my local regiment, the Royal Gloucestershire, Berkshire and Wiltshire. The way I saw it, it was a way to get out of the mess I was in.

I was still too young to join, as I had to be sixteen years and nine months, but I remember my Grampy, who had once served, saying, 'You'll have a roof over your head, always have food, meet some great friends and you'll get paid for it.' In my mind, I was sold. 'In the meantime, you will stay with us,' he said, 'and labour for your uncle Andy to earn a few quid and keep you from moping around the house.'

I can't remember exactly how many months I stayed there for, but what I do know was that they were some of the fondest times of my younger years. I loved them so much for helping me, feeding me, and all round being a solid rock when I really needed it.

While I was waiting to sign up, aside from the physical element of working with my uncle, who was a repointer, I would spend my evenings and days off running up and down Britwell Hill, where a scene from *Chitty Chitty Bang Bang* was filmed. The fact that I was now being well fed meant that I looked so much healthier in myself. However, I had no idea if I'd been training hard enough for what I was about to do.

At sixteen years and nine months on the dot, I signed up, and the time came for my first week in training. I remember getting to the train station at Lichfield, nervous but so excited, and feeling a real sense of purpose again.

On the first day, after an evening of getting all of our gear and equipment dished out, we had our fitness test: a one-and-a-half-mile sprint, two minutes of press-ups, two minutes of sit-ups and as many pull-ups as we could do. The corporal assessing us was wearing a maroon beret. I asked what regiment that colour was. He came right up to my face and said, 'Something you will never get into, you skinny fuck. This is the Paras. You should be kissing my fucking feet just for being in my presence.' I wasn't going to argue with that! I stared at him in awe, wishing that I could be one.

Eager to impress, I felt sick with nerves as we stood at the start line waiting for the whistle to blow to start the run. When it did, I sprinted off with everything that I had. I knew that I was leading but when I turned around, the next man had not even come around the corner, some

200 yards behind me. I missed breaking the Lichfield record by just a second. Before the next man crossed the line, the corporal from the Parachute Regiment came up to me and said, 'If you can do the same in your press-ups, sit-ups and pull-ups, would you be interested in joining the Parachute Regiment, not this shitshow you've just signed up for?'

'Yes, Corporal, I would.'

And this is how I came to be in the Parachute Regiment.

As I sat in the hotel reflecting, it became quite apparent that these few years before joining the Paras had been pivotal in shaping my mentality and the way I would do things for years to come. I was strong-minded, incredibly independent and knew that I had it in me to take on any challenges that were put in front of me. Living in a tent, scraping by and surviving one day at a time and finding my own way from such a young age would help me to build up a resilience, resourcefulness and confidence in myself that would be key in helping me on this walk. However, although some of my biggest strengths, some of these traits were also to become my biggest weaknesses in the years leading up to it.

Back on my coastal walk, I ended up staying five days in Liverpool. While walking around the city centre, I stumbled across a homeless guy who had a piece of cardboard with his name, rank and army number written across it. I walked over and asked if he didn't mind if I sat down next to him for a chat. He was a lovely guy, about twenty-five years old, and his name was Gary. After around an hour, I had a good rapport with him and he rolled back his trousers and showed me an infected hole in his groin. It looked awful. I can only assume it was drug-related. I asked if we could meet again the next day. The following morning, after a deep night's sleep in the Hilton, I stuffed my hotel breakfast in a bag under my jumper to take to him. Although I had a purpose, I was also homeless, and I think that helped him to warm to me. I turned up at the place where Gary slept at night, opposite a Tesco Metro and a newspaper building, and though his stuff was still on the pavement, there was no sign of him. Some builders had just turned up and were starting to erect scaffolding right over where all his gear was, so I asked them, 'What are you gonna do with all this guy's stuff?'

In a very cocky and heartless kind of way, one responded, 'Well, if he ain't back in half an hour then it's going in the bins.'

'That's someone's belongings,' I replied. 'And he's a homeless veteran.'

Without even turning around to reply, he said, 'Not my problem, mate.'

I'm not usually an angry man, but I could feel my blood boiling. A stiff breeze could have blown me over in my skinny state, so a man-slap was out of the question against three scaffolders. Instead, I ran into the newspaper building, explained the case and asked for some bin liners so I could bag Gary's stuff up. They obliged and I went straight outside to pack up his sleeping bag and a couple of other loose items. As I stood up holding the bags, I just couldn't help myself.

'You really are a bunch of twats, do you know that?'

The more feisty, full-of-himself member of the team turned around and squared up to me.

'So,' I said, 'in one morning, you're gonna throw away a homeless veteran's belongings and then the three of you are going to beat up a homeless ex-Para who's walking around the UK coastline to raise money for our veterans? Aren't you the tough guy! I've taken pictures of the name of the company you work for and there's a newspaper building over there that would love this. Make my fuckin' day, I beg you.'

He stared blankly at me. I turned around and walked off, half expecting a punch to the head from behind. It didn't come, but as I walked away and crossed the street, I heard him shout, 'Dickhead!'

I searched all day for Gary, holding onto his stuff, but without joy. I took his gear back to the hotel and asked for it to be washed and cleaned. In the morning, I set off early and made a few calls to get him some help from SSAFA. I was desperate to find him, as this would be my last day in Liverpool. I asked every homeless man I saw if they knew him or had seen him. Eventually, I came up trumps. He was back outside the mini Tesco where I'd first met him. I returned his clean gear and we made some calls together to make a visit to the SSAFA and apply for some housing through the charity. He was incredibly grateful and humble. We shook hands and said our good-byes and that was the end of that. Around two months later, I received a call letting me know that he had been housed and was now back on track. I smiled all day.

The next morning, I left my hotel and made my way towards Preston and the Lake District. I had a massive day pumping out a good distance, but that night the weather turned. I found a tidy camp spot in some woodland to get cover from the winds, but sadly, at around 3 a.m., the flimsy poles in my tent snapped and the whole thing collapsed over the top of me like a soggy blanket. The rain water seeped in and soaked everything, including my sleeping bag. It eventually stopped at around 8 a.m., at which point I packed up quickly so I could get moving to keep warm and give myself a chance to air my stuff before camping up again later that day. I'd put a post out on my page saying that my pole had snapped and I'd be going into Preston to try and get it fixed. Not long after, a guy called Wayne Koda Mills got in touch via my Facebook page to say he wanted to meet me in a bar in Preston as he had a treat for me. I was excited at the prospect of this.

When we eventually met up, he got a pint in for us both and then pulled a bag from under the table. Inside was a grey, two-man North Face tent.

'Here you are, mate, this should solve your pole problem.'

I couldn't believe it. This tent was twenty notches above any of the ones I'd had to date. I couldn't wait to get inside it. I gave Wayne the biggest hug and he dropped me back to the coast where I'd left off, pointed me in the direction of a nearby spot he knew where it should be safe to camp, gave me fifty quid to live on and said his goodbyes. He was a great bloke and I really took to him.

About 11 o'clock that evening, I was woken by some nearby teenagers clearly getting drunk close by. One of them had clocked the tent and I heard them say, 'Look, someone's camping over there.' It was a muggy night and I'd stripped down into nothing to get into my sleeping bag. I could hear them approach, laughing and finding it incredibly funny that they were about to disturb me. I slowly unzipped my sleeping bag and grabbed my walking poles, which were lying by my side. Still totally naked, I slowly unzipped the tent and waited to see if they were going to leave. About thirty seconds later, while I was crouched and about to do the hundred-metre sprint, something hard hit the back of my tent. *Fuck it*, I thought. With my poles, I burst out of the tent as naked as the day I was born and screamed, 'Come on, then!' They ran away so fast, it was a joy to watch. I put my clothes on and moved my tent into a different location in case they came back for more. It was a bottle of Budweiser they had thrown at me and, sadly, it was empty.

The next stage of my journey would take me through Blackpool, Fleetwood and on to Lancaster. One seaside town blended into the next. The never-ending struggle to eat and find good spots to camp away from any humans continued. I'd lost a ridiculous amount of weight and I was mostly still boiling basmati rice, often with nothing else to go with it. As the days grew shorter and the nights got colder, my need for fuel became more and more urgent. I was definitely becoming more and more resilient when it came to camping and living outside, although my crap army roll mat gave little in the way of comfort. I'd wake up so stiff and hurting, it was a nightmare. My back was even starting to hunch. Each time I dropped my pack off my shoulders, I would stand there for at least five minutes just shaking them off to try and relieve some of the tension.

I skipped fast through most of the big towns to find safer spots to camp, although I did still find time to do some PR for the charity whenever I could. I was excited to reach Lancaster, as that meant I was nearing the Lake District. Although it was starting to rain a lot more and the winds were really picking up, as the days shortened and got colder, it made the walking itself easier. I enjoyed cooler temperatures – not constantly dripping in sweat as I had done during the height of the summer. Another bonus was that, with less heat, my body demanded less water, so I wasn't having to carry as much and my kit weighed a lot less. I always tried to find a little positive like this to boost my morale.

As I made my way through Cleveleys, Fleetwood, Knott End-On-Sea and Bank Houses, I eventually arrived in Lancaster. I really struggled with the amount of farmhouses and private property, and every time I saw a sign 'Private Property: Keep Out!' it would really bug me, as it would mean I would have to turn back and be forced to take the road, making me feel like I wasn't keeping true to my word. On occasion, I'd just go for it. More often than not, I'd get away with it, but on a few occasions, I did have a run-in with a farmer, and I would always just play dumb and pretend that I hadn't realized I was trespassing.

I was licked when I arrived in Lancaster. I got there in the evening and needed a rest to plan my next move and find a place to camp. I made my way to a little bar to charge my phone for an hour and got myself a cordial. After a quick chat with some locals expressing my concern about finding a place to camp that would be out of sight and out of mind, one of the fellas had a banging suggestion. 'Dude, there's a church just over there, next to the school. Surely they wouldn't just turn you away.'

'Not a bad shout at all,' I said, and made my way over

and found a spot in the back of the graveyard to pitch up. I'm in no way a religious man, but couldn't help paying my respects to the dead, telling them I meant no harm and thanking them for having me!

After Lancaster, I headed into Carnforth and the beginning of the Lake District. It was amazing to see the mountains in front of me, as for the last month the coastline had been particularly flat. Autumn brought a change in the weather; the mornings started to get frost on the ground and the nights were closing in faster and becoming much colder. It rained a lot, but I was starting to have some early winter cold yet sunny days, which were great for walking.

Often, I'd just lie in my sleeping bag on the shorefront and hope that it didn't rain, use the occasional bus stop and, for the first time, out of desperation and just needing some sleep, I camped in the middle of a massive roundabout that had a small plantation of trees smack bang in the centre. It was so obvious; it would be the last place anyone would find me. I just hoped that some alcohol-fuelled driver didn't fly straight over the centre of the roundabout in the middle of the night!

8

Scafell Pike

In order to raise more money for SSAFA, I decided that I would walk through the centre of the Lake District climbing as many of its peaks as I could, ending with Scafell Pike. Climbing on your own comes with a certain anxiety in wild places. There is no room for error if anything goes wrong, nobody but you to make a call to the emergency services, and it's an incredibly vulnerable feeling. I plotted a route on the map through the centre of the Lake District that would bring me back to the coast into a place called Ravenglass. From there I would get the train back down south of the Lakes where I left off just before Grange-over-Sands. The route I plotted meant I could climb ten mountains on the way, aiming to raise £100 for every peak that I climbed, with every intention, November weather permitting, of camping at the summit of each. Also, this would mean that I would end up in the beautiful valley

79

of Wasdale, where England's highest mountain, Scafell Pike, is situated. This meant I could climb the highest peak in a second country, knocking off another mountain in the famous Three Peaks Challenge, leaving only Ben Nevis in the Scottish Highlands.

During my time in the Paras, I had become an accomplished map reader, spending years perfecting the art of navigation. If you're not clued up on how to read an OS map and adept with a compass, you shouldn't even be there. Many have made this mistake and not lived to tell the tale. Nature is beautiful but brutal. It doesn't care about us and gives nobody a second chance. It simply must be respected.

I climbed my first peak on day one in the Lake District and, after descending, I immediately made my way to the second mountain, called Sergeant Man. At 2,415 feet high, it was a four-hour hike up and down. I felt strong and full of energy after a few days' rest and a good feed. I made my way up, even stopping at a beautiful little waterfall with a shallow pool at the bottom for a rest. I stripped off to have a bath and take in the amazing scenery around me. After, I soon reached the summit, only to see on the opposite side of the mountain a weather front coming my way. Experience had taught me that I only had a few minutes to find a safe spot to take refuge. Knowing the wind direction, I hid behind a big rock to avoid the oncoming mist and strong winds, made worse by the fact that I was so high up. A human's natural instinct would be to try and get down as soon as possible to avoid it, but this is a big no-no and the reason so many who are unprepared lose their lives in the mountains. Thankfully, I had food, a tent, and knew how to get out of the winds to avoid the tent being smashed up. In no time, the top of the mountain was engulfed in what is called a whiteout: a thick mist where you're unable to see an arm's length in front of you, which is incredibly dangerous to keep walking in, exacerbated by some big winds. Normally, people climb in pairs or groups. Being alone brings a whole new fear factor to the situation. It's quite frightening being alone on a summit in a whiteout. I spent three hours crouched behind a rock while nature's wrath did its thing. After three hours, there was a break in the clouds and a drop in the winds and mist. I figured I had around fifteen minutes to retrace my steps and find the path that I had come up on to make my escape. I didn't run in case I tripped and got injured, but walked briskly, getting as far down as quickly as I could. Fortunately, I was facing west and, as I descended, I was kept out of harm's way from the easterly winds and mist. In no time, I made it to the bottom gasping a sigh of relief. I kept walking a few more miles, often looking back at the forbidding mountain with a cheeky grin, knowing I'd done exactly what I should have. I was growing in confidence all the time and, boy, would I need this over the coming years.

Over the next few days, I climbed and descended the peaks edging nearer to Scafell, my final summit in the Lake District. It took me about three and a half to four hours to climb England's largest peak, on 8 November. Having scaled a smaller yet harder peak in the morning before doing Scafell, it was becoming evident that the amount of walking I'd done up to this point was really paying off, as in no way did I struggle going up. Even after my descent, I still felt like I had plenty more in the tank.

Scotland was edging closer by the day, and I knew that its rugged terrain would be my biggest challenge of all, mentally and physically. The next day I woke and took an early train back to where I left off, just shy of Grange-over-Sands. As soon as I got disembarked, I did the nine-mile stretch, eventually arriving in the beautiful little town. My phone was out of battery, and I noticed a Victorian pub and hotel popular with climbers called the Commodore Inn. It was right on the coast and I popped in to ask if I could charge my phone and, as usual, buy the cheapest drink – a cordial. The staff were amazing. I quickly became friendly with them and told them what I was up to. Lesley Flynn, a slim, vivacious lady in her early fifties, had moved to the town thirty-odd years ago, met her now-husband and had decided to stay for good. They were a lovely couple and we are still friends to this day. They offered me a room for the night before heading off the next morning. I really loved it there.

Lesley mentioned a friendly homeless guy who often slept in a little shelter on the promenade, and I decided to go and visit him. When I arrived, a well-spoken, gaunt-faced but otherwise healthy-looking man greeted me. He had his roll-mat out and was sitting minding his own business with a guitar leaning against his side.

'Fella, do you mind if I come and join you for a bit?' I asked.

'Of course, I'd be grateful for your company,' he replied.

I took a seat on the bench inside what I can only describe as a coastal bus stop, but with no buses. We got on well and really opened up to each other, and soon enough he was telling me about his children whom he no longer saw. This was not because he didn't want to, and I could tell by the way that he was telling me about it that this had broken him. He told me that he had been on the run from the police and admitted he had done something silly, but it wasn't domestic violence or any kind of abuse. I believed him wholeheartedly. He had split from his partner a year ago and, in doing so, had ended up on the streets. Out of desperation – and I can relate to this – he'd simply needed to eat. He stole from a shop and got caught. When the police came, he did a runner. I could see how he had built a picture up of himself as worthless or irredeemable.

'Dude, this is breaking you – I can see it. Please think about this . . . sometimes it's good to hear it from another person's perspective, and I mean this with the best of intentions and absolutely no insult . . . You're telling me that in your mind you don't believe you deserve to see your children because you stole a fucking chicken and mushroom pie?

'You are not a bad person because you stole. Desperate people do desperate things. Being homeless and needing to eat is not a crime. The worst that's going to happen to you is that you will get some time in jail, more because you ran away from the police and resisted arrest. If anything, for however long you have to do time for, you get food and your own room, even if it is a cell!'

We both chuckled. I could see that he was tearing up and gave him a huge man-hug.

'Look, I'm gonna go now, and I'm chuffed that I finally met somebody who smells worse than me,' I said. We both laughed and said our goodbyes.

As I was walking away, I turned around and said, more seriously, 'Jay, go hand yourself in, pal. They won't bite. In a few months, after showing your ex that you want to turn everything around, you could be sitting here with your kids. Think about it. Goodnight, pal.' And with that, I walked back to my tent, which was pitched at the edge of town.

The next morning Lesley appeared holding a guitar in front of me.

'What the hell is this?' I said as she passed it over. I turned it around to find a message engraved in the back of it:

Thanks for the advice, Chris – off to jail. I leave this for you, Jay.

I couldn't believe it. Lesley and I both looked at each other and smiled as tears crept down my cheeks. I found out a few months later that he had done only a tiny stint in jail and was released ready to go out and get his kids back. I don't write things like this to say, 'Look at me and what I've done.' There's a selfish side to it; doing something nice and lending an ear can really make a difference. I know this from experience. It makes me feel great doing simple little acts similar to those that I had been the recipient of in the past. It felt good being able to pay that forward.

Almost all my time in the Lake District was spent getting wet. In fact, barely a soul seemed to venture outdoors, so I spoke to very few people. That being said, I really enjoyed my own company and the space that it gave me to think about my life and what was coming next. I can't remember

Week one, day one. With my mother Sam and stepfather Dave, plus
Chris Carree and his parents Dave and Liz. I can't tell you how awful
I felt this day! But every adventure has to start somewhere.

Just before starting my challenge, I looked so gaunt
and stressed. I truly believe the walk saved my life.

On the edge of big coastal towns or cities I would search long and hard for a safe spot to bivvy up. I'd leave the tent in my bag so as not to attract any unwanted attention, going to bed at last light and waking up at the crack of dawn.

I'm not sure I ever want to see a tin of tuna again after this walk! Burning so many calories each day meant eating anything I could that gave me nutrition. Here we have a classic dinner of frozen butter, tuna and ready-made mash.

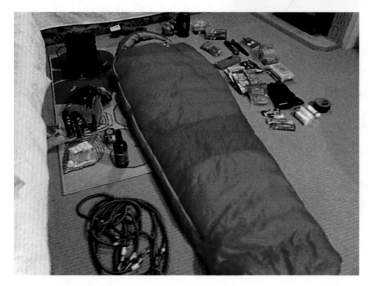

A new lease of life thanks to Kevin Farrington. People really are so kind.

Jet and I have slept in the most unusual places. I made the mistake of building a fire in here. The smoke flushed out hundreds of spiders in the evening that fell directly on top of us.

Working our way around the west coast of Jura was a real highlight of my walk. Nothing but wilderness, beautiful views and a few thousand deer to share it with!

The last of our Three Peaks Challenge: Ben Nevis, Scotland's highest mountain.

Looking over at Glenbrittle on the Isle of Skye. We had about eight days left of gruelling yet incredible terrain to get through until we finished it.

Above: Traversing mountains around the coastline was no easy task. Jet was at home in these places, sniffing out deer tracks and forging a path through. Memories of those days will stay with me forever.

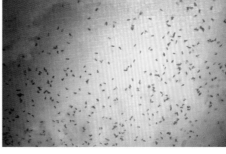

The Scottish midges – and these are just the ones I killed!

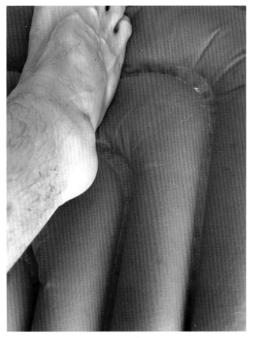

You really get a feel for who you are as a person when things go wrong in places you really don't want them to. I remember thinking: anything but my ankle! It's amazing what one can achieve by remaining calm and focused.

Taken from the bothy on the remote Isle of Rum in the Inner Hebrides.
Running through the mountains was the river that Jet and I had to
cross after being stranded for days.

Christmas Day 2018 on the uninhabited island of Little Bernera,
off the west coast of Lewis. Tim, Kath and their son Josh turned up
armed with a Christmas dinner and plenty of good whisky!

Navigating the beautiful west coast Scottish sea lochs. In my eyes they are some of the most, if not *the* most, stunning spots in the UK.

After a gruelling day of heavy hail and monumental winds, this bus provided the perfect shelter. Notice the broken back window where I had to throw Jet through and climb in after.

The east side of the Isle of Lewis. On cold winter nights with clear skies, the stars dominated the sky like I have never seen before. I cried from pure euphoria at such a spectacular sight.

I would sit for hours just mesmerized by the sight of a winter sky on the Outer Islands. It was my television, and the sound of the birds my radio.

any other time I'd been so soaked both day and night. Even with my sleeping bag and dry kit inside a waterproof bag inside my bergen, overnight the gear became more and more damp and eventually unbearably wet. It rained so hard at times that, at night, the water level exceeded what my tent was able to handle. It was awful. I remember doing a video and posting it on my page one evening when I was walking through fields in the middle of a valley with water so deep that it reached above my knees. The runoffs – the ditches dug by farmers – had completely flooded over.

I knew that I had to get higher up, so I waded through the water to a small bridge crossing over the river at the end of the estuary. It was impossible to camp, so I had to keep moving. I had my head torch on and stopped in the middle of the bridge to look at the raging, swollen river. It was scary. I found a road and followed it up the hill for about three miles. I couldn't even get my phone out to check the maps. Shivering, I huddled under a tree and took out my waterproof OS map.

Eventually, I spotted a small wooden shelter which had some hay inside and just enough space for my tent. Now, out of the rain and desperate to get my clothes off, I stripped naked and hung them up to drip-dry over a beam that was holding up the roof. It was pitch-black, but I did have my head torch on. Naked as can be, I started erecting my tent as quickly as I could, but as I put in a peg to hold my tent down, my torch beam picked out a tiny pair of red eyes inside a small hole in the corner of the shelter. I slowly walked towards it and, in doing so, noticed a further eight holes in the ground all around where I'd pitched. On the floor in a corner where the straw had been moved aside, I also noted a load of droppings. *Rats!* I thought. *Bollocks!* I used straw and waterproof bags to stuff the holes as best I could while I made my food. Still naked, I went out into the rain and left my cooking pot in the middle of a puddle. Rats hate water, and I wanted no food around me giving them an open invite. I pretended they weren't there and climbed into my sleeping bag to get some shut-eye.

9

Borderlands

I'd made it past Barrow-in-Furness, and for the first time I now had Scotland in my sights. It was the middle of November, and it was becoming noticeably colder. The winter was really closing in, and I was getting cold at night now, too. It worried me, knowing I'd soon be in Scotland in the worst of the winter weather, dressed like a complete amateur. The gear I had – charity shop clothes and a sleeping bag only suitable for the height of summer – was no match for winter weather only thirty-five miles from the border.

Often in the mornings there was a cold, hard frost on the ground, which meant that once I'd drunk my coffee and packed up my gear, getting the tent pegs out of the ground was a real mission. I didn't have any gloves, so I'd pull out a frozen tent peg with my bare hands and then run around the tent, my hands under my armpits in agony, clenching my teeth and grimacing as I collected the rest. Once the cold gets you, you're done for – the pain is horrific. It was the worst part of my day and I hated it with a passion.

I was becoming a good camper and my skill had improved tenfold living outside, but my gear didn't reflect my abilities in the slightest. Not far from a town called Workington, about thirty miles from the Scottish border, the weather took a turn for the worse and a huge storm hit. The landscape was flat and completely exposed to the elements. That evening, with no protection, I took a massive beating. My North Face tent that had been gifted to me by Wayne back in Preston was completely destroyed – and my soul along with it. It was the only half-decent bit of kit I had. At around 4 a.m., the storm died off and I crawled out of my tent, which by now was nothing more than a flimsy blanket lying over the top of me, and saw four different breaks in the poles, one of which had pierced through the outer skin of the tent. I had stayed up all night in case I had to bail with my kit packed, ready to move if need be, and Workington was still a good distance away. I emptied the last four sachets of my porridge into my cooking pot to give me the energy to get there in one push, and then I left at around 5.30 a.m.

I found the going a bit boring to be honest, because the landscape that day was so flat and unremarkable. I was also soul-destroyed that my tent was ruined and anxious as to where I would sleep that night. I arrived in Workington later that evening, knackered. By this time, my donations and following had both gone up, not by much, but I now had about £3,000 in the kitty and about 2,500 followers.

I was satisfied that at least it was going in the right direction – as was I. Getting to Workington was a game-changer, because I met a great guy called Kevin Farrington, who had been following my journey and awaited my arrival. He owned a recycling centre, which he gave me a tour of. I really admired the success that he had made of it and the work ethic it had clearly taken to get him this far. He'd obviously done very well for himself and was incredibly humble with it.

He asked me if I would like to go into the local town with him and his father, Tony. We parked up in a beautiful little town and headed straight for the pub where Tony got a round in. We had a great laugh, but as we were just about to finish our pints, Kevin, with a more serious tone of voice now, said, 'Chris, I so admire that you're doing all of this with absolutely no funds, but your gear, given the size of the expedition you have undertaken, is, quite frankly, awful. I looked through your page and noticed that you have no "Go Fund Me" button or that "Buy Me a Coffee" thing people use; so many charity fundraisers do, even when they have plenty of their own money. It's amazing that you've got this far, but I will say – you look like shit!' We all laughed and I agreed.

I gave him my usual speech about finding it hard to accept anything from others, and Tony shook my hand and said, 'Good for you, lad! Chris, the reason I have asked you to come here today is because I really want you to let me help you get kitted out. You're about to enter Scotland in the height of winter and if anything were to happen to you, knowing that I could have done something to help, I would never forgive myself. And, of course, I just want to help.'

After a big hug, I agreed to accept his help. We walked to the local camping shop – none of this 'Go Outdoors' for summer campers nonsense, but a proper shop in the Lake District. Kevin immediately walked over to where the sleeping bags were hung up and called me over. 'Chris, I want you to choose whatever you want from here. Don't look at the price; just get something that will keep you warm.' I couldn't believe it. While I looked, I checked the prices on the sly and picked the cheapest one I could find – which was still a massive improvement on the hanky that I'd been using.

'This will do!' I said.

Kevin had a feel of it and in a stern northern voice said, 'No chance, fella, it's not gonna be me that's gonna be freezing my arse off in a tent up in Scotland. Just choose what you bloody need.'

Around forty minutes later, we left the shop with me as happy as a man can be, the proud new owner of stainless steel pots to cook in, a £300 Rab sleeping bag, a £250 pair of Meindl walking boots, six cans of gas for my stove, my first pair of gloves and some new socks, as well as a Jetboil stove. To say I was chuffed is too weak a phrase – I would literally have kissed his bare *arse* if he'd asked me to! I couldn't wait to make use of it all, especially the sleeping bag and the Meindl boots. For the first time on this walk, I had some genuinely decent kit, and was beginning to feel more like an adventurer rather than a homeless man walking the UK coast.

I remember my penultimate night in England looking over the estuary at Scotland. For the first time, I decided to get my phone out and check ViewRanger (the app that

I had recently started using for my map) to see what all the fuss about Scotland's coastline was. If I was navigating a mountain range, I would always use a detailed Ordnance Survey map, but for just scuttling along the coast I knew it was hard to get lost so long as the sea was always on my left.

I zoomed out on ViewRanger and looked at Scotland's west coast. *Holy shit!* The amount of lochs, ups, downs and sideways I had in front of me was unreal. Not only that, but on closer inspection, it was incredibly impressive and daunting to see how much of Scotland's west coast is completely wild once you hit the Highlands. I found myself staring at the coast in front of me with a glint in my eye, thinking, *Bring it on, Scotland. I'm ready for you!*

The closer I got to Scotland, the more I'd hear from locals about the different laws with regards to camping. There, I would have the 'right to roam'. Essentially, this meant I'd be able to pitch my tent pretty much anywhere so long as I was respectful to locals and the environment around me. I found it hard to believe that I'd go from a situation where I'd spend so much time in the evening searching for a camp spot to keep away from trouble and not be seen, to suddenly being able to pitch the second I got tired without having this worry. I couldn't wait for the chance to see if this 'right to roam' was real.

On 6 December 2017, my last day in England, I woke up tucked into a small cove only metres from the high tide in just my sleeping bag. It was working an absolute treat – I was so happy with it, so even though I was still without a tent, I was warm enough at night. I headed slightly inland to Carlisle in the hope that I could try and get my poles taped up at the very least, and going straight to the nearest camping shop and explaining my case. The staff were amazing and helped me to patch up my poles with masking tape that we wrapped around all the parts that had split. In the afternoon, with only around six miles before I'd reach the border into Gretna, excited, I smashed the miles out in no time. This was a huge milestone. I sat on my bag on the border in disbelief that I'd made it into Scotland.

That night, I thought I would put the 'right to roam' law to the test, eager to see if this was for real. God, it would make my life 100 per cent easier if it were true. I pitched up about a hundred yards from the pub in a place where I could easily be seen. I made my food and settled in for the night. The following morning, I woke to a lady outside the tent.

'Hello? Is anybody in there?' came the voice. I stayed still for a minute.

Shit! I thought to myself, realizing that what I'd been told was a load of crap. I sat up and took a deep breath, my eyes still half closed. *Here we go*, I thought. I unzipped the tent, already halfway through explaining myself, expecting a grilling from a local about camping here. I stuck my head out to find a mother and her young child standing there, holding a small bag.

'We saw you pitch up last night and were really worried for you,' she said. 'It went down to about minus two last night – you must've been freezing. We're sorry for disturbing you while you slept but we wanted to bring you a couple of bacon rolls we've just made with a nice hot coffee.'

I was like a rabbit in the headlights – totally stunned. I couldn't thank them enough for such a kind gesture.

'Also, if you need a shower, we live just over there,' she said, pointing to her house. 'You are most welcome.'

I got out of the tent and thanked them and they walked away. I sat eating my rolls, delighted that I didn't have to boil water and go through the same process that I'd had to do every single morning. *So it* was *true*, I thought. This would be one of the many reasons I would soon fall head over heels for Scotland. The Scottish adventure that lay ahead would change everything, and I'd learn more about myself in these next few years than I had in my entire life. Although I didn't know it at the time, this is where the adventure truly began.

10

The wisdom of beards

The first morning I woke in Scotland was a sobering, eerie experience. Before me was a frozen shoreline, the ice darkened by seaweed beneath. The next stage, and my initial section of Scotland, would take me some 125 miles west to the Mull of Galloway, before heading north once more and passing through Annan, Dumfries, Dalbeattie, Kirkcudbright and Gatehouse of Fleet.

The weather was definitely on the turn, becoming increasingly colder all the time. Getting up and out of the tent each morning was a real effort, pulling my pegs out of the frozen ground became my worst part of the day and for the first time in my life, I would see sections of the shoreline's seawater icing over. If I woke up and it was raining, I would consider that a bonus, as low cloud cover traps the earth's heat, making it much warmer. Without clouds, heat escapes into the earth's atmosphere, the temperature drops and up north it can be nothing short of brutal if you're in a tent.

Each day, I'd take every opportunity to air out my gear. A few days before arriving in Gatehouse of Fleet, however, I made a terrible mistake – one I would learn from very quickly. It was a beautiful cold, crisp, windy day and the sun was shining, so I decided to stop for some grub and air my kit out, mainly my sleeping bag. Once I'd hung it on a fence post, the wind filled it like a wind sock, so I put some noodles on and sat down to chill out while it dried. Around half an hour later, I turned to check all was okay with my gear and noticed my sleeping bag had dropped down towards the floor. The wind was still as strong; I couldn't quite understand it. I went to investigate and when I got closer, I found the thing was near soaked through, inside and out. While I was struggling to process how this had happened, there was no question of what it meant. With no way to dry it out and the temperatures set to plummet into the minuses that evening, I was in a really bad position.

I put my gear back in my bag and sat facing the wind, my fingers running through my beard in contemplation mode, thinking, *What am I going to do?* Then I noticed my beard hair was damp. Suddenly, it clicked – the hair was picking up tiny particles of moisture invisible to the naked eye. I stared down more intensely to see if I could see them, but I couldn't. I knew the damp was there though; my beard was the clear indicator. That evening, I had the worst night of my entire walk to date. It was so cold, and since my sleeping bag and kit were now damp and unusable, my only option was to stay up and forage as much firewood as possible so I could sit the entire night next to some kind of warmth.

Sadly, there was nowhere near enough driftwood here, and no trees. I had gathered enough wood to last around two hours, so I deliberately didn't get the fire going until the coldest part of the night – actually the early hours of the morning – as that's when I knew I would need it the most. When the fire wasn't alight, I ran around in circles, shaking my hands and jumping up and down – anything just to generate some body heat. It would have been too dangerous to have walked in the dark, which left me with no choice but to wait until light to get going again.

My hands and feet were unbearable – I couldn't have undone a zip if I tried. The whole thing was horrific and I promised I would never let this happen again. Every time from this point on when it came to drying out my kit, I would stand and look up or turn and face the wind for a good few minutes and afterwards run my fingers through my beard. If my beard was dry, then I knew it was all good to hang up my gear. If there was the slightest bit of damp in it, it was a no-go. I would use this system all the way around and it never failed me. It was a lesson I'd learned the hard way, but I'd learned a fantastic survival skill.

The next night, before I arrived in Gatehouse of Fleet, I found a lovely secluded spot on the shore where I noticed wood lying around the rocks in abundance. I cut my day short and got to work, eventually grabbing a huge pile of fallen wood and driftwood. It took me a while to get it going as it was so damp, but I had the perfect wind on my side to help start it and soon enough got it blazing. I hunted around for a piece of rope, as you often find on the seashore, to improvise a makeshift washing line, and used my walking poles as a stake to put in the ground. I eventually found some washed-up blue rope and unravelled it to the perfect length to hang my wet sleeping gear over. I tied the rope to each pole, near enough to the fire but far enough away so as not to burn, making sure it was upwind to keep it away from the smoke. Sadly, it would not be enough for my sleeping bag. It was too far gone; only a tumble dryer would sort that one out, but at least soon enough my clothes would be dry and I could put them on before the cold of the night encroached. I stripped naked and dried out what I was wearing just to make sure I could cover myself in every layer of clothing that I had. It worked a treat.

Again, the evening was bitterly cold, but the experience was a far cry from the night before. I stayed in the same spot all night keeping the fire going and warming up my bones, huddled around the flames in just my bivvy bag. I put a huge pile of wood next to me and went to sleep. I would only wake when I became too cold, meaning the fire was starting to die out, but with plenty of embers still on the floor, I'd grab a heap of wood, throw it on and, minutes later, the fire would be re-energized. I repeated this process probably once every hour, all night. After I threw a fresh lot of wood on the fire, I'd lie back and stare up at the stars reflecting on how beautiful they were. I remember thinking to myself, *This is exactly what I set out on this journey for*. It was just me, nature, the skills that I had learned so far and a chance to get away from the intense speed and clutter of modern-day Western life. I loved it. Best of all, the comfort of knowing that I couldn't be moved on or told off for being here was pure bliss. I think this was my first night on the walk that I felt totally safe and free. From now on, every opportunity that I had, I would leave the tent, build a fire and just bivvy up around it.

I arrived in Gatehouse of Fleet the next day, determined to find someone I could ask to use their tumble dryer for my sleeping bag. It was an absolute must; I simply couldn't move forward without it. Desperate, I banged on a random door. An elderly lady, probably in her seventies, who I remember having the most amazing smile, greeted me with open arms.

'Of course you can use my dryer!' Elda said with the most wonderfully strong Scottish accent. 'And would you like to come in for a cup of tea?'

I gladly accepted the offer. While my sleeping bag regained some health in the dryer, we chatted away, swapping stories and having a great time. After I'd had around four cups of tea and had a belly full of McVitie's biscuits, my sleeping bag was ready. I packed up and we said our goodbyes.

On New Year's Eve, I arrived at a small village called Creetown. After being welcomed into a pub, I listened to somebody playing the bagpipes for the very first time. Melancholic and soulful, their notes touched a deep nerve within me as the room fell quiet with pride and rapt attention. I should've known I was going to fall in love with Scotland.

Over the next five days, I passed through Newton Stewart, Wigtown, and the Isle of Whithorn, eventually reaching the Mull of Galloway. The weather had changed again; the rain had stopped and although it was absolutely freezing, I had some beautifully crisp winter days. As I packed up my things to start walking the Mull of Galloway, a retired sergeant major called Kenny Patterson drove up in his van, introduced himself and asked if he could walk with me for a few days. We did the entire stretch together, sticking rigidly to the coast, constantly jumping electric and barbed-wire fences.

Kenny had two dogs – Cole and Toby. They were such beautiful mutts, and I adored them. Sadly, the cows in the fields didn't feel the same way and we would often find ourselves running as fast as we could to the nearest hedgerow or fence line to avoid curious herds. In the UK, cows kill more humans than any other animal does, usually during spring in calving season. They are incredibly protective and sometimes some unfortunate dog walker will get stamped all over. It was genuinely quite a frightening experience and one I would have to cope with all the way around the UK through spring and summer.

We made our way down from the hills to a rocky shore that backed onto a farmer's field in order to avoid the cows. Sadly, the way the currents flow in these parts meant that it had become a collection point for rubbish from Northern Ireland. We couldn't see for washed-up fishing nets and all manner of plastic. There were even wheelie bins that had been brought over by sea from Newtownards near Belfast. This particular stretch of coast is not somewhere anyone would walk, seeing as it backed onto a farmer's field and was miles from a road, so the rubbish is just allowed to accumulate. To this day, it is by far the worst example of sea pollution I've ever seen. As we walked along the beach, discussing how bad it was, Kenny's dog Toby came over to us with a plastic bottle in his mouth. To our disbelief, it contained a message.

As soon as I opened it, I was bowled over by the awful smell of fish from the ink on the paper that had been trapped inside the bottle. The letter read:

Hello Bottle Finder,

My name is Brian Sullivan. I am thirteen years old. I am from Northern Ireland and I have a brother, Kyle. He is ten. I have a sister, Lindsey. She is seventeen. I have lots of hobbies which include football, reading, birdwatching and I'm also into rave and pop music. Me and my friends go to the local rave disco once a month. We have a good craic there and we meet lots of new people. My favourite football team is Manchester United. I have a pet dog. She is a German Shepherd and her name is Trixie. This is not my first message in a bottle, as I call it. Are you a boy or a girl? What age are you? Where are you from? I'm very curious about your hobbies and interests. If you decide to write back, I will be very happy to hear from you. One thing that I have not mentioned is that I am part of the RSPB. I have ten mates – Gilly, Daniel, Roger, Si, Peter, Tom, Smithy, Paddy, Gilesy and Ant.

I hope you write back,
Your friend,
Brian
This is my address . . .
Goodbye for now.

The note was dated and we quickly worked out that the message was twenty-five years old. I felt a deep urge to find the now thirty-eight-year-old Brian to return his letter and jokingly tell him off for throwing litter into the sea! I actually wasn't far away from where I could catch the ferry over to Northern Ireland.

11

Troubles

I have a history with Northern Ireland. Not only did I serve there with the Paras, but I also lived there on a few occasions. Northern Ireland also gave me my first child, who is half Northern Irish.

My first time in the province was in 1998, on my first tour at the age of eighteen in east Tyrone; a place called Dungannon. Still very young and relatively politically unaware, for me it had felt like entering a different world. It was incredibly strange, as it's only a stone's throw away from the peaceful west coast of Scotland. Northern Ireland has had its problems for decades. To put it in a nutshell, at the time I arrived, it had been in a political and civil war since the late 1960s, divided into Unionists and Nationalists (Protestants and Catholics). The Unionists wanted Northern Ireland to remain as it is and continue being part of the United Kingdom. The Nationalists wished to see Northern Ireland unified with the Republic of Ireland, otherwise known as Southern Ireland.

For decades, there have been riots, bombings, murders . . . you name it. The Republican activists commonly known as the Provisional IRA (PIRA) each year would fight the Unionist groups such as the UVF (Ulster Voluntary Force), the UDA (Ulster Defence Association) and the UDR (Ulster Defence Regiment) in a brutal fashion.

I remember my first riot on Limestone Road in Belfast very well. Not knowing what to expect, I admit, I was slightly nervous as we arrived and the back doors of our armour-plated vehicle (a Snatch) opened, and all I could see was carnage. It immediately became apparent that the army and the police (at the time called the RUC – Royal Ulster Constabulary, now the PSNI – Police Service of Northern Ireland) were smack bang in the middle of it all trying to keep the peace between the two fighting sides.

All of us, armed with massive body-length shields, a hand baton and our rifles (SA80s), would separate the two sides and stand right in the middle of them while they threw bricks, petrol bombs, any solid tools and the occasional pipe-bomb. It was unreal to see it first hand, and the rioters on both sides were so young. It was clear to see the violence and hatred were real, with burning cars being sent down the streets in our direction. Very early on, I had a gut feeling that neither the Catholics nor the Protestants wanted us to be there, as we often got a battering from behind and in front, but we did our bit and whether it was the riots or just standard patrols, we would arrive back to camp during the early hours of the morning, highly strung and full of so much adrenalin it was almost impossible to sleep.

It was on this tour that I met my now ex-wife, and soon enough Caitlin was brought into the world. I was very young and very naive when it came to women, and Jo was my first ever girlfriend. By the age of twenty, I found myself married and a stepdad to three children, as well as a biological father to our newborn, Caitlin. I think it's safe to say I'd dived far too deep, far too soon into a relationship that would inevitably start seeing cracks very early on. If I'm honest, it was never going to last.

Around 2001, the Paras upped sticks and moved from our base in Aldershot up to Colchester in Essex to form a group called the 16 Air Assault Brigade. By this time, I was a PTI (Physical Training Instructor). I was incredibly proud of this and knew that I was doing my bit to train and keep fit one of the fittest, toughest, most disciplined regiments in the world. I worked alongside some top lads: Chris Coney, Dan Field, Sandy Geddis and Daz Liney, to name but a few. Daz, in particular, is probably one of the hardest men I've ever met in my life – he had a face like Mike Tyson and the build to back it up! To this day, one of my proudest achievements is beating Daz in a pull-up competition!

Sadly, after just a few tours, my time with the Paras would soon come to an end.

Jo, my ex-wife, had a hard time after giving birth to Caitlin. She had asked me to apply for what is called a compassionate posting, which would mean me leaving Colchester and heading back to Northern Ireland. Her mother and father lived there, and they would be able to help with the kids while I was working. I was so incredibly torn; I'd worked so long and hard to earn this incredible cap badge and the thought of having to leave my beloved regiment (2 Para) and being thrust into a new regiment that I knew nothing about, nor anyone in it, made my blood boil. However, if Jo was going, taking Caitlin and my three step-children with her, I had no choice; I simply had to go.

Before I knew it, I was back in Northern Ireland in a place called Palace Barracks in Holywood, attached to the Argyle and Southern Highlanders Regiment, who at the time were on tour here. I became a member of their gym staff. I loved working with the Scots and took to them straight away. They were a great bunch, and I loved their sense of humour, but I had a real feeling that the CO (Commanding Officer) was not my biggest fan.

About six months into the tour, things had come to a head between Jo and myself. Caitlin was only one when we eventually split. I was immediately moved into the single men's accommodation, while Jo stayed inside the house we'd lived in inside the camp for a few more months, giving her enough time to find herself and the children somewhere to live. Sadly, the split would not be a clean one. To this day, I'll never know why, but I was stopped from going to the house inside the barracks to see Caitlin. This was made clear by the Families Officer. I was mortified, as I had done absolutely nothing wrong, apart from the fact that it had been my decision to break up.

Around three weeks after we'd split, I still felt so hurt at not being allowed to see Caitlin and the fact that I'd had no say in the matter whatsoever. I was unable to take it and decided the Families Officers could all go and stick it. They were all sitting at home with their kids every evening; it was all right for them. *She's my daughter and they can all fuck off*, I thought.

I walked up to the house just to try and talk to Jo to see if we could work things out peacefully. To my horror, the house was empty; they'd gone! Jo's phone number had also been changed. I now had absolutely no idea where they had moved to or how to contact them. I sat in my room the entire night just staring at the wall, completely numb.

To make matters even worse, that week I was called up to the CO's office, escorted by the Company Sergeant, regarding some complaints that had been made against me. I marched into the office, stamped my foot and gave a salute.

'Lance Corporal Lewis,' said the commanding officer, 'we've been receiving calls and letters saying that you have been harassing your wife and family. We are on tour in Northern Ireland and I have enough on my plate without having to deal or put up with your personal life.'

If I'm honest, the man had a very valid point, except for the fact that the accusations were all wrong.

'Sir,' I answered, 'I have no telephone numbers or any knowledge of the whereabouts of my daughter, my wife or her other children. It's simply impossible for me to have done what's been said – I can't harass people if I have no idea of their whereabouts. The telephone numbers have been changed.'

With a brief pause, the CO looked at me and clearly saw how distressed I was by the whole situation. My eyes were watering, and I felt a mixture of sheer sadness and pure rage that this was happening to me.

'Lance Corporal Lewis, I'm afraid to say that if this continues and we receive any more complaints about you, we're going to send you back to Colchester, back to your regiment. I do feel for your situation, but maybe you should lean on your regiment to help you through it.'

By this point, both of my fists were clenched and I was fucking angry. In a stern and sombre voice, I said, 'Sir, all I want to do is see my daughter. Ever since I realized they were gone, I've been driving down to Bangor where my wife lived before, at every opportunity, in the hope that I might see her or one of my step-children, so I can somehow find out their address in order to start court proceedings to gain legal access to my daughter. I cannot control letters or phone calls that come your way and beg you to just ignore it or rise above it.'

'I feel for you, Lewis, I really do, but I meant what I said,' he replied.

By this point, I was livid, and my best option was just to leave the office. I cut him short and saluted him, did my about-turn and walked out. I felt so unsupported and on my own with this injustice, it was unreal. The sergeant who escorted me to the CO's office was standing outside and had heard everything. He asked if I was okay and if I needed the afternoon off.

'Fuck this,' I said. 'I'm leaving the army.'

I was very fortunate that it was just the right time for me to decide whether I would continue my career in the Forces or simply leave. I walked down to the office of my good friend, Corporal Mark Menhennit. I signed off there and then, meaning that in one year, after serving out my notice, I'd be out of the army. My one hope was that in that year, I didn't get sent back to Colchester and lose my chance to fight for the rights to see my daughter and also say my farewells to Jo's other children, whom I adored.

I continued to go to Bangor every day that I was off, or after work in the evenings, in the hope that I'd see Jo or any of the children. About three months in, I hit the jackpot. Out of pure luck, as I was walking down a road in Bangor, I saw one of her children walk out of a front door. I now had an address. I got in touch with a solicitor immediately and started formal proceedings to gain access to my daughter, which I succeeded in doing. Twice a week, I'd pick Caitlin up and bring her back to camp where she would spend the evening with me. I absolutely loved it; I had missed her so much.

Soon enough, my seven years in the army would be over. I decided to do a resettlement course – a course that is offered to anyone who has served over a certain number of years in a chosen field of interest to help them get work once they leave the army and re-enter civvy street. I decided to do a close protection course to become a bodyguard for the rich and famous. If I'm brutally honest, I really didn't think this through. After I finished the training, I was offered a number of jobs, some extremely well-paid, but which involved me being out of the country for long periods of time. I wasn't prepared to leave Caitlin, however.

Instead, I took on a flat outside the small seaside town of Bangor and did every job I could to bring in some money. I worked on building sites and also got a job as a private investigator, which involved travelling to all different parts

of Northern Ireland, doing everything from following teenagers whose parents believed they were taking drugs, to
women who were believed to be having affairs.

As much as I didn't particularly enjoy following people
around, especially teenagers, I found the whole thing hilarious and a real insight into how desperate people can be
to satisfy their suspicions – and how much money they
would pay to do it. I would often joke to myself that for
all they knew I could be sitting in a car park catching some
zzzs and making it all up with a simple phone call after a
good night's kip in the car; 'Yes, ma'am, your child is a
drug dealer!' Fortunately for them, I was very professional
and even bought myself a pair of James Bond-style shades
to look the part.

Two friends of mine had also recently left the army. Phil
and Jamie – Northern Irish and Scottish respectively – were
both boxers and invited me to the local boxing club in
Bangor, knowing how much I loved to train. I was a very
well-built guy and fitness had always been my life. I would
go down to the boxing gym to train and spar with other
fighters, soon enough earning myself a bit of kudos among
the lads as well as the owner of the club, Sonny Dice.
Sonny had only one leg. From what I'd heard he had been
blown up in a car bomb for reasons still unknown to me,
but one thing I did know was that in the club and around
Bangor, he was a well-respected man. Sonny also ran the
doors in Bangor in all the clubs and bars with a slick and
well-organized band of hardy Northern Irish boxers as
bouncers. After my sparring session with Jamie, a fierce
boxer and a true no-nonsense Scotsman, Sonny pulled me
to one side.

'Chris, if you like, I have a few nights where you could come and work the door for me, and obviously I'll pay you.'

At the time, I jumped at any chance to earn some extra cash, and soon enough, I was working the door in various different bars in and around Bangor on weekends. Often, myself and the other lads, including Jamie and Phil, would spend these nights breaking up some seriously big fights. We even once had to deal with a small riot in a hotel just outside of Bangor. I still couldn't get it out of my head that here I was, an ex-Para doing door work in a country I had once walked around wearing a military uniform. The Paras are not the most loved of regiments in Northern Ireland, especially after the continuing Bloody Sunday investigations, so to work the doors like this was quite a ballsy thing for me to do given the history.

After about a year of bouncing and taking part in a few boxing matches for Sonny to earn some extra money, my time in Northern Ireland came to an abrupt end. We'd had quite a few nasty fights to break up during this time, some of which involved individuals who were members of one of the warring factions, and you genuinely didn't want to get on the wrong side of them.

The flat I was renting at the time was just over a mile's walk from Bangor town centre where I worked. Each night after the pubs closed and everybody had left, the staff would normally share a pint together before heading off home. I liked to walk back to the flat to clear my mind and lower the levels of adrenalin, depending on how the night had gone. As a result of my military background, whenever I walked home it was hardwired in me to take a different way home so as not to make my route predictable. One particular evening, I was hungry, and not far from where I lived there was a twenty-four-hour garage on a dual carriageway. I would often stop here for late-night snacks before going home to bed. It was around 1 a.m. and I was walking past the cricket and football grounds just outside of the town.

All I remember was three men and the threat 'Fucking leave Northern Ireland' being shouted at me as they gave me a good beating. I could handle myself one on one, that much I know, but with three of them, they got the better of me. Helpless to retaliate, I crouched onto the floor, protecting my head with my hands and arms, but the rest of my body was open season. I have the scars on the left side of my head to this day as a permanent reminder. When I came around, I tried calling Jamie, but by this time he was asleep. I managed to get myself back to the flat and passed out on the bed. I think I must have slept for at least a day and a half. God, did it hurt!

After this incident, I disappeared off the face of the earth. Sonny and all of the other boys, including Jamie and Phil, had absolutely no idea. I didn't tell a soul. Angry and clueless as to what to do, I hid away in the flat for around three weeks. I had quite a few knocks at my door but I just kept quiet and pretended I wasn't in while I figured out my next move. The last thing I wanted to do was bring any trouble to any of them, but more importantly, to Caitlin. I had to make the hardest decision of my life: did I stay in Northern Ireland living in fear of it happening again or, worse still, something happening to the person I loved most in this world, or did I leave with only one aim in mind, to protect her?

A month after the assault, having only left the flat for supplies, my face was pretty much healed and my injuries were barely noticeable. My decision, however, was firmly made. Behind on my rent, jobless and in an all-round shitty place, I used what little money I had left and went to Belfast International Airport. I couldn't afford the plane ticket to go back to London, but after a few hours, I got myself a cancellation seat and boarded a flight. How I felt on that hour's journey to London is something I'll never be able to fully explain. I was numb with anger – not only with the people responsible, but also myself – as well as fear and, worst of all, the thought of being a huge disappointment to Caitlin. I loved her so much but, out of necessity, I'd left without telling a soul that I was going or where I'd gone. Looking back, I was slightly broken, but I still had a plan: I would disappear and let the dust settle until such time I deemed it safe to return and rebuild my relationship with Caitlin.

12

Whiskey galore!

The last night before I headed to the ferry over to Northern Ireland, Kenny and I slept in the back of his van. We parked up on a strip of land that disappeared into the sea; it was almost like a sandbank but with a track that ran straight through the middle of it for about half a mile. Kenny, his two dogs and I went to sleep for the evening after a bit of food, but at around 11 p.m. we both woke up to the sound of a vehicle pulling up alongside ours and two fellas talking.

When they started trying to break into the back of the van, Kenny and I shouted out and flew out of our sleeping bags to fend them off. A van loaded with an ex-Para, a hardy Scottish ex-sergeant major and two loyal dogs was certainly not what they'd expected! We burst out of the back of the van to see the little scrotebags already halfway down the track. Oh, how much we enjoyed watching them scuttle away! I got back into my sleeping bag with a serene smile on my face, enjoying a huge slice of karma.

The next day, on 26 January 2018, after four days in his excellent company, I said my goodbyes to Kenny and walked the stretch from Stranraer up to Cairnryan, ready to cross the pond and be reunited with Northern Ireland after fifteen years. The security at the docks recognized me from my Facebook page and were all asking for photos to be taken with them and wishing me luck for my Northern Ireland adventure.

Weeks before this, I'd been contacted by a beautiful couple, Graham and Doreen Galt. Graham had served with the RUC (Royal Ulster Constabulary) during the height of the Troubles in Northern Ireland; a top guy, he couldn't do enough to help me. He'd pre-arranged a visit to a whiskey distillery and had also contacted friends who would help me around this stretch of coast. Northern Ireland was the same as England and Wales when it came to the laws of camping, which would make life very difficult for me again, but that was the least of my worries. Although by this point, a peace process had been put in place in the province, certain areas still had pockets of angry Unionists and Nationalists with unfinished business that would probably love to get their hands on me, an ex-Para – made worse by the fact that my Facebook page was public and, by this point, my following had grown to around 6,000 and I'd started to receive a lot of local media coverage.

We had devised a plan that I would start from the north-west point of the coast – Londonderry/Derry – and work my way south to Newry, the most south-westerly point of the province. I had decided that I would always post my photos and vlog about a place two days after I had been there, meaning that if one rogue fool tried to make a name for himself and intercept me, I'd already be two days ahead and he'd be waiting a long time.

As I walked through certain areas, I would be escorted and followed by a car and then be picked up if needs be. The amazing people who would help me through this stage of my journey would be Graham and Doreen Galt, Randal and Kathy Scott and Nikkie Sailes, most of whom were retired police and knew the country very well. I would be dropped off in the morning, walk as much as I could and be picked up to sleep at their houses each evening. The next morning, I would be dropped off where I'd got to the night before and continue. I wasn't too worried about my personal past experience in Bangor catching up with me; I now had a big beard, was a lot thinner and all around a lot more hanging than I was the last time I was here. The only thing that would identify me was my name.

Despite my past in these parts, and obviously the Troubles that I have written about, Northern Ireland is such a beautiful country – as are 98 per cent of the people that live in it. Nowhere in the UK have I seen a more family-orientated nation, nor one so laid-back. This time around, I hoped to see the real Northern Ireland and not get caught up in any of the drama.

I met up with Graham, Doreen, Randal, Kathy and Nikkie to discuss some plans and get acquainted with each other. Graham had arranged for us all to be taken to the Bushmills Distillery in County Antrim. What lovely people they were and what fun we had! After a tour of the distillery and a few free samples at the in-house bar, Graham had organized as a surprise for us to be taken into what's called – I believe after a visit from Barack Obama and various other high-profile guests – the President's Room. Grant, the rep Graham had been in contact with, took us into what I can only describe as a small aeroplane hangar laden with barrels of whiskey stacked on top of one another, some of which were seriously old. There was one particular keg in the middle of the room that we were all asked to stand around. Grant kindly said a few words of encouragement about my walk and that they were honoured to have me here and, as a thank you for what I was doing, presented me with two bottles of twenty-five-year-old Bushmills Whiskey, again organized by Graham. On the front of the two bottles, the label read, 'Bushmills 25 Years Old' and 'Chris Walks the UK'. I was so humbled by the wonderful gifts and, after making a quick speech myself, promised that every year on New Year, I would toast the new year with a glass of the whiskey that I'd just been presented with. This was a great start to Northern Ireland.

My next stop would take me back to Bangor on a small detour to meet up with Brian and hand over the bottle he had left his friendly message in. Prior to this, after posting that we'd found the bottle, I had heard from a lovely lady who worked for the press in Northern Ireland at the *Mirror*. With the address on the letter, she'd been able to track Brian down and arranged a meeting between all of us so I could return the bottle with the press there to capture the moment. We met Brian on the coast just outside Holywood, in between Belfast and Bangor. Brian was incredibly appreciative that I'd come to return the message in the bottle he'd thrown into the sea all those years ago.

We had a great chat and the press took photos with our backs both turned to the camera so our faces could not be seen. Brian presented me with a wonderful bottle of bubbly as I handed him back the bottle. He told me he was going to frame the letter and keep it for his children. We were both delighted that I'd found him and said our goodbyes; job done!

I loved this part of the coast. Having been a massive fan of the *Game of Thrones* series, I got to see a lot of the dramatic and beautiful coastal places where it had been filmed.

A standout for me was the Giant's Causeway, formed some 600 million years ago and made up of around 40,000 hexagonal-shaped columns made of cooled lava that contracted and cracked to form these shapes. It's a spectacular work of art by Mother Nature.

The legend goes that the Irish giant Fionn mac Cumhaill, from the Fenian cycle of Gaelic mythology, was challenged to a fight by the Scottish giant Benandonner. Finn accepted this challenge and, it's said, built the causeway across the North Sea so they could meet for battle.

One evening after a day's walk, Randal and Kathy took me to a hotel for a gathering with some veterans and others who wanted to meet me. I was amazed to walk into a room of around eighty to a hundred people who all cheered and clapped as I entered. I was introduced and then gave a small talk about my adventure, adding how much I appreciated the warm welcome and how much I was loving my experience in Northern Ireland so far. I was handed a small envelope with £380 cash inside that had been collected by all in the room to help see me on my way. I was completely choked. I stood and chatted with all the guests, shaking hands with them one by one, showing my gratitude for what they'd just done for me.

That night on my own before bed, I couldn't help but feel a little bit proud of myself. Looking back to the beginning of the walk, I couldn't believe the difference in my confidence; I'd been almost too nervous to even walk into a shop when I set out, and yet only six months later, here I was standing in front of a crowd of people giving a talk.

Over the next few weeks, Graham, Doreen, Randal and Kathy would take it in turns seeing me safely around the coast. Next it was Nikkie's turn to take the baton and see me through my last section down to Belfast, ending in Newry. Before I eventually finished the coast of Northern Ireland with the help of these lovely people I could now call my friends, in the back of my mind there was one thing bothering me. The tent I had was still broken and the poles still taped with duct tape. I was going to have to use the money I'd been given by all the wonderful people back in Port Stewart to deal with this problem. Deep into winter soon, I'd be out of the comfort of staying in their houses after every day's walk and into the tent once I was back in Scotland. Being inside tents is not the best place to be, let alone one that was about to see the end of its days at any time now. I had to up my game when it came to my accommodation.

I went to Newtownards and the only decent camping shop I could find there and came away with a one-man, four-season tent. There is no describing how happy I was about this. I'd been sleeping in the spare room at Nikkie's up until this point, but as soon as I got the tent, I saw out the rest of my time in Northern Ireland camping in her back garden. The first thing I noticed about the tent was how light it was, and yet it had three times the strength of any tent I'd owned prior to this. I would constantly practise putting it up and down again as quickly as I could to get ready for the oncoming slaughter when I returned to the Scottish mainland for the rest of the winter. I was very professional at this by now, always going through my gear, checking I knew where everything was off the top of my head, only ever packing for emergencies. I had no gimmicks or things to make life comfortable; no books or any entertainment other than my phone.

In my mind, I would imagine the worst-case scenario and make sure I was ready for it. If I was to snap a leg in one of the wild sections of Scotland edging around a mountain, I would work out what I would need and that would be all I took. My foraging skills were something I was getting much better at, and if I had Wi-Fi, I'd always be jotting down tips in my journal and then putting them into practice. My mindset and approach to this walk was certainly becoming more serious. I was still determined not to cut any corners or skip any sections just because they were wild, pathless or incredibly difficult, regardless of the time of year. Each season has its own challenges. I now had some decent kit and felt more ready than ever.

It took me around a month to complete the coast of Northern Ireland. Bag-free, good meals as well as being picked up and dropped off each day gave me a chance to get plenty of miles in. On 20 February 2018, I was taken to the ferry to head back to mainland Scotland. That morning, all my new friends, whom I'd now named 'Team

Northern Ireland', drove down to Belfast to see me off. It was an emotional goodbye for us all; they had all been so kind and I really felt like I'd made some friends for life. I had mixed emotions as the ferry started to pull off. After my last time here, I'd vowed never to return again – but this time I'd seen it in a completely different light. I'd loved my time there and would leave with wonderful memories.

As I sat on the front of the boat reflecting on the past month, I thought back to the beginning of the walk, though this time with a smile. I turned around to look at my bag, tucked away in the storage unit fifty yards behind me, chuckling to myself at how awful my gear had been when I first started. I'd known back then, deep down, that one day, as long as I just kept driving forward, good things could happen, and they did! Now, I had some really decent gear to continue my journey north and had no doubt that it would all be tested very soon. Having just spent the last month house-hopping down the coast, as much as I appreciated and loved the company of my new friends, I realized how much my tent had become more than just a place to sleep for me. Each night, regardless of how treacherous the weather or however difficult the day had been, the whole process of pitching a tent, collecting water, making a fire and cooking food – in essence, stripping right back to basics in a nomadic lifestyle – was fast becoming a far more inviting, freeing and peaceful way to live. I had nobody to answer to, no schedule to keep. Being hosted all the time, wonderful and kind as it is, can quickly get too much. I needed my space back, as time to myself was what was helping me to achieve on a personal level what I'd set out to do at the start.

As we pulled out of Belfast Docks, to the north I could just make out the tip of the Mull of Kintyre, and to the east, the Mull of Galloway, the direction in which I was heading. Excited and with butterflies in my stomach, I was suddenly hit with a realization: not only had my gear grown in quality as my journey had progressed, but I too had improved. Here I was, a more focused person, more in tune with my own mind, with a purpose and a glint in my eye. I knew I still had a long way to go in myself before I felt I was healed from the ghost that I had become, and to eventually feel whole again, but it was evident that with each step I took, each day, week and month that passed, the once dim ember still just about burning inside me was growing into a healthier, more robust flame. My confidence and self-belief were now at a level that I had not experienced for years. The walk was working. I still had no idea exactly what it was I was searching for on my walk to self-discovery, but I was starting to see that it was all heading in the right direction.

13

A dog called Jet

One of the greatest aspects of a completely unplanned journey, living day by day, is the surprises it can bring. Arriving into Irvine would not only change the direction of my walk, but would help to change the direction of my life.

The next stage of my journey would take me further along the west coast of Scotland, heading north through Girvan, Ayre, Prestwick, Troon, Irvine, Ardrossan, West Kilbride, Largs, Greenock and into Glasgow. One of the great things about heading north into Scotland is that you don't suddenly find yourself on the coast in the middle of nowhere – it happens gradually and, for me, this was great. Having the ability to camp where I wanted in between towns gave me real time to practise what I would need as I made my way into the more remote Highlands.

Each night, regardless of the cold or rain, I'd spend

hours studying fire, gaining understanding of the foresight one needs to gather vital kindling, how to get it and build fire even in rain. As always, I was constantly prepared for the worst-case scenario. If I were to get hurt and have to wait days – or weeks – before I was found, for example, I'd have to know how to forage from the sea and be able to make fire in any weather in order to cook. It was around the time when the UK was hit by the 'Beast from the East', and so it was incredibly cold, snowy and windy. Eager to test out my gear, when it was snowing at night, I'd even practise bivvying up (sleeping outside in just your sleeping bag with a waterproof 'bivvy' bag over the top and nothing else) for the night without the tent.

I worked so hard practising these skills and, boy, I would not regret it. I'd collect limpets, whelks, mussels and razor clams – all manner of shellfish on big beaches with big tides. Condiments or suchlike to add any flavour were a luxury I also couldn't afford, so I would simply have to put up with boiling and eating them as they were. I couldn't stand them, but always felt satisfied after a good few, knowing that by having them alongside some vegetables, I was maintaining a healthy diet; crucial to keep me well in both body and mind.

When it came to my route, even if there was a road right next to the coast, so long as there were rocks to the side of it, I would always clamber, scale and climb them instead of traipsing along the flat tarmac. It would take at least three times as long, and so much more effort with my huge bag on my back, but I knew it was necessary training to see me through the north. Deep down I was preparing myself to achieve this walk in a way that no other had done before. It was in no way to prove anything to anyone, not even myself. Rather, it was the culmination of a lifetime's desire to seek real adventure and experience a connection with the wilderness and the wildlife that inhabits it.

I wanted to be away from the white noise of modern life and embrace untouched nature for what it really was. I wanted to feel free and undo the shackles of society. The wilderness was just the place to find out who I really was, what I was made of and hopefully arrive at an organic inkling of what I wanted to do with the second half of my life.

I'd heard through the grapevine of a family who were looking for someone to adopt a dog. She was a lurcher; a cross between a greyhound and a saluki.

In March, I'd arranged to meet Jet's owner, a guy called Jim, in Irvine. Obviously, I'd never met Jim before, nor Jet for that matter. I was nervous about the whole situation, wondering to myself if adopting a dog on this journey was a bad decision. Jim and Jet pulled up in a van outside a pub where I'd arranged to meet them. He came outside, introduced himself and we stood chatting for about ten minutes. He opened a door to the van and out jumped a beautiful white lurcher with a brown patch of fur on her left side by her shoulder and a small brown mark in the middle of her tail as well as two brown patches on each ear. I took the lead from Jim, walked her across the road and sat on a bench.

The first thing that I noticed was how incredibly thin she was. I had learned that working dogs (which I'd been told Jet was) are often like this to keep them fast and nimble for hunting. I looked into her eyes and I could tell she was slightly scared and stressed in her new surroundings, but as I watched her I saw something that I had never seen in a dog before; she looked wise and full of spirit. I smiled and wrapped my arms around her and she just stood still, accepting my token of affection. I knew at that moment that this was not a good decision; it was an amazing decision. Little did Jet or I know that we would create a bond stronger than either of us had ever had before. I walked back with her and told Jim there and then that I wanted her. He left pretty much immediately, clearly upset to be parting with her, while I had just acquired the best friend that I would ever have.

That evening, once the tent was up, I decided to stay awake all night just stroking her and talking to her to reassure her and gain her trust. She lay at the bottom of my sleeping bag with her head between my legs looking up at me. Restless, she would sleep for a while and then wake up and just stare at me. By morning, I was covered in hair and absolutely stank of fox poo. I got out of my tent at first light. Jet followed immediately and stood right by my side. With the lead in my hand ready to put on her, I walked forward a few steps and she followed. I then jogged a few more steps and again she followed, standing right by my side. The bond was immediate. I kneeled down on one knee so I could be at her eye level, looked her in the eyes while stroking the back of her ears, put my nose next to hers and said, 'Jet, would you like to come and walk the rest of the United Kingdom coast with me?' She looked at me and gave me my first lick to the face. 'Then it's settled, let's do this!' I said by way of reply.

The next leg, accompanied now by my new four-legged friend, would take us up into Glasgow. It was after Glasgow that the Scottish coastline came into its own. Nowhere in the UK has a coastline like it. In fact, few countries around the world have a seaboard so jagged and broken, with huge sea lochs pretty much around every corner. The coast is riddled with them all the way up to the very north-west tip: Cape Wrath.

After Glasgow, the bigger towns had pretty much stopped. This is where the real fun would begin, heading into miles and miles of much wilder coast with much smaller towns and little hamlets dotted around the end of each loch. Nervous and excited for my first real taste of Scotland, I felt completely ready for it. My foraging, fire-making and my ability to read and feel the weather systems were growing stronger all the time. Jet and I started to tackle the maze of lochs and our first Scottish islands around these parts: Great Cumbrae, followed by the Isle of Bute.

The problem I had, as always, was funding. If I didn't have the money to catch a ferry to an island, then I would just continue along the coast of the mainland until a time when I could afford the fare and hitch a lift back to the ferry to get to whichever island I'd missed. My very first would be the tiny island of Great Cumbrae, taking me only a single day to walk its coast with a circumference of just six miles. After this, my second island would be Bute, but before we got there, we'd have to attack the first of our sea lochs.

Now, you can do this one of two ways: cut off the entire loch by road, or edge around it. Navigating the coast around each loch tends to be a lot wilder, and given there are so many, it would be very easy to just cut them off using a road to reach the other side rather than walk around them. To give you an example, there are certain stretches in Scotland where you can use a road only around six miles long and, in doing so, avoid around three weeks of insanely wild walking, edging around mountains with no coastal paths, and all-round hard graft. Cutting these sections off also means you can get to shops far more frequently and easily for supplies.

Throughout my journey, I had heard of a good few coast walkers who had walked the coastline of mainland Britain, but there is only one man who I know stuck rigidly and completely to the coast even in the toughest sections of Scotland. This is because most of these sections are unpathed, meaning you have to forge your *own* way through dangerously isolated areas where you might spend an entire day grafting only to conquer a mere few miles; edging up and around completely overgrown valleys, traversing the sides of coastal mountains in ankle-breaking territory, all the while praying you don't make a mistake and injure yourself in parts impossible to get to unless by helicopter search and rescue. It's tedious, energy-sapping graft with absolutely no room for mistakes.

To help put this into context, most of the other walkers took around a year to complete their coastal journeys. Back in 2015, another homeless veteran named Christian Knock decided to walk around mainland Britain for the charity Help for Heroes. As hardy, fit and determined as they come, similarly with no funds and camping wild as I was, it took Christian two and a half years to complete his journey. That's the difference between sticking strictly to the coast or using only coastal paths and roads. This is not to take away anything from any other walker; I have the utmost respect and admiration for anyone who takes on such a massive and daunting task.

Everyone's journey is different, but I believe that given the circumstances in which Christian and I both left for our walks and the fact that we were both ex-Forces meant that we shared the same mentality of refusing to cut any corners. This wasn't to prove anything to anyone but ourselves. I believe we both needed the solitude these sections offered as a means to well and truly get away from it all and rediscover our sense of selves. Neither of us had a plan. Christian and I would become good friends and stay in touch throughout my entire journey. He was the only person that I could in any way relate to when it came to walking the west coast of Scotland in terms of the walking itself, sleeping rough and wild camping.

It would very soon become apparent that coast paths were a distant luxury. Jet and I were having to forge our own path along the jagged west coast. Scotland has a massive logging industry, meaning a lot of the coastline is thick, dense ferns, making life very difficult depending on the time of year. By now, it was safe to say that I'd survived my first winter. We were now heading into spring and very soon summer. I was so excited by the thought of this, but still, I had a lot to learn when it came to Scotland. Little did I know how incredibly hard my second summer on this walk was going to be.

After passing through Succoth, Carrick Castle, Ardentinny, Blairmore and Sandbank, we soon made it to a town called Dunoon. It was already clear that my good friend Jet had completely taken the bull by the horns on this adventure. She loved it, being completely free to run around and sniff out rabbits and deer tracks. I could see how much more content she was, but the thing that really stuck out the most was her complete devotion and loyalty to me. If I stopped, she stopped. If I sat down to take five, she sat down next to me. We were starting to understand each other very well and I would soon learn to read her inside out. For example, if Jet walked close behind my heels for any more than twenty minutes, it was her way of telling me that she wanted to stop for the day. Often eager to continue and press on, I wanted to show the same devotion and loyalty to Jet as she showed me and would stop for the day anytime she asked. I adored her spirit, looks and thirst for the great outdoors. She literally had the perfect dog's life, with all of my attention.

My routine each time we stopped would be, firstly, getting the tent up and unpacking all of the gear we needed for the night. Then I'd immediately feed and give water to Jet to get her rested up. I'd then scope out a good spot to collect driftwood or fallen wood from the trees for fire. The second I was out of Jet's sight, however, she would bolt from the tent to be next to me. I felt so bad for her, as I just wanted her to rest up. Her loyalty often didn't do her any favours on this front, so each night I'd pitch the tent facing in the direction of where I'd collect wood so she could see me at all times. Only then would she be content to stay put and keep warm and rest. God, I love her!

By the time I reached Dunoon, I'd received a few

messages from other walkers warning me of the next loch I was about to tackle: Loch Striven. One guy told me he'd attempted it, got lost and sat helpless, crying, completely disorientated and petrified of the position he had got himself into. Others simply cut the whole thing off. You can look at the maps all you like, but until you're there, you have no idea just how dense, overgrown and rocky it is in places. All I could see was forestry on quite a sheer slope. If I'm honest, I was foaming at the mouth to get my teeth into it; this kind of challenge was why I was here in the first place!

The day before I went for it, I was made aware of an accomplished walker who had attempted this loch some seven years ago, having completed the Munroes (a range of mountains over a certain height in the Highlands). She'd fallen badly and broken her leg smack bang in the middle of one side of the loch. She had then crawled into her sleeping bag to wait for help, but wasn't found until some four years later by the crew of a fish-farming boat. It was an awful and tragic end for the poor lady, but I just kept telling myself, *I'm not her*. The least I could do was give it a go.

After camping up the night before, hidden away in a small dark block of forest in the hills above Dunoon, I set off to do Loch Striven. As I approached, I gained some higher ground as a viewpoint so I could clearly see both sides of the loch. There was no doubt how incredibly dense it was. I set off scrambling through the low branches of the pine trees, getting constant whips to the face, scratching and cutting me on any bare skin that was showing. It was infuriating and bloody hurt, so I came up with a new plan.

In my bag, I had a length of rope that I would use for a washing line to dry my gear or anything else it would come in handy for. I kneeled down and tied the rope around my waist, then attached it to my bergen, now heavier than ever due to the amount of dog food I had to carry for Jet. I got on all fours and started crawling my way through the dense forestry, dragging my bergen behind me. Once in a while, I'd reach a small opening where I'd stand up, stretch off and take a breather. Jet, for the first time since having her, went in front of me, sniffing out barely visible deer tracks for us to forge a passage through. It was hard graft but I was in my element.

What would have taken me only an hour to walk along a road would take me seven hours' navigating only one side of the forbidding body of water. Eventually, I reached the first end of the loch, ecstatic that I'd made it through and having had so much fun in the process. Still running on adrenalin, I decided to knock off as much of the other side as I could, giving me enough time to pitch the tent and cook before dark. Immediately back in the dense woodland, we made our way skirting rigidly to the coast, clambering rocks, making sure I could see the sea water at all times so as not to get lost or disorientated. We eventually stopped for the day in a spot called Arobey Point, a small opening of grass opposite the side where I had started. I was delighted with our progress, as that left us only another two miles till we'd come out of the other side onto a dirt track that edged along the coast. I pitched up the tent, made a fire and had a lovely, relaxing evening under the stars at the bottom of a 1,634-foot peak.

Jet and I woke at the crack of dawn, eventually making

it out the other side. It took me four hours to do two miles. As we joined the track, I spotted my first house with a couple outside chatting. When I approached, he asked, 'Have you just walked around that loch?'

'Yes, mate, it was amazing to walk,' I replied.

'You're only the third person I've ever known to complete it!' he exclaimed.

I laughed. 'I'm not sure what all the fuss is about – we loved it!' And with that I walked off, actually rather exhausted, with still another six miles before I made it to Colintraive, where I would catch the ferry to my next island, the Isle of Bute.

Loch Striven had taught me a valuable lesson, not only about the walk, but about life in general: I can't tell you how many people warned me of this place and told me not to do it, but I had realized by now that people can only advise you or tell you how difficult something is based on their own limits or what they believe they are capable of. Just because they are scared or unwilling to at least try something, doesn't mean you might not be able to do it. I would never again let anyone try and put me off something that I truly believed I could do. Ironically, this would be a walk in the park compared to what the next few years was going to bring. I'm not saying it was easy, but I knew I had so much more in my tank. It's all about mindset and total belief in one's abilities. I'd been getting a lot of advice based on hearsay rather than personal experience, but deep down I knew that, as much as I appreciated the concern and care for my wellbeing, anyone who had not at least tried it was in no position to tell me not to.

I sat that night around the fire thinking to myself that

there are two types of people when it comes to pushing limits: people who need to be encouraged and told they can and people who need to be told they can't. I am definitely the latter, and if I'm honest, I always have been. Telling me that I can't do something makes me more determined to prove that I can, but only to myself. It added fuel to my fire and made me want it even more.

14

The King's Cave

As well as the mountains, the west coast and islands of Scotland have lots of bothies, which can be anything from an old open wooden structure to croft houses situated in remote places around the country. Bothies give hikers, kayakers, or any adventurer for that matter, respite from the rain and winds, and they soon became my favourite places to sleep. Most of them are owned by the MBA (Mountain Bothy Association) and around once a year, a group of people go to each one to make any repairs needed or just do general upkeep. Every time I knew I was approaching one, I was always incredibly excited, as there was something very special about them.

In early April, Jet and I were walking the Isle of Bute, a relatively small, well-populated island around fifteen miles long and around three miles in width. One afternoon, we arrived at one particular bothy that consisted of a small wooden hut with a compost toilet and a fire pit, mainly used by kayakers who would island-hop from the mainland.

We were both completely soaked, as it had rained seriously hard that day. The ground was totally sodden and the dead wood I was hoping to make a fire with was completely unusable. Each piece I picked up would be rotten and immediately snap in half as soon as it left the ground. With very few small trees, driftwood would be my only chance. The tiny bothy came into view, and before even looking inside, I threw my bag down, ran to the shore only fifteen feet away only to find no driftwood at all. I was absolutely gutted, as this would probably mean a couple of hours tracking back in the pissing rain to find whatever I could scattered along the shoreline.

With no gas to cook, I made the decision to call it a day, strip off and eat what food I had with a cold coffee rather than go on the hunt. I was soul-destroyed. Then I turned around towards the bothy and noticed a pile of bone-dry wood stacked inside, leaned up against the wall. I couldn't believe it! Instead of a cold, wet night for Jet and me, this meant a warm meal, hot coffee and the chance to dry all of my clothes and Jet's soaked fur. Jet slept in the bottom of my sleeping bag every night, and so when her fur got wet, it was a damp night for us both. I was so happy this wasn't the case tonight. And I wouldn't have to wake up tomorrow and put on soaking wet gear. I learned the bothy code immediately; if you use the wood that somebody else has made the effort to gather and leave for you, then you make sure, that night or the following day, you replace it for the next people who come and may need it as much as you did. It was a great system, and one I would abide by in every bothy I used.

The Isle of Bute now finished and back on the mainland, my next stretch would take me around another sea loch down towards Tighnabruaich and Kames, then on to Scotland's biggest sea loch, Loch Fyne. I loved the stretch down towards Kames; it was wild and gifted with the most beautiful coast path. It was easy to find firewood and I did a lot of foraging on this section of the walk. I felt good; probably the strongest I had on my journey to date, but Loch Fyne would prove to be incredibly stressful.

As I mentioned earlier, Scotland has a huge logging industry, on the west coast in particular, and I would often see cut-down pines piled onto the back of lorries destined for the south. The roads in these parts are the main veins out of the Highlands and can be absolutely treacherous. Sadly, one of these roads, one side stretching some thirty miles long, is right on the shoreline, with big hills on the opposite side. Alone, I could have banged this out easily in a couple of days, but there was no way that Jet could do that. The road was a main route for the trucks carrying the logs and they would hurtle down so fast, leaving little room for Jet and me. It really was terrifying.

In the end, I decided to wait out the daylight hours and walk at night so the roads were less busy and I could hear any oncoming vehicles, giving us either enough time to scramble to the opposite side of the road or cling onto the rocks as they passed. Worst still, Jet had to be on a lead, which she hates, purposefully slowing down in resistance, genuinely annoyed that I had to put her on it. I hated it too.

To make matters worse, I could only carry so much food for Jet before my back would snap in half, meaning I had around three days to reach the next town or village in order to stock up. We made it into Inveraray exhausted, stressed and soul-destroyed. I gave us a day's rest before eventually making it into Lochgilphead, a bigger town where I could stock up with the £15 that I had on me, kindly gifted by a follower I'd met in a nearby village. It's safe to say that Jet and I were both completely fucked. It would be the first time that I'd feel incredibly guilty for having Jet on the walk with me.

Another of life's precious lessons awaited me the evening I stayed in Lochgilphead. Growing my social media following was something I never really cared about apart from the fact that it raised my donations. As always, no matter how tired I was, I would make a huge effort to speak to people and promote the walk and the charity, SSAFA, and it was starting to grow more and more. I was getting more press attention all the time and was starting to get recognized in pretty much all the smaller towns, villages and even hamlets I passed through. Messages had started to come in thick and fast, and it had got to a point where it was becoming impossible to reply and save my battery and data.

One guy in particular called Michael, who was in his thirties, had been trying to get in touch with me for a few months. He lived in Lochgilphead and had been sending me messages once or twice a week for the past two months asking me if I could come and see him when I arrived. He really wanted to meet Jet, and had also invited us to stay in his flat for the night. To be honest, I just wanted to eat, pitch my tent and rest for the evening, but given how persistent he'd been, if I did that, I'd feel really guilty.

'Jet, pal, we need to go and see this guy or he'll never leave us alone! It's only a few K – another half an hour, tops. Let's just do it and we can rest and go to sleep afterwards.'

So, early that evening, I arrived to see Michael standing on the second floor of a balcony of very well-kept flats. He waved and pointed us towards the stairs we needed to climb to get to his front door, and I was relieved to discover he was softly spoken and in no way an intense human being. We didn't really speak for the first few minutes; he just kneeled stroking Jet, speaking to her like he had known her for ever. I was impressed by how quickly she took to him, even following him into the flat without checking me for a look of approval, as she normally would. We spent a good few hours just chatting and laughing, talking about my adventure and also how wonderful dogs are. He made us feel so relaxed that I even admitted that I almost couldn't be arsed to come up because we were so tired, and the last few days had been awful.

I admired how calm he was and noticed how intently he listened to every single word I said and would always reply so genuinely. He is the first and last person Jet has had enough trust to lie down on their lap, and I joked to Michael that I felt completely betrayed, but, equally, I was incredibly happy to see her do it. After a few hours and a couple of coffees, uncontrollably yawning, I told Michael we had to go as the evening was closing in and I wanted to pitch up before it got totally dark. He offered us the sofa for the night, but I politely declined, telling him we just wanted our own space to turn off the thinking for an evening.

'No problem, Chris,' he said, 'I totally understand.'

As we were leaving, Michael walked into the kitchen and pulled from the cupboard some huge bandages. 'Bloody hell, mate, what are they for?' I said, intrigued.

He replied, 'It's for the pain. Would you like to take a couple for your lower back? I attempted to pick up your bag when you weren't looking. With all that weight, it must be ruined!'

I laughed. 'It's okay, you keep them. Hopefully by the time I'm sixty, technology will have come on enough that I can nip to a chemist and buy a new spine!' We said our goodbyes with a big man-hug and a strong handshake, and I walked away down the steps from his flat that led directly to the coast. Later that evening, now camped up, fed and getting my head into my journal, I grabbed my phone to see what time it was, noticing that stuffed inside the inner pouch of my bum bag, which I'd put on the kitchen counter while at Michael's, was a folded-up piece of paper. It was a note . . .

Chris, I really didn't want to say anything whilst you were here, so as not to make you feel awkward or feel sorry for me, but I'm not very well and haven't been for some time. I just want you to know that following you and Jet and watching you both never give up, has been a real light in my life over the past ten months. Make sure you don't take your hat off while you're on the walk – it's how we know and have come to love you! Good luck. Your now friend, Michael.

I later found out that he was terminally ill with cancer. He was probably only in his early thirties. Now it made sense why Jet had stayed so close to him all evening – she knew he was ill. A few months later, while camped up in the Hebrides, I received a text message informing me that Michael had passed. I'd only met the man once, but would often think of him as he left such a lasting impression on both Jet and me. Sat in my tent, I vowed that from that moment on I would honour his wish and keep my hat on for the rest of the walk, regardless of the seasons.

Sad but also happy that he was no longer in pain, that night I'd learned a valuable lesson; there are too many people out there, probably more so on social media, who whinge and whine about the most humdrum, insignificant things. Even my problems were miniscule compared to what Michael must have gone through. Life is such an amazing gift – and so short. He knew this and I believe he made the most of his last few months on earth. He accepted his fate with such humility and just went on being kind to everybody in the process. Wearing the hat would come to mean much more to me than just a promise. If I had a bad couple of days, or just felt a bit sorry for myself, the hat would always remind me that I had nothing to complain about. So thank you, Michael. Rest in peace, my friend.

For my next stage, from the top of Scotland's biggest sea loch, Loch Fyne, I had to head south, tackling the Mull of Kintyre, which involved walking twenty-one miles south to reach Tarbert, then another twenty-eight miles south to reach Campbeltown, followed by yet another fifteen miles just to reach the most southern point of the Mull of Kintyre. Once I'd walked those sixty-four miles, I then had to swing around the corner and walk all the way back up the opposite side of the peninsula until I was level with the top of Loch Fyne again; in all, around 120 miles over three weeks, just in order to stick to the coastline, but without making any more progress northbound. To help put this into perspective, this is the equivalent of walking from the beginning of the Thames estuary near London directly across England until you hit the coast at the Bristol Channel.

On the way down to Campbeltown, we jumped aboard a ferry that took us to the Isle of Arran. I loved this stretch. Heading down past Campbeltown to the very south of the Mull of Kintyre, I would spend the night camped behind the walls of a lighthouse. Once we had pitched, we climbed back up to find and visit the memorial of a Chinook helicopter that had flown over from Northern Ireland on 2 June 1994 and sadly ran into thick fog; unable to see, the helicopter slammed into the hills, killing all twenty-five passengers and the four crew members on board. I sat and watched the sun set next to the monument, once again reminding myself how fragile and precious life is. At times, I'd get slightly annoyed at myself forever getting so worked up about things that genuinely were not important. I made a toast with my cold coffee to all those on board and made my way back down to the tent ready for a good night's kip.

I was chuffed to be on Arran, as it looked beautiful; 2,500-foot mountain peaks running through its centre (hence the name 'Mini Scotland') and a road that hugged the coast pretty much the entire way round, making it very easy walking. The island averages around ten miles in width and nearly twenty miles in length. It's a haven for cyclists, relatively easy to circumnavigate in a day with some beautiful coastline to enjoy as you go. I loved walking this coast. I was starting to get stopped a lot by locals and tourists alike, who had either seen us in the papers or clocked us on social media. One of the people I met there was a woman called Shona and her children. In a few years to come, Shona would prove to be a huge help with my Instagram account once my Facebook page alone had become too much to handle, let alone Instagram and Twitter!

My real excitement here though was the history, and Jet and I ploughed on, eager to arrive at the famous 'King's Cave'. The sandstone caves were given the name due to a Scottish hero, Robert de Bruce. Most of us have seen the film *Braveheart* and would normally associate this accolade with William Wallace. However, the film is widely known to be historically inaccurate – not to diminish the valour of William Wallace, but the real Braveheart was in fact Robert de Bruce, King of Scotland.

After the death of Wallace, de Bruce began the quest to reunite the clans of this proud and rugged country. After years of English dominance in the north – subjecting the Scots to tyranny and injustice under the rule of England's kings, Edward Longshanks and his successor, Edward II – de Bruce finally defeated the English at the Battle of Bannockburn, driving them out of Scotland once and for all. It was a monumental achievement.

His attempt to reunite Scottish commoners and nobles to form an army strong enough to beat the English and regain the lands taken from them had taken years prior to this epic victory, and de Bruce had travelled far and wide across Scotland and its islands; no easy feat. After years of trying with little success, in 1307, de Bruce found himself on the Isle of Arran having just lost a battle with another clan which had wiped out most of his men.

Retreating to what is now called 'the King's Cave', injured and demoralized, de Bruce looked up to the ceiling of the cave and fixated upon a spider. For hours, he sat and watched the spider struggle time after time to swing from one side of a rock to the other. Relentless in its will to reach the other side, the spider eventually made it, spending all night spinning the perfect web. The tenacity and determination inspired Robert de Bruce to never give up, and eventually he succeeded in what at the time must have seemed an impossible quest: to beat the English back to where they came from. After his death, Robert de Bruce's heart was put inside a box and kept in a church for safe-keeping as a symbol of hope for Scotland, hence the name, 'Braveheart.'

After spending hours in the sandstone cave mesmerized by Iron Age carvings on the walls and many other fascinating historical carvings, including a sword that is said to have been carved by de Bruce himself, I got the roll-mat out ready to sleep inside. Looking up at the roof, I tried to imagine what he must have been feeling and what courage it must have taken, more so back in the days when life was so brutal and unfair depending on your title or position in society.

As I contemplated his feelings all those centuries ago, my thoughts soon turned to my own challenge. Although nowhere near as daunting a task, it was epic in its own way, and I smiled at the thought that never once had the notion of quitting this walk ever crossed my mind. I visualized the web and saw mine only half spun. I thought about the relentless perseverance of the spider and how obstinately determined I too would have to be in my pursuit of happiness and the challenges that still lay ahead on this walk in the months and years to come.

It's always baffled me how, these days, many people's ideas of heroes and idols are celebrities – namely singers and actors. Mine had always been people like Wallace, Robert de Bruce, Shackleton or anyone else who had the courage to achieve monumental feats of endurance while putting the lives of others before their own.

I adored Arran and was sad to be leaving. The camping was great and I loved my night sleeping in such an extraordinary cave with a lovely fire at the entrance so as not to smoke myself out. In all, it was a truly wonderful and unforgettable experience. Arran now finished, I caught the ferry and made my way back over to the coast where I left off. At this point, I was unable to afford any ferries to take me to Jura and Islay, so I cracked on, heading north in the direction of Oban. It was on this stretch that I really started to see what Scotland had to offer in the way of startling beauty. It is simply *stunning*; slowly but surely, the bigger hills began to morph into sizeable mountains. To the west I started seeing more of the Inner Hebrides isles coming into view. Even the poor weather had started to turn clement, and I was blessed with some warmer days as well as some incredibly wet ones. The stretch to Oban had its challenges, and never had I been so happy to have made the decision to learn how to forage. I'd leave small towns with the two pouches on the side of my bergen full of dog food to make sure I never ran out for Jet, while carrying only vegetables and stock for myself to eat alongside my main source of nutrition: shellfish.

15

How quickly things can turn for the better

As the crow flies, it's only thirty miles to Oban, but the actual coastline dictates otherwise, again often sending you south, down smaller peninsulas, one of which took me to Kells, another to Aird and the last to Lower Ardentallan, adding on twice the distance. It would be a big push for Jet and me to make it in time in order to restock with more supplies before we ran out. Once again, completely knackered, Jet and I staggered into Oban on 6 May 2018 for my thirty-eighth birthday. Completely out of battery and with only 42p to my name, I headed to a pub called the Oban Inn to recharge my phone and get half an orange cordial.

It was utterly soul-destroying watching people come in ordering meals that looked so delicious. One family sat down at the table next to me and ordered steak n' ale pies all round – my favourite. I was *so* hungry! Seeing as it was my thirty-eighth birthday, I'd be a liar if I said I didn't feel a little bit sorry for myself. I made my half cordial last for around three hours, by which time the evening had started closing in and the bar had started to get busier. It was a Saturday and soon enough, the place was nearly full. I decided to get myself, Jet and my big bag that was taking up so much space out of there to find a spot to camp and forage for some whelks, which, by now, I was already sick of the sight of!

As I was leaving, I held the door open for four gentlemen, one carrying a banjo, one a guitar, one a ukulele and the other a fiddle. Once they were all in, I let go of the door and made my way around the corner.

Next minute, one of them ran back out and shouted, 'Chris, fella!'

I turned and said hello, to which he replied, 'Mate, I wondered where I recognized your face from . . . You're the guy walking the UK coastline, aren't you?'

'Yes, pal, I am indeed. I'm just heading off to camp up for the night.'

'Chris, please stay a bit longer and let us buy you a pint. What you are doing is insane and we would be honoured. By the way, my name's Spence.'

I agreed and went back in to join them. I asked what time they were going to start playing. 'No, mate – we just go from bar to bar with our instruments playing Scottish music,' said Spence. 'We do that a lot up here in Scotland.'

'That's bloody awesome,' I said. 'I love to play too. I really miss my guitar.'

'Well, we're gonna have a jam very shortly and the pub's got its own guitar on the wall over there. Join us if you like!'

'I'd love to!'

Spence got the pints in and soon enough we started to play. By the time the bar was full, Jet was given a blanket to lie on under the table, relax and fall asleep. Given the fact that I hadn't eaten and was all-round exhausted, the Guinness went straight to my head in no time. They were all great musicians, and I could also hold a tune. After about half an hour of playing, I said to the band, 'Let's spice this up. If I start playing something, can you just go with it and play along with whatever I do?'

'Take it away, Chris!' one of them said.

I got up off my chair and stood on the table with the guitar and shouted, 'Folks, do me a favour,' aiming it at everyone in the bar, 'let's have some fun!' Everyone cheered. I started to play 'Mr Brightside' by The Killers and in no time the whole bar was up on their feet singing at the top of their voices while the lads played the most amazing backing, Scotland style!

We played Bruce Springsteen, Stereophonics and Pink Floyd – it was just incredible to be a part of such a special moment. As the evening drew to a close, one of the bar staff presented me with a steak n' alé pie with mash and pies as well as some garlic bread. 'You deserve this! Enjoy!' she said. Next minute, the whole bar was singing 'Happy Birthday' to me, egged on by one of the band members whom I'd told it was my birthday earlier that evening. I was overwhelmed and nearly in tears.

I left the bar in no fit state to walk, let alone pitch a tent. But I do remember having a brief moment thinking how this was the epitome of what my walk was really about – arriving at a town with no money and no food, leaving later that evening having had the best evening and best birthday one could ask for thanks to the kindness of strangers. I was beginning to realize just how quickly things can change for the better, and it was one of the things I loved about this unplanned, totally unpredictable journey.

I stumbled my way to a patch of grass outside a huge building and got to work pitching my tent. Needless to say, it was definitely not my best attempt yet! Shortly after as I lay inside, a police car pulled up and two officers got out and approached me.

'Do you realize you have pitched your tent in the garden of the Civic Centre?' one asked.

I did my very best to explain what I was doing and related the events that had occurred earlier that evening, at which point they both laughed. One of them said, 'Look, it's okay. Just make sure you're up and gone before 9 a.m.! We have coffee in the car – would you like some to help sober you up a bit?' I agreed and they stayed and chatted with me for a while, laughing at how totally pissed I was before shaking my hand and leaving.

The next morning, I got up bright and early, feeling like the inside of my head had just been dragged around a cactus, and started to make my way towards Fort William. This stretch was without doubt the most scenic and beautiful coastline I'd seen to date. Fort William is known as the gateway to the Highlands, with around twenty-eight miles of pure, breathtaking nature. As I walked, I could see the mountains of the island of Mull to my left, mountains in front of me and two beautiful sea lochs. It would also be the place where I'd get to climb the last of the

Three Peaks, Wales, England and Scotland's highest mountains; Fort William being home to Ben Nevis.

I arrived on 13 May, a great time of year to climb the 4,411-foot-high mountain, with warmer weather but still ice and snow as you reach the summit. The following day would give us a rare sunny day, with perfect visibility to climb it. It took Jet and me around three hours and forty-five minutes to reach its summit and, boy, it did not disappoint! It was perfect. From the top of Ben Nevis, you can't see a single town or village – just mountains as far as the eye can see. We couldn't have asked for a better day. As we made our descent, Jet ran around in the snow as happy as I'd ever seen her, utterly in her element. It was joyous to watch!

That evening, camped up just outside Fort William next to a castle ruin, I lay there excited about the notion of doing another island. I couldn't get the thought out of my head that I should walk to Mallaig and catch the ferry over to Skye. This would mean I'd have to cut off a big section to get me to Loch Aline, where I would get the ferry over to Mull, another Scottish island. Knowing I still had Islay and Jura to complete further south, I could do Skye then return to Fort William, walk the section I'd missed to Loch Aline, get the ferry to Mull, then find a way to do the islands that I'd missed. It was settled: I was off to Skye!

The walk to Mallaig is simply gorgeous. Surrounded by mountains, incredible beaches and an abundance of deer and other amazing wildlife, here I also saw my first golden eagle. Soaring high using thermal air to conserve their energy while hunting, they are so majestic and graceful to watch. I was in awe – it was a real moment. I stopped to just sit and watch a pair do their thing, smiling the entire time. I thought back to when I first came up with the idea of walking the UK coast, imagining myself in the mountains watching eagles, and here I was. *Here I was!* Once trapped in the claustrophobic confines of my city flat and depression, I was now amid the wilds, witness to these rare, incredible creatures. They represented the kind of freedom I had longed for and now had. We are what we dare to dream.

Not long after, I would pass by the famous Glenfinnan Viaduct, made even more famous having featured in the Harry Potter movies as the train route for the *Hogwarts Express*, and what a sight it was! Soon after I arrived, I found the most perfect spot to camp a few hundred feet up the side of a mountain overlooking the viaduct and a huge memorial on the seafront commemorating those who fell in the 1745 Jacobite Rising.

I got a fire on the go to cook and, to my surprise, that evening, someone below played the bagpipes, giving me an hour of what I'd dreamed Scotland would be like. Surrounded by hills, mountains, perfect greenery all around, and a calm glassy sea loch reflecting sunsetting clouds with Jet fast asleep, fed and watered, I was now in my sleeping bag feeling incredibly happy. Nothing could have ruined the calmness that I felt.

Arisaig is a small village only six miles south of Mallaig. It would be the start of a not quite so calming experience for Jet and me. Throughout the whole winter and spring, I'd been excited for the coming of summer, but sadly, a new harsh reality was about to hit, and things were about to drastically change. It would be my first introduction to the dreaded Highland midges. Yes, I'd been warned about *the midges* throughout my journey in Scotland, but like any other warning I usually just took it with a pinch of salt, telling myself, 'It can't be that bad – I've probably had far worse than having to deal with a few flies.' How wrong I was!

That evening, in late May 2018, I pitched my tent in a small block of woodland about a mile out of Arisaig. Once pitched and with Jet fed, I sat on a rock, snapping photos as the evening drew in, the sun disappearing behind the mountains in a mellow haze. Soon enough, we would be covered by shade. Suddenly, out of nowhere, I could feel sharp pinches, with my face and arms absolutely covered in midges. It was like somebody had turned on a tap gushing with insects. I turned around to see Jet as hellishly uncomfortable as I was, sneezing and rubbing her eyes. We were getting bitten all over. I sprinted to the tent, as always left open so that Jet could see me, only to find the inside swarming with them. I couldn't believe what I was seeing! I moved quickly, shaking off our sleeping bags, using a T-shirt to get rid of as many of the flying blight as I could while getting bitten in the process, and then dived inside with all my gear and zipped up the tent.

Inside, it was still teeming with them. I had to kill each and every one – it was that simple. I covered Jet with my sleeping bag to stop them going for her eyes and spent the next few hours tediously terminating them off one by one, using my thumb to crush them against the material of the tent, the whole time getting eaten alive. All through the night, I would wake up to more bites from those I had missed. It was dreadful. It makes me itch even now as I write this, just thinking about it!

Never again would I make the mistake of leaving my tent open. I immediately had a strong hatred for these little airborne assassins. To make things worse, every time Jet needed a wee, I had to open a gap in the tent just big enough for her to squeeze out of, and when she'd come back in, her white coat would be swarming with them, bringing a new wave of hell back into our tiny one-man tent; again it would take me hours to painstakingly kill them off, one by one. I remember thinking, *How on earth are we going to put up with this all summer until September, when they finally begin to disperse?!* It would change everything.

Sitting in a boiling tent in a part of the country where it didn't get dark during the summer months until after midnight was not my idea of fun. Unable to cook food outside after a certain time or even just to enjoy my surroundings, it was a total destruction of my soul. I needed to learn everything I could about these critters – areas they liked the most, what time they appeared and how to kill them. The fight was on!

The next day, looking like I'd just contracted measles, my aim was to head to Mallaig to catch the ferry over to Skye. That was until we got to a place called Morar Sands, where I stood at the top of a 280-foot hill called Beinn an Achaidh Mhoir and witnessed the most beautiful bay I'd seen so far. The sea was a turquoise blue with a freshwater river flowing underneath from a huge loch called Loch Morar, just the other side of the bay, adding to the incredible colours. The sand was the whitest I'd seen yet.

I stopped and sat to just drink it in, reminding myself, *Once in a while, I'm allowed to take some time to really enjoy what I'm doing.*

So, I decided to stay for the night and found a perfect secluded cove, cut off by the sea at high tide. That night, I learned something new about the despicable midges – it only needed a few miles an hour of wind to keep them away. There was a perfect warm breeze which allowed us to sit outside the tent for the evening. Once I'd got Jet sorted, my face completely covered in bites, I stripped naked and bathed in the sea water, hoping the salt would help get rid of the incredible urge to scratch my arms and face from the meal they'd made of me the night before. It worked a treat.

In the shallow clear water, I noticed some good-sized crabs scuttling around the nearby rocks. Unable to catch them with my hands, I went back to my tiny cove and got busy making a spear. I found a great length of thin branch lying in the trees, grabbed the duct tape that I carried to repair any holes in the tent, and fastened my fishing knife to the length of wood. Stealthily, I headed back into the water with some small sea snails I'd found and removed from their shells as bait. I perched myself on the rock they were hiding under, dropped the sea snails and waited patiently. It took some time but, a few hours later, I came back with two sizeable velvet crabs. I love crab; it's one of my favourite meats. To bulk things up for my evening stew, I picked more whelks and limpets. It's so satisfying to hunt your own food when you really need it; the feeling of being full on a good, nutritious meal in a situation like mine makes the world of difference.

The day after next, we made it to Mallaig after a very different evening to the one before! I made the grave mistake of camping up in some heather that evening and the restaged attack by our newfound friends was absolutely brutal. In the morning, pocked like a pincushion, I was in despair at the thought of leaving the tent.

Once on Skye, we arrived at a small bay called Armadale on the south-west tip of the island. It took about a week and a half for me to complete my first section, ending up in Skye's biggest and main town, Portree. I walked the section that took me past Skye Bridge, Broadford and eventually the last nineteen miles back into Portree. I will admit that I found it genuinely hard. As beautiful as the landscape in Skye is, the days were getting hotter, the nights longer and the midges unbearable each night and morning.

By this point, I figured out that on the really sweltering days, Jet and I needed to wake up early, an hour before light, then walk as much as we could before the heat of the day became unbearable for her, then repeat this in the evening when it got cooler, hiding from the heat of the day in a shaded spot. The midges in the morning are as horrific as they are at night, but they start to disperse once it gets too hot – so it was kind of out of the frying pan and into the fire!

However, as soon as they go and it gets hotter, just to make sure you don't rest on your laurels, out come the *cleggs* – horseflies. It seemed like one endless torture! Hot and sweating, covering every inch of my body with clothes, constantly slapping myself across the face after each bite and in sheer frustration, by the end of the day, it would just be too much to bear. Knowing the midges would very soon be out again, I was finding it really difficult to enjoy my first few weeks on Skye.

To make matters even worse, I would soon learn how unbelievably quickly *burns* (streams) from the hills and mountains dry up, leaving very little to drink. I physically couldn't carry all my gear, Jet's dog food and at least ten litres of fresh water a day for us to drink, cook and use to cool her down throughout the day.

We arrived in Portree on 1 June thirsty, hot and bitten messes. I made a pact to myself and Jet to spend a couple of days there to regroup, find out local knowledge of the island and give my girl a good rest with plenty of water. I noticed some tents camped up on the shore of Portree, and while normally I would do everything to keep away from the crowds, on this occasion I decided to go and mingle. I pitched my tent and very soon four guys – a French Canadian, Dault, a German, Chris, a young Scottish fella, Brian, a Slovakian, Sven – and a younger Italian girl, Angela, came over to see me. We all hit it off really well, and in the end spent four nights camping together, foraging mussels on the coast and making dinner over a huge firepit each night. It was the first time that I would feel like a real traveller, with people around me from all walks of life and their own adventures to share. One evening, Dault asked if we had ever heard of the 'midgey test' before. None of us had.

'You strip naked, spread your legs, put your arms out in the air and see if you can stand it for one minute while the midges devour you,' he said.

'Fuck that!' Chris the German said.

Brian, a lot younger and game for anything, said, 'I'm up for it, pal!'

'I'm in!' I added.

Chris soon caved and agreed. Angela was sleeping in a hostel and had already retired for the evening. Once the midges were at their most ravenous, we all stood in a line using Dault's phone as a stopwatch. At this point, even with our clothes on, it was already unbearable.

'Let's just do this!' said Chris, clearly unamused.

We all stripped off as fast as we could, ready to take the punishment. Now, I've seen the films with over-elaborate torture techniques. What a real waste of time all of that is. Stick someone in a room with 100,000 midges and, believe me, you'll extract all your information in no time. Each of us breathed heavily through our noses so as not to ingest them, swearing uncontrollably with constant shouts to Dault – 'How fucking long left?!' – only to regret opening our mouths as they poured in, evil opportunists that they are!

Impressively, we all made it to sixty seconds. As soon as the time was up, no words were spoken. We all ran out from behind the bushes like we were fleeing for our lives, all in our birthday suits, shouting and slapping ourselves in a deranged frenzy; unzipping our tents and diving in with a desperate sense of urgency. All we could hear was one another swearing, slapping our bodies all over, from our feet, legs – even our manhood – all the way up to our faces and hair. After about half an hour, German Chris shouted in a rather disgusted manner, 'That was an *effin'* awful idea!' We all laughed and refused to leave our tents again for the evening. This is my only good memory of the midges.

The rest of Skye would be a very similar story: a constant struggle for water and long stretches before being able to stock up on food for Jet. Already, I was looking forward to autumn. As much as I'd longed for summer, ironically, I now spent every day hoping it would rain or be really windy.

16

Careful where you stand!

Not long before finishing Skye, I would be ill for the first time on the walk. I made my first mistake when it came to foraging. Mussels are a great source of food, but you must be very careful when to pick them during the warmer months. Ideally, you want to select ones that have been submerged in water most of, if not all of, the day. You wait for the tide to be out and pick them when they are still stuck to the rocks and submerged in seawater. Ones that are closer to the shore may have spent many hours out of water depending on the tide size. Essentially, the hotter months create more algae, and toxins emitted by the algae may be digested by the mussels and contained within them, as with any shellfish. I learned this the hard way.

I was on the north-west of Skye in a bay not far from a place called Portnalong when I started to feel very ill. In no time, I had a seriously violent bout of vomiting and diarrhoea. I pitched the tent early next to a freshwater stream, having just had two days of rain, and spent the whole afternoon being sick and offloading my bowels next to some bushes. It was awful! To make matters worse, I knew in the next few hours that the dreaded midges would be out for the kill and I'd be running in and out of the tent to do my business, horribly ill, sweating and getting eaten alive during the process.

Confident I was far enough away from any unwanted attention, allowing me to be left to suffer alone, to my disbelief, I heard a vehicle pull up just metres from my tent. I'd literally just got back in after leaving another unwanted surprise on the floor. I heard some foreign voices talking and, so as not to be rude, unzipped my tent to say hello. Looking gaunt and pasty, I said hello and asked if everything was okay. To my horror, it was photographers and two female models, one from America, the other from France. They had come to do a photo shoot!

Completely oblivious to my situation, they set up the shoot, the girls standing where my rear end had just unleashed hell. After half an hour of shooting, the photographers, now aware of my story, asked if I would come and stand between them for a photo. I was so desperate to go to the toilet again, it was unreal. I asked them to wait a second, telling them I needed to put some clothes on. About to explode, I reached for the pot that I make my food in and, almost in tears of shame, squatted and let rip inside the tent, shitting in my very own food bowl. After I was done, I stepped out to get a photo with them in the knowledge that, unbeknown to them, the models were standing directly in my excrement!

Near the end of Skye, I arrived in such a beautiful spot called Glenbrittle, right by the mountains. Dault and Angela had asked if they could walk with me for a few days and we hiked around the mountains, making a visit to the magical fairy pools – a stunning mountain stream with many small individual pools, smoothed by the gushing winter rains that flow through the valley. Despite it being insanely busy with tourists, it was a truly spectacular spot.

We ended up in and around the mountains of Skye when Storm Hector hit us with some real force. We camped that night at the bottom of the mountain, getting a serious beating from the winds. It really hit us hard. This was not the first storm, nor would it be the last I'd endure, and I'd experienced a lot of heavy winds on my walk so far, so I felt at ease, but I could really sense a fear in Angela; she wasn't really a camper and had never experienced anything like this before. She was in good hands though, with two very experienced campers by her side. The next day, we said our goodbyes and I set off to complete the last stretch back to Armadale where I started.

I was given a lot of good advice by locals about how to stop midges attacking: products such as Avon Skin So Soft, Smidge, various oils as well as fires and other smoke-radiating products. This was all well and good if you're taking a stroll, a day hike, a short camping trip, or if you're in a safe place to make fires, but for Jet and me, there was a huge difference: we didn't have the comfort net of knowing that soon enough they'd be a distant memory, nor could we jump into a car, put the air-con on and drive to our accommodation to make a quick escape. Believe me when I say, there is a huge difference! For us, there was never any escape. It was a constant battle throughout the entire summer.

And when it came to products, Jet and I were on a mission. The heat of the day would have me in buckets of sweat, the result of which was that any product would simply stream down my forehead into my eyes, burning them and making it almost impossible to see. Also, lighting fires during summer in places where the ground is covered with dry grass and heather is a complete no-no. The grass catches fire so fast and before you know it, you've got acres of land up in flames, killing off all the native wild-life in and around it. My only option was a head net and gloves but, sadly, as I learned in Skye, that wouldn't work for me either. One evening, I kept Jet inside the tent while I sat outside with my head net on. Jet, loyal as she is, unable to see me, panicked and clawed her way through the fly sheet of my tent leaving a gaping hole, and for the entire night, the midges had free reign to swarm in and annihilate us. With all the hardship we were yet to endure, it remains without doubt the hardest night of my entire walk.

I was also learning about the layout of the Hebridean islands. Depending on the size of the island, the average one would normally have one main town or village, but other than that shops were very few and far between, making it harder to restock on supplies. I had learned the hard way that during the summer months accessing water was going to be a huge problem, and I'd have to dedicate hours of the day to source it. But now as I became a competent survivalist, I was able to take a calm step back, distilling water from the sea and constantly foraging. I also realized that I would never again take for granted a running tap or the ease of simply nipping to a shop.

It dawned on me that the constant struggle for the basics in life – food, water and safe shelter – as well as the physical and mental endurance aspect of the walk, had now consumed my mind. As difficult as it was, I was really starting to enjoy the constant battle for the only things that humans really need, which, in turn, took my mind away from the not so positive thoughts that had consumed me for so long: be it debts for things I never needed in the first place, frustration with the amount of negativity that seems to plague society, and the feeling of entrapment, of living in a system that's been created where I saw everybody as cogs in a machine, that I too had unwillingly found myself a part of. My world, though not easy, had become simple, and although it had always been there, my appreciation for the things we so often take for granted was beginning to change my entire perspective on life.

I returned to Fort William ready to tackle my next big leg. This would take me around a sixty-mile section eventually reaching Loch Aline. It would be my longest, most desolate section yet, passing only a few buildings on the entire stretch and without a single shop in which to stock up with food for Jet and myself. Excited for the challenge, I knew it wasn't going to be easy. It was July; infernally hot, and the cleggs were out in abundance, but my main concern, as ever, was the water situation. Checking the maps and marking every single burn, I could only hope that it rained, filling them up for us. If not, I would have to spend hours making a fire and distilling sea water.

Obviously, one can't drink seawater. The salt content is

incredibly high and will pretty much immediately make you sick, dehydrate you and eventually kill you. Using simple science, I'd fill my pots up with seawater and bring them to the boil over a fire, their lids over the top at a slight angle with my mugs sitting underneath. Slowly, the fresh water separated, creating a steam that gathered underneath the pot lids. That steam then dripped into my cups underneath, giving me fresh drinking water. It was a long and slow process, but a lifesaver. Without it we would have been in big trouble and unable to have completed this stretch. It took us six days to make it to Loch Aline. One day, we had a huge downpour of rain, blessing us with a day and a half of fresh burn water. Jet and I drank as much of it as we could, to the point where I felt physically sick.

Putting the heat, consistent bites and lack of water aside, this was such a stunning section to walk, with mountains dominating the landscape, incredible valleys, and the occasional forest to pass through, teeming with wildlife and giving Jet and me a perfect place to rest in the shade. I was really proud of her and myself for making it through this section unscathed. Stupidly tired yet overjoyed at the thought of a day's rest and relieving myself of the crippling weight of my bag off my shoulders, we arrived in Loch Aline, our final stop before heading on the ferry to Mull.

As our popularity grew, help from locals and followers started to come in thick and fast. When we arrived in towns or villages, the offers of a plate of food or even a few quid to help us with supplies to see us on our way were improving. I realized that it wasn't just because our profile was growing that helped to this end, but just how friendly, kind and generous the Scottish are.

It always made me feel a little better about accepting their offers when they told me how much they loved following the journey, and that through my photos and videos, they were getting so much joy, seeing not only my adventure, but also parts of the UK coast that they had never visited before, and often never knew existed. I found some comfort in this exchange, given I was the only one who knew how hard I had to work to get these photos.

After a two-day rest, we took the ferry over to Mull, followed by isles Iona, Staffa and Lunga. Mull has 300 miles of more jaw-dropping coastline, its climate moderated by the Gulf Stream with mountains running through the centre. I loved it! In no time at all, we were blessed with the sound of sea eagles hovering high, stalking out their prey. The locals referred to them as 'flying doors', they were so big. We headed north-west along the coast, passing through Salen before eventually making it to the colourfully quaint town of Tobermory. Pink, blue, white and green houses create the most wonderful, clean-looking seafront I had ever seen – it was like walking into a postcard. We spent two days finding out local knowledge of the island and its coast, locating shops as we circumnavigated its coast and, of course, PRing for SSAFA.

By this point, pretty much every local newspaper and radio station wanted us for interviews. News travels fast around the islands, and given the effort that I was putting into chatting to locals and promoting our story, in every town or village we passed through on the coast, Jet and I would be stopped by passers-by who'd heard about us. It was lovely at first, but became quite tiring after a while, repeating the same story and answering the same questions time and again, especially after a hard day's shift.

In essence, from the second I woke to the second I went to bed, I'd be constantly working. I tried to remind myself that every single time somebody asked me a question, it would be the first time for them. Questions were always asked with real curiosity and, despite being tired, I'd always be more than happy to chat away, appreciating the well wishes and kind words.

From Tobermory, we made our way to the northernmost tip of Mull, navigating that most difficult of terrain: felled trees. I could walk up, down and around mountains all day (I love it!), but this was a different ball game. When a pine forestry block has been cut down, you are left with huge expanses of land completely covered at least two feet high with broken branches and snapped logs, with every step a potential ankle breaker. For Jet, it was almost impossible. Scared that a single wrong move from her could result in her being impaled by a protruding stick, I decided that the best thing to do was to carry her. On flat ground, it would have taken me about fifteen minutes maximum. Through this, it would be an easy half-day's worth of meticulous navigation, carrying a four-stone dog and a six-stone bergen laden with our gear and dog food.

It was brutally hard work, stopping every ten minutes to rest my arms, only to look back and realize we'd hardly covered any ground at all. At the same time, I was sweating buckets and getting bitten by the relentless cleggs. It really tested my patience and willpower. I remember getting to the end, shaking like a leaf from the weight I'd been carrying, dropping to my knees and throwing up all over myself – a sure sign of heat exhaustion. It was soul-destroying. Unable to do any more, we walked to the nearest burn and found a spot to camp up for the night. After pitching, I walked to the burn and must've drunk about two litres of water. I got naked and lay in the icy mountain water for as long as I could to cool down. Sadly, my respite was cut short with the shade of evening encroaching; it was time to make food and retire to my tent before the inevitable influx of midges. All I wanted to do was sit by the sea, listen to the calm water, have a sea bath and write in my journal. Instead, Jet and I would both overheat, confined to our tent until it got dark at around midnight. It really was torture.

We made good progress around Mull after this, passing through Dervaig, Calgary and more of the island's exceptional coastline. I met a lovely fella called Bob just south of Calgary Bay, who offered me a shower and a much-needed wash of my clothes. It had been about a month since I'd had such a luxury. Crusted sea salt, small twigs, clumps of dirt, dead flies – you name it – ran off my body into the basin of the shower. I'd had no idea just how many cuts, scratches and bites I had, as well as small burns all over my hands from making fires. I had got a particularly bad slash under my left arm while carrying Jet through the felled woodland. I had tripped and twisted my body so as to break the fall for her, then felt a really sharp pain. In the shower at Bob's house I could finally take stock of my injuries and realized that this one was a deep gash. The walk was really taking its toll on my body.

17

The big pop!

From Mull, we caught the tiny ferry over to the serenely pretty island of Iona. With aquamarine water lapping at icing-white sandy beaches, it was beyond idyllic. I spent a day there resting up and giving Jet some time out from the heat and constant walking. It then only took me a day to walk it. I stashed my bag so I could explore the idyllic coves and small beaches weight-free.

While I was on Iona, we were offered a boat ride to visit and walk two uninhabited islands: Staffa and Lunga; both neighbours of Mull and havens for birds. As we boarded the boat, the wonderful skipper gave me and Jet a perfect floor seat next to the open door for the whole ride. Better still, two Scottish ladies armed with a fiddle and a guitar serenaded the boat with Scottish music. In all, it was such a perfect day.

The two islands were covered in puffins, Lunga particularly. One of the first things you think when you see a puffin up close is how much bigger you thought they'd be, when in fact they're tiny, incredibly cute birds with the most amazing vividly coloured beaks. As for Staffa, what can I say? It's an absolute must-see! Just like the Giant's Causeway, Staffa's cliffs tower high as a cathedral, their basalt rocks forming perfect hexagonal columns that look like church organ pipes. Staffa is also famous for mystical Fingal's sea cave, a geologically Gothic marvel, the only access to which is by boat. Resident grey Atlantic seals, twice the size of a common seal, surrounded us on ledges and rocks protruding from the sea, barking loudly as they sunned themselves.

Soon enough, our time around the beautiful island of Mull had come to an end. Like Skye, it had been tough-going. The heat and the midges made us work for it all the way round, but keeping a promise I'd made to myself that 'Chris Walks the UK' would always be a positive page, I never once moaned about my adversities on social media. Rather than drone on about my frustrations when I found things really tough, particularly during a stage like this when it would be so easy to vent as I sat boiling in a tent fighting off the dreaded midges all night, I just kept my hardships to myself. I wanted my page to showcase the beauty of our coastline, revealing uplifting stories of people at their best, as well as interesting history videos and footage of places that took my breath away. Yes, I wanted my page to be honest and reflect the reality of my experience, but it's both my choice and my nature to show how I overcame adversity with a positive mindset. Perhaps the social media page's ever-increasing positivity was reflecting my own positive transformation and growth as a person.

After finishing Mull, I arranged a lift to take me back down south near the Mull of Kintyre again so I could get the ferry to Islay and Jura, the islands I'd had to miss previously due to a lack of funds. It would be Islay first and then, from there, a ferry-hop to Jura.

I arrived on Islay on 6 August 2018. Known as the 'Queen of the Hebrides', it's the fifth largest Scottish island, with around 130 miles of coastline, and is also famous for its whisky distilleries. Despite being only twenty-five miles long, it holds nine active distilleries. Sadly for us, the first day walking on Islay did not go quite as planned. We arrived off the ferry in a small port called Askaig, in the absolute arse-end of nowhere. It boasted just one small pub and an even smaller shop. As I sat in the beer garden with my usual cordial, planning our next move, I suddenly found myself surrounded by a flock of candyfloss-pink sheep; an absolute first for me!

After a chat with some locals, as always gleaning some much-needed local knowledge, I was shown a camp spot just past the small village. As ever, keeping the sea to my left, the next morning the plan would be to head in the direction of Port Ellen, Islay's biggest and main town, some fifteen miles south. Jet and I had worked hard to finish Mull. Both of us were physically and mentally tired, and I knew Port Ellen would be a much better place for us to rest up before heading around the rest of the island. We both badly needed a break. Only that morning we'd been in Mull and had to wake up at 5 a.m. to walk two hours to get the ferry back to the mainland; once there, we thumbed a lift south to Largs, from where we had to catch another ferry over to Arran; and from Arran, we had to walk the eight-mile stretch to the other side of the island to then catch *another* small ferry that would take us north of the Mull of Kintyre. It was then a five-mile walk crossing over from one side of the peninsula to the other (from east to west) to catch the final ferry, eventually taking us to Islay. After a few big days prior to this, in order to finish Mull, it was safe to say we were now both absolutely shattered.

By the time we arrived on Islay, we had very little light left to play with. I made the call to make tracks ASAP to get a few miles in, leaving us less to do the following day. This was a stupid mistake on my part. When you're both physically and mentally tired, exacerbated by the heat and frustration of constant attacks by cleggs and midges, slowly but surely you start to make mistakes. Thinking logically becomes harder and you become clumsy. Signs of this become obvious in your sloppy decision-making. As I walked, my ankle slipped on rocks slick with seaweed that I would never usually attempt to walk on. All my weight and that of my bag fell sideways, with my ankle still lodged between two rocks as I fell. I felt and heard the big *pop* and was immediately in excruciating pain. 'Oh fuck!' I said to myself.

After lying down reminding myself to just remain calm, I then sat up to check out the damage to my ankle. It wasn't good. I sat leaning on my elbow and had a look around, knowing I had to pitch the tent immediately as it was getting dark. I needed to stop, reassess my situation and make a plan as to what to do next. I saw a patch of grass about thirty yards away, perfect for the tent. I tied the rope in my bag to the top of my bergen, crawled over to the patch of grass and then used the rope to pull my bergen over me so as not to carry it. With great effort, I pitched up, made some food and sat for a while contemplating our next move. I had paracetamol and ibuprofen but knew they would not be enough.

Back in Arran, I'd been given a hip flask full of whisky by a lovely follower. I had yet to sample it. I held the painkillers in one hand and the hip flask in the other. I remember thinking to myself, *Screw the painkillers! If anything, the whisky will give you a good night's sleep.* It was a no-brainer. I took a huge swig of the whisky, put the painkillers back in my bag and started to get very merry as I constantly swigged away.

I thought long and hard about this journey and why I'd started it: the ups, the downs and all my challenges so far, and how far I'd evolved as a person. I was in this to test my limits and learn what I could about myself as a man. I'd always believed that I was capable of great things, regardless of how ridiculous that sounded to anyone else. I wondered what else I would learn about myself in the coming months. Also, in the back of my mind was the very real possibility that if an accident like this was to happen to me in places like the Outer Hebrides or Shetland in winter, it would be important to know that I had the minerals to get my injured self to safety.

I thought about a book that I'd read called *Touching the Void*, a true story about a man who fell into a crevasse in the Peruvian Andes and managed to pull himself out with a severely broken leg, dragging himself six miles to safety through perilous ice and snow. It's a wonderful, miraculous story of determination and survival. Mine was no comparison to this, but I could at least try and see if I had it in me.

The next morning, I woke early and got to work making a crutch from driftwood and washed-up rope from the shore. I folded up my jumper and put it under my armpit to provide some cushioning for the crutch. I then packed up my gear, again tying my bag around my waist so I could drag it rather than carry it, relieving my ankle of any extra weight. It would be nine miles before I hit a road or any signs of life and most of this section would have me clambering over rocks with cliffs and mountains to my right and the sea to my left. It was so difficult with the crutch – my bag dragging behind me snagging constantly on rocks. Often, I'd just sit on my backside, using the palm of my hands to push against the ground and drag myself along, then pull on the rope to drag my bag to where I'd got to. I'd repeat this process until the palms of my hands couldn't take any more and then revert to using the crutch.

My ankle was badly swollen, felt burning hot and the pain was searing. With every drag of that bergen, it was a constant reminder that I'd done some serious damage to it. Within my boot, I could feel both a looseness and fluid inside. To make matters worse, in order to avoid hitting my ankle on the rocks, I would have to lift my right leg constantly. After miles of doing this, my thighs cramped up with intolerable pain, and I had to stop to stretch them out; by the end of this nine-mile stretch of hell, it felt like someone had taken a baseball bat to my thighs.

Throughout this long and arduous process, I took frequent breaks, Jet constantly licking my face out of concern. I thought a lot about my daughter, Caitlin, and felt shit for being so down and stressed before starting this walk, and the effect it must have had on her. Tired and in agony with a swollen ankle, I would often cry with anger at myself, constantly thinking I was a failure to her. This would make me so furious that I'd immediately start moving again, determined to keep edging myself forward.

Looking back, perhaps I was punishing myself, but also venting in a cathartic sense. I knew I couldn't change the past but, so far, this whole journey had been a healing process for me. If venting my self-loathing was what I needed to do, then so be it. In all, the biggest challenge would be to prove to her and myself that I'd overcome my demons. Dragging my arse with a buggered ankle across nine miles of rocks still seemed like a far lesser task.

What would normally have taken me three hours to walk would ultimately take two whole days to eventually hit a road. Exhausted, I just lay down beside it, waiting for the first car that came by to hopefully help us get to Port Ellen, my trusty four-legged friend never more than a few yards away from me. About half an hour later, to my absolute joy, a taxi came into sight. I stood up and flagged it down with my last shred of energy.

'Chris,' the female taxi driver said, 'you've had us all worried to death! People have been out looking for you. Get in – I'll take you to Port Ellen to get you sorted out.'

The last few days had been a personal experience the like of which I didn't want to talk about. I did my best to act like nothing was wrong, put on a brave face and accepted her offer of a lift. We had a good chat, all the while me covering the palms of my hands so she couldn't see how slashed and sore they were, so as not to attract any unwanted sympathy.

She introduced herself as Donalda.

'I've never heard of that name,' I told her.

'Out here, a lot of children tend to adopt their father's name,' she replied. 'My father's name is Donald. Stick an 'a' on the end and you have my name!'

I was amazed and quite loved the idea.

We finally arrived in Port Ellen and Donalda refused to take any fare from me. Ever grateful, I thanked her, and we said our goodbyes. I was so relieved to be here, back in the embrace of comparative civilization. Despite the fact I was probably a quarter of my usual size, so skinny from relentless walking, it was evident that my body, still wiry as sea-rope, was in good shape; as after just two and a half weeks' rest, the ligament damage to my ankle had fully recovered and I was ready to go again.

A local fisherman, Dave, had offered to take me to an uninhabited island called Texa, around a mile off the coast of Islay. Excited at the prospect, I jumped at the chance. On his small fishing boat, Dave dropped me off and told me he'd come and pick me up in a few days after the bad weather subsided. I spent three days on the island in an old, abandoned house. The wind speed was such that it would be at least that long before I'd even have a remote chance of being collected again, the sea now rough and forbidding. It was a small island and didn't even take us two hours to circumnavigate, but my biggest problem was, once again, water. I'd been told of a tiny freshwater spring that is only accessible when the tide is out, but as my bad luck would have it, I'd been pointed in the wrong direction as to where to find it. I searched all day with no joy, finally having no choice but to give in and get to work distilling sea water.

The next day, desperate not to use up all my gas just boiling sea water, I searched every nook and cranny for the elusive spring. Eventually, my tenacity paid off and I did discover it; a precious tiny trickle of water seeping between two small rocks. I was able to fill up my water flasks just in time before the tide covered it up. To say I was happy was an understatement. There's something extremely liberating about staying alone on an uninhabited island out at sea. Having begun to make friends with the demons and shadows in my mind and started the long process of patching up my heart, I felt solitary island dwelling was something I wanted to do more of in future. In all, I had a fantastic three days.

As the sea calmed, I returned to Islay and found it such an incredible coastline to walk – spectacular high cliffs, beautiful waterfalls you could stand behind and more eagles to feast my eyes on. One evening, I camped in a spot called the Singing Sands, a beach made entirely from broken shells that make a noise when you walk on them – hence the name. A wonderful woman, who had been following my progress and reached out to me, had made me a cheesecake to devour after I'd made our staple food. I got to work collecting driftwood to get my grub on, only to return to the tent to find an empty box with just a few crumbs left for me. I looked out of the flaps to witness five sweet-toothed rams looking rather pleased with themselves! I'd walked three miles there and back just to get that bloody cheesecake – I was so mad at them! Lesson learned.

I loved Islay and had already made a good rapport with some of the locals, especially those in Port Ellen, who'd kindly given me some great historical information and places along the coast that are must-visits: fourteenth-century tombs with the most incredible stone carvings, beautiful beaches, and Port Charlotte with its singing seals. One evening, thirsty as hell, I banged on a door to ask if I could fill up my water bottles. To my surprise, the young lad told me nobody on that street had, nor ever had had, running water. Much as I was gasping for a drink, I loved this; it was fascinating, even comforting, to see folks still living the old way, collecting their own water.

One thing that had really started to strike me was the extreme lack of trees. As time went on and I progressed on my walk, I would see that a lot of the islands had absolutely none. At night, sitting in a tent, I was puzzled as to why this was the case. I was told that it was because the weather on the islands was too brutal for the trees, but that didn't seem right to me. The more logical conclusion in my mind was that, long ago, the trees must have been used for housing, building boats, making tools, burning for warmth and any other necessity trees are incredibly handy for. Soon enough, I would walk many other islands which were covered in vast expanses of peaty moorland, especially the Outer Hebrides and Shetland, where peat is essential for heat in the winter months. I was often told about peat digs where ancient forest stumps would appear perfectly preserved in the peat, meaning at some point trees had once existed.

What this meant for me was that my only hope for making a fire would be wood carried by the tide from all different parts of the world onto the shores of the Hebrides: driftwood. Summer months made life difficult, as tourists and locals would also gather as much as they could, leaving little left for Jet and me, but over time, I started getting good at locating pieces of tiny branches scattered in and around the beaches and rocks where nobody else would think to look. By now it was September and fire was not just a luxury around which we could sit and relax on a cool evening; it was a necessity for us, as we needed it for food and warmth. I simply had to become adept at locating wood.

My last stretch in Islay would take me six miles south from the most northern tip, Ruvaal, past a lighthouse occupied by a couple who seldom left, only ever to get food. It was a stunning stretch down to where I started on Islay back down to Port Arisaig. It was also exciting looking over to my next island, Jura, on my left. I could see the mountains, the Paps of Jura, and was itching to get in and among them. We made it safely to Port Arisaig on 27 August ready to board the tiny ferry and cross over the half-mile stretch of sea to Jura.

18

I left my heart in Jura

I was by now starting to get a bit of national press rather than just featuring in local newspapers, and it would not be long before I realized the monumental effect this would have on my fundraising. Before crossing over on the ferry to Jura, I did an interview for *The Guardian* about my travels. Just that interview would become one of the many reasons that, up until this point, Jura became one of my favourite islands – and still is to this day.

The island is around twenty-seven miles long and averages around eight miles in width, with a total area of 142 square miles. Its name comes from the Old Norse word for 'deer', and with a population of only 200 humans and around 6,000 deer roaming free, I could see why the Vikings had chosen such an apt name. Craighouse is the small main town and holds most of the population, with random houses and farms scattered only up the east coast. The west coast is completely wild, bar one estate owned by Lord William Astor.

It just so happened that I arrived on the island only a week before the Jura Music Festival – a small and intimate affair where Scots from different isles and the mainland come to hear traditional music and to drink. It really couldn't have been better timing! Arriving in Craighouse after a five-mile walk from the ferry, I did my usual and headed to the pub to have a chat with the locals, get a feel for the island and, of course, soak up what was always the best local information. No pamphlet or book can give you even a glimpse of the knowledge that a local can, which is partly why I always did my best to make connections. Arriving just before the festival, I was witness to the most amazing sense of community, unlike anything I'd witnessed so far on the other islands – everyone helping one another and doing their bit to set up and prepare. It was incredible to see and evident that this wasn't just because of the festival – they looked after each other all year round. There was such a strong sense of community spirit that, sadly, I believe is long gone in most places, certainly where I come from.

I immediately took to them and had a feeling they had also taken to me. After telling them my plans and how rigidly I was determined to stick to the coast all the way around, including the completely wild, uninhabited west side of the island, I was made aware that nobody had ever done that before. There were two bothies on the west side of the coast, and people would cut straight across from the east coast of the island to the west to stay in them, do some exploring and then return the same way they came. Even asking some of the indigenous folk, I realized even they were unable to advise me what it would be like to walk the entire west coast stretch. Obviously, this made me more determined than ever.

Jura is split into two sections. About halfway up the island is Loch Tarbert, a sea loch around six miles each side which basically cuts through the entire width of the island, bar half a mile of land on the east side. My plan would be to do the flatter east coast first, heading north until I reached the most northern tip of Jura, and then head down the north-west coast, which would eventually bring me to the north side of Loch Tarbert. I'd then take a few days' rest to enjoy the music festival and, afterwards, head down the south-west side of the island, bringing me back round to where I'd first arrived on the ferry.

As it was now September, to my absolute joy the midges had started to disperse and it was coming to what I like to call 'storm season': a mixture of still sunny, warm days which could then suddenly turn into ferocious autumn winds. Loaded with supplies, courtesy of the locals, and with the incredible support of a farmer called Grant who I will forever be grateful for meeting, we made our way to the northern tip.

I stopped for a while to marvel at Europe's third largest whirlpool, 'Corryvreckan'. The Gulf of Corryvreckan is a narrow strait between the islands of Jura and Scarba. On a strong tide and good conditions, the tides push fast-flowing water through the narrow stretch between the two islands. Underneath is a huge slab of rock, around 650 feet below, helping to cause a massive whirlpool. It really is incredible to see its power. I sat for half an hour just marvelling at yet another of nature's wonderful creations, but my joy at watching such a sight would soon be cut short.

Things quickly got real – or surreal – as, all of a sudden, strong winds came from the west, bringing the rain with them, leaving us totally exposed. Any normal person would probably have just said, 'Sod this – let's come back when the weather's better!' but, determined to get this cracked, I stood up.

'Come on, Jet, let's do this.'

In my mind, regardless of how tired and wet we'd be, I knew at the end of it we'd be rewarded with a beautiful bothy around six miles south. I stood on the vantage point and had a good look around to see what we were about to embark upon. As astoundingly beautiful as it was, the hills smothered in beautiful purple heather, I could immediately see that this stretch was going to be an absolute nightmare to walk. Given my recent ankle dilemma, I won't lie: I was slightly nervous. I knew that I just had to make the call and commit. As far as I could see, it would be some of the most awkward ground to walk on. It was a never-ending landscape of tussocky bogs and one big hill after another. Tussocks, sometimes referred to in the military as 'baby-heads', are clumps of ground that stick up, leaving (in most cases) a foot's drop in between each one with boggy peat water below running in between: essentially miles of stepping stones that bend and sink each time you step on one. With all my gear, I knew that we were in for a ride! All it would take would be one bad fall and then pop went the weasel; my already weakened ankle would be finished.

It was incredibly slow-going, taking around two hours of graft to walk only half a mile, but I kept reminding myself progress *was* being made.

The road on the opposite side of the island would be around eight miles in equally difficult terrain with nothing but sheep and deer. I knew there was absolutely no room for error. The concentration levels required with every step, thinking, *For God's sake don't slip here or you're a goner*, was much more mentally draining than the physical aspect. Around eight hours in, four miles done and around two miles left, with the bothy occasionally in sight as I headed in and around the nooks and crannies of the west coast, it was clear that Jet and I needed some respite from the constant rains and brutal westerly winds, as well as a moment to rest the brain given the intricacies of the coast-line we were walking.

I happened to notice a cave and knew it was the perfect opportunity to escape and give my brain, legs and back a break, as well as Jet's paws. As I was about to walk into the cave, I suddenly observed two sheep and a deer taking shelter inside.

Surprised and delighted they didn't startle and scarper, I didn't want to disturb them from their temporary respite, so I took my time and started talking to them in the softest, most unthreatening voice I could muster. We edged slowly into the opening of the cave just enough to shelter ourselves from the rain and wind. The sheep and deer kept their eyes on us, ready to bolt at any time, but I kept talking softly to them, reassuring them we were no threat. I sat down and Jet lay down next to me, then I reached for my ready-made sandwiches and started to eat . . . very quietly!

I'd often look back to the months leading up to my grand walk and smile at how far I'd come, both in terms of distance and mentally, but this encounter really was a chart-topper! Here I was on the wild west coast of Jura, in brutal weather and sharing a cave with my dog, two sheep and the most elegant, beautiful deer; I felt so privileged to have been trusted by them all. Never in my life had I felt so connected to nature. It was such a rare, precious and beautiful moment and will always remain one of my all-time favourite experiences.

Around half an hour later, we said goodbye to our new friends and walked what seemed like the longest mile ever, ending up at a bothy with a red roof in an idyllic cove. We'd made it! I immediately got to work collecting wet driftwood for the fireplace inside, to warm us up and hang our clothes near so they'd dry out quickly. I made a hot cup of coffee, fed Jet and put my feet up. I was incredibly proud of us both; it had been an endlessly hard shift. I decided to write a letter to Caitlin and stash it in the bothy in the hope that one day I could return with her to retrieve it. I folded it up neatly and put it in a box on the fireplace with a note asking for it to be left undisturbed. Some years later, another walker sent me a photo of it to let me know it was still there and safe.

While I sat writing, I thought I heard the sound of a boat. *No it couldn't be*, I said to myself, *not in this weather.*

I went to take a look, and sure enough, it was the coastguard. One of the crew was making a dash towards the bothy while the other waited for him.

'Chris!' he shouted. 'We're doing a training exercise and we wanted to stop off to check that you were okay. That's no easy feat what you've just finished. You had us all worried!'

Obviously, I had been – and still was – completely out of phone signal, and I knew people were quite worried about us doing this section.

'We're fine, fella,' I shouted back against the high wind. 'That's such a lovely thing for you to do. I can't tell you how much I appreciate it.'

'Do you want us to take you back? The weather's getting even worse tomorrow.'

'That would be cheating,' I said, laughing.

'No problem. Just be safe, you crazy man!'

We laughed as I stood and waved the crew off, Jet standing by my side.

True to his word, the next day the weather was awful. I packed our stuff and we left the warmth and dryness of the bothy to make our way to the north side of Loch Tarbert that would eventually bring us to a road where we could return to Craighouse, ready for a few days of fun and good music. I also found this section really hard. The day before had completely drained both my mind and my body, as I'm sure it did Jet's. My legs felt stiff as logs. It would take us yet another two days and a night spent in our second bothy on the north side of Loch Tarbert before we were done. That said, I believe there's always a silver lining if you look for it, and the bothy was situated in the most magical location in Jura. I spent the night replying to the crooning seals that were singing in the nearby sea loch, reciprocating with the same noises they were making. There's no way it wasn't a two-way conversation – they just happened to sing better than me!

We finally reached the road the next morning and were back in a signal zone. As it was still raining, I took Jet's coat off, dried her as best I could with the clothes from my dry bag and wrapped her inside my sleeping bag, covering her with the outer skin of my tent to keep her warm and dry. Soaked to the bone and stupidly happy to be back on the safety of a road, knowing that a human might pass at any time, I revelled in the fact that we'd made it.

I lay down on the road and took ten minutes. Using my military poncho to cover myself, I pulled out my phone and turned it on. It began to ping endlessly with notifications and messages for at least a minute and a half before eventually stopping. While I had been grafting round the west coast of Jura, *The Guardian* had published their article about me and my walk. I'd arrived on Jura with £12,000 in donations for SSAFA and, overnight, unknown to me, my followers had been helping my donations climb to an incredible £47,000! The second I saw it, I jumped onto my feet, shouting 'YES!' at the top of my voice, accidentally scaring Jet.

I'd received at least 300 messages of congratulations and still they continued to flood in. National news channels and papers were asking for my story as well as friends, family and loyal followers consistently messaging, asking if I was okay and if I'd seen the news. The first thing I did was wrap my arms around Jet.

'See, girl, hard work does eventually pay off!'

With a bit of graft, in three hours we would be warm and sitting in a pub celebrating our efforts with a pint. We arrived in Craighouse and were greeted like I'd never been before. As well as being relieved that we were back safely, all the locals were now aware of our story and the recent jump in donations and publicity. It was a happy time all around, and to my disbelief, endless pints had been left behind the bar for me as a congratulations for reaching nearly half of my final donation target: £100,000.

The festival would start the next day, and the local football pitch and surrounding areas were completely filled with tents. I was surprised by just how many of the visitors had been following me with such encouraging words of support and received a massive hug from each and every one of them. It was quite surreal, being simultaneously happy, tired and overwhelmed, and yet provided the perfect kickstart to a few days spent with wonderful Scottish people at my first ever Scottish festival.

Over the next few days, Jet and I did our very best to rest up, take our mind off the walk and just drink everything in. We watched some incredible music and a well-loved Scottish band called Skipinnish who played the most amazing, upbeat Scottish music. I was presented with a bottle of Jura whisky from the distillery opposite the pub as well as being asked to play a music set in the bar with a couple of locals. I felt so honoured.

Later that evening, as a local band played on the main stage, the entire place erupted; the atmosphere nothing but pure joy and fun. The band performed a cover of Coldplay's 'Fix You' and, during this song, I had a real moment. I stood next to the stage looking all around me while Jet was looked after by a couple of islanders, though she had me in her sights the whole time. As I glanced at everyone having fun, dancing and singing at the top of their voices, I looked over to my loyal and best friend, as she looked at me. I smiled at her in the most loving way that I could, so proud to call her my friend. Only we knew what we had just done.

This moment would be undoubtedly the happiest I had experienced in so many years. I had a real reason to feel proud of myself and, for once, not feel like a complete failure. I ran over to Jet, gave her a hug and took her outside to spend an hour with her, sitting by the shore, just the two of us. Jet sat in between my legs as I stroked her, while I looked out to sea relishing this feeling – pure happiness – that I had longed for for so very long.

An hour later, a local ran outside.

'Chris, the ceilidh band are about to start. Please come and join us!'

I said I'd never been to a ceilidh before. 'I have no idea how to move to it. I'll be a disgrace to your dance moves!' I joked.

'Who cares!' he said. 'As far as we're concerned, you're one of us. Anyway, we'll guide you. Now, come on!'

I walked back to a much quieter, more relaxed atmosphere in the large gazebo, where people sat back drunk in chairs, half asleep with their heads on their chests.

'I'm not sure there's a band in the world who could get this lot going!' I joked, and yet a minute later the ceilidh band started their explosive set; pipes, fiddles, ukuleles and guitars creating an upbeat and joyful sound that awakened the slumberers like a tonic. Never had I seen so many pissed people spring into action so quickly and spend the next two hours dancing with more energy and expertise than I could ever dream of mustering – it was like Lord of the fucking Dance on speed!

My hand was grabbed and, soon enough, I became part of the swirling teetering dervish. We swung each other round in circles, jumping from one partner to another, listening to the most upbeat traditional Scottish music, just as I could imagine them doing hundreds of years ago. Not for a single second did I stop laughing or smiling. My God, how I was falling in love with Scotland and its people.

Jet and I left the next day to complete a two-day stretch around the south-west side of Loch Tarbert and finally down to the place where I had alighted the ferry to start walking. Although not such a difficult section, the autumn rains had returned along with the winds and were happily giving us another beating. I edged my way around the Paps of Jura – three mountains whose name originates from the Norse word *pap*, meaning 'breast', which I can confirm is very apt. No matter where you are on Jura, the Paps are always in view, giving you a useful navigation point. I would pass some of the biggest raised beaches in the world. It really was spectacular.

Only a few miles away from catching the ferry and now back in signal, I received a phone call from the BBC to tell me that I'd been nominated for the Pride of Britain awards. It was a perfect way to end what had been an incredible time on the beautiful Hebridean island of Jura. It will forever remain a very special place to me, and I can't wait to go back one day and revisit.

19

At the table of a lion

Oban is about thirty miles south of Fort William, the
gateway to the Highlands, and is the main artery for ferries
heading to the Inner and Outer Hebrides. I had £18 on
me and headed to the ferry terminal as soon as I arrived,
smiling at the memory of when I'd drunkenly pitched my
tent in front of the Civic Centre and been wished goodnight by the friendly policemen.

'I have £18. Where will that take me?' I asked the lady
behind the desk.

'Well, we have a ferry going to the Outer Hebrides in
an hour – an island called Barra.'

'That will do. Barra it is!'

I was so excited at the prospect of going to the Outer
Hebrides. It was 28 September and, after four months of
torture, the midges were finally subsiding. I couldn't help
but wonder how winter was going to be in the Outer

Hebrides, or even what part I would be walking during this season.

Geographically, it would make sense to continue further up north after I had completed Barra, taking me to the Uists, then Harris and finally Lewis. Unfortunately, this is not the way it would turn out. I arrived in Castlebay, Barra, some five hours after getting on the ferry. It was a beautiful small little port with a medieval castle perched on a rock cut off by the sea, named after the Norse word *Ciosamul*, meaning Castle Island.

Six miles wide, the small island has roughly thirty-five miles of beautiful coastline, which is followed by a single-track road. I had a good reception in Barra, and I made my way to the local bar as ever to suss the place out. I soon got chatting to the locals and loved their accent; it was so strong and different to any I'd heard before.

One local who was having a pint in the Castlebay Hotel approached and we got chatting about the walk and our shared interest in music. He was in a well-known Scottish band called the Vatersay Boys, named after a small section of Barra called Vatersay, where they lived. In no time at all, he got out his accordion and played me the most incredible rendition of a song called 'Promontory', famous as the main theme song to the film *Last of the Mohicans*. I loved both the film and the song, and already I now loved Barra. It struck me as such a powerful motivational tune, so I recorded it and it would become the song I would put on every single morning when the weather was brutal to motivate myself to leave the tent; I did this for years! Thanks, Vatersay Boys.

Inspired, I decided to head to Vatersay first. Now, I had

seen some beautiful beaches so far on my journey, and as much as I'd like to be biased, having set off from Wales, none so far had come close to some of Scotland's. This next one, however, was on a whole new level. The white sand partly comes from glacial deposits, but most of it is made up of tiny shell fragments as well as an assortment of broken-down spines and other remains of marine animals, along with algae, leaving you with creamy white sand, perfect turquoise water and as clean and well-kept a beach as anyone could wish to find. I could never have dreamed of seeing such places on my walk. I had no idea the Outer Hebrides held such gems.

It didn't take long to walk the island. I headed up north, eventually arriving at Barra airport, where I was welcomed with kindness and a meal. Barra airport is unique: it's the only airport in the world where commercial scheduled flights use a huge tidal beach as its runway on the shallow bays of Traigh Mhòr. It's surreal to watch a plane land on the beach. I stayed an hour to see one land before heading off down the west coast of Barra, which was scattered with more stunning white beaches and very easy walking. Then, out of nowhere, disaster struck.

Scottish islands are renowned for having all four seasons in the space of an hour. One minute it's calm, the next a huge cloud passes over, bringing brutal winds with it. Jet's metallic dog bowl was fastened to the outside of my bag; it got used so much that it was just easier to unclip it from the outside rather than have it take up space on the inside of my bag. Just like that, a huge, powerful gust of wind came from behind and caught the metal bowl, hurtling it into the right side of my face with such force that it cracked one of my teeth in half! I dropped to my knees, blood dripping from my mouth, at the time oblivious as to what it was that had hit me. Shaking like a leaf, I decided to pitch my tent so I could assess the situation. I used my phone camera to see the damage, gargling water to flush out the blood, but had to wait until the bleeding had stopped before I could see anything.

I just so happened to be in one of the only sections on the island where I was unable to seek immediate help – on the other side of a 1,089-foot mountain peak and completely out of signal. Heading back to get help would have taken hours and I was in far too bad a state. I knew I'd have to deal with it myself.

I'd carried an old guitar string pretty much from the start to use as a snare for hunting if ever I got desperate, and while I waited for the bleeding to subside, I got out the snare and tied it around a rock. Soon enough, I was able to see that one side of the tooth was still firmly in place, while the other was piercing into my gum, putting unbearable pressure on my nerve endings. It was so painful it's hard to describe. Toothache times a million, it felt like someone had clamped a vice around my gums and was constantly tightening it. It was a pain unlike anything I'd ever felt before; utterly excruciating.

My eyes now watering uncontrollably from the agony, I grabbed my hip flask filled with Jura whisky from my visit and swigged away like it was apple juice, each time gargling it over the tooth. I was shaking so much it made it hard to get the tiny snare hole around the smaller broken piece of tooth that was now wedged into my gum. It took me about ten minutes to finally get the tiny hole in the snare to grip and tighten around the broken section of tooth, although it felt like an eternity. Each time, if it so much as even touched my tooth, the pain was so intense that I would let out a howl from the depths of my stomach. Once I could feel it had a good enough hold, I had another large gulp of whisky for Dutch courage, and let go of the rock. As the tooth came out, it ripped through my gum, dropping to the ground. The pain was so extreme that I fell to the floor and threw up. But the second the pressure was taken off my nerve endings, the shock of my ripped gums some-what subsided, the pain more than halved – it was such a relief! Soon enough, it was evident that I had sunk the whisky faster than I probably should have, but at the time, remaining sober didn't even cross my mind. Now half-drunk, with a smile on my face knowing the problem was sorted (at least for now!), we got some sleep.

I packed up the next morning and carried on to finish Barra. I tried to continue for as long as I could, but an abscess where I'd ripped the tooth out was growing and the pain was insufferable. I hated to break off the walk, but I could tell this was serious. On 6 October, rather than carry on further north into the Outer Hebrides, we were forced to return to mainland Scotland where the nearest hospital was. I urgently needed antibiotics.

After a few days, fit enough to get going again, we made it back to Oban, where I made the call to head over to the islands of Coll and Tiree before heading north back to the Outer Hebrides.

Coll and Tiree are two separate islands about twelve miles west of the Isle of Mull. I made my way first to Coll, my ferry paid for by a wonderful follower, Maisie, who lives in Oban. It was a strange boat ride for me – the press had kept on coming and people sat on the boat staring at Jet and me while reading the paper. We had full-page spreads in *The Sun*, the *Mirror*, the *Daily Mail* and *The Times*. Person after person was approaching asking if it was us. I was being asked for photos the whole way and even to sign someone's map! Happy as I always was to talk to people, to be recognized for our efforts and to know that the time and hard work I'd put into PRing the charity seemed to be paying off, I'd never been one for attention and, to be honest, just couldn't wait to get camped up back in my own little space again.

Once on Coll, I was greeted by a wonderful man called Rob, who had been asked to keep an eye out for me when I arrived. Some people you can immediately tell are good eggs, and he offered to put me up in his caravan – separate from his home on a lovely beach – while I walked the small island. At around thirteen miles long and three miles wide, it was home to roughly 200 residents, with views over Rum, Eigg, Muck, Skye, Mull and the Paps of Jura. It was a great location and a very easy island to walk compared to some I had done. If you're lucky, on the three-hour boat journey you may be treated to basking sharks, seals, dolphins and – if you're *very* lucky – the odd killer whale.

Keen to get my teeth into Coll, after settling into the caravan, Jet and I set off to the north-east side, and the wildest, but only five miles long. The stretch took us over a few hills and the odd lovely bay, through Sorisdale and around the coast to Arnabost. My favourite section was the south, with two big sandy bays either side of a half-mile stretch of land. It took us no time to finish and on our last night, Rob invited Jet and me to his home to meet his family and join them all for a lobster dinner. His two children were so polite and his wife was a pleasure to be around. I made the regrettable mistake of joining them for a glass of wine, which made me feel so ill with all the antibiotics I'd been taking.

After dinner I noticed some pictures of Rob on the wall playing rugby and took a closer look. Then it clicked – it was Rob Wainwright, former Rugby Union player, capped thirty-seven times for Scotland and also capped for the British Lions as a flanker. I felt privileged to be eating food with him and his family. What a gentleman he is!

The next day, we jumped onto the ferry and headed to Tiree, our next island before eventually returning to the mainland and back to Loch Aline, ready to finish the section we'd missed. It would take us around more wild coastline with big stretches of mountainous wilderness as we made our way towards Strontian and then to mainland Britain's most westerly point: Ardnamurchan.

We had gone days without seeing anyone, the only sign of habitation when we eventually passed a big stately home. In fact, the whole section from Bonnavoulin was incredibly peaceful and wild; forging paths, traversing the sides of mountains and scaling up and down valleys through seriously dense forestry – definitely not for the faint-hearted, I'll say that much. The ominous Loch Striven I'd walked way back down the south of Scotland was *nothing* in comparison to this – a mere taster! It was extremely testing but the heat had at least subsided and the presence of more rainfall made fresh mountain drinking water easy to get hold of. Best of all, on the non-rainy days we were finally able to sit outside and enjoy a fire with the tent open should Jet feel the need to go to bed before me.

We had the occasional storm, but nothing we hadn't camped in before. Reading the winds and always being one step ahead helped, pitching behind rocks in case unpredicted weather came in while we slept. As long as you know the direction of the incoming weather and prepare, one can rest easily. Living outside in wild places is all about foresight and knowing your stuff. Wilder weather certainly had its challenges, but we much preferred it to summer.

Out walking, we passed the estate out in the sticks and from nowhere a Land Rover pulled up to ask what I was doing, probably to check I wasn't poaching deer. I explained my case and they were fine. They even told me to keep an eye out as I passed, since the latest James Bond was being filmed there. I could see the iconic silver Aston Martin DB5 glinting in the sunlight, and got a photo, but I didn't manage to catch a glimpse of Bond unfortunately.

We would soon have our second whiteout while scaling around a mountain called Monadh. It was hard-going as it was, but with mist covering us for hours, on these sections I'd always use my Ordnance Survey maps and a compass to navigate. I trusted them so much more than an app. We moved on in the thick mist, fortunately without the extra burden of wind. I loved navigating through the dense woodland and would stop every few hundred feet to get my bearings. The sheer silence was like nothing I'd ever experienced before. I shouted and listened to the echo of my voice rebound like a skimming stone. It was eerie but so peaceful: no cars, no buses, no sirens, no humans – just pure uninterrupted deafening silence.

We made it up the nineteen-mile stretch, taking us to the mainland's most westerly point, Ardnamurchan. We had some incredibly beautiful camping spots along this stretch. It had rained all day when we arrived and after a visit to the lighthouse we made our way to Sanna Bay to find a refuge from the rain. There was nothing apart from a disused red telephone box. We stuffed ourselves inside and sat for an hour, Jet lying over my legs – not the most comfortable of sanctuaries, but it kept us dry. I was really keen to get back to Mallaig, where we would catch a ferry to the next islands: Rum, Eigg, Canna and Muck, so we didn't hang about.

Now heading down the north side of Ardnamurchan Peninsula, we began striking back up north, constantly walking in and out of sea lochs, always heading west then east again, then north, west, east and so on – never was there a straight section! We passed through Kinlochmoidart, Glenuig and eventually back to Mallaig. By road, you're talking a two-day walk, but with all the wild, unpathed sections, it took around a week. I was chuffed to have arrived. We had been to Mallaig before to get to Skye, but now I'd covered both the islands and the mainland I'd had to previously miss. From here, it was the isles of Eigg, Muck, Rum, Canna, the rest of the west coast of Scotland and the Outer Hebrides. It was northwards from here on.

The first of these islands would be Canna: five miles long and a mile at its widest, with a population of just fifteen people, making it, if I'm right, the smallest population of all of the Scottish islands. I arrived and made my way to the local shop. I took a look around to see what I might eat that evening but couldn't find anyone to serve me. I must have sat outside for an hour waiting for someone to turn up. Just then, a gentleman walked in.

'Hey, pal,' I said. 'Do you know who owns the shop? I've been waiting ages!'

He laughed at me. 'Our shop is an honesty shop. You pick what you want and put the money in the tin over there,' he replied.

I felt so foolish. 'Wow! I've not seen that before, at least not with so much lovely stuff. Does that mean I can steal what I like?!'

We both laughed. I got a few bits, found a spot to camp and waited for the next day to walk Canna in one.

The island, owned by the National Trust since 1981, is a little peach, flat on the east side with contrasting high cliffs on the west. I spent some time in a cracking spot high on the cliffs looking down at a grave in the shape of a Viking boat or a fish. It was hard to tell, but it's said that it belongs to a king of Norway. I never could find out who, but I wondered what kind of life he'd lived and what stories he must have had to tell. How had he ended up on Canna? What were the circumstances that led to his death? Either way, I couldn't help but think to myself what a wonderful spot it was to be buried – looking out to the Atlantic sea from a tiny island. The beauty and serenity of the place really spoke to me; it was exactly the kind of spot I would choose if I were to be buried, I thought. As planned, we finished in a day and waited for the ferry to take us to the biggest of the four islands: the Isle of Rum.

20

Marooned on Rum

Rum is about eight and a half by eight miles long and the fifteenth most inhabited Hebridean island, home to around twenty to thirty people. It boasts stunning mountains around the south and south-west of the island, combined with huge valleys and more mountains to the north. Something else that excited me was the two perfectly distanced bothies to take shelter in; one in Dibidil on the south-east side, and another in Kilmory on the north-west side, around eleven miles apart. We had camped so much over the past three months and, as much as I love camping, months on end without a break can start to take their toll during relentless bad weather or a summer of midges. Constantly lying on my side using my elbows as a lean-to meant I'd started to really hurt my left elbow in particular. I'd always be leaning on it to look out of my tiny one-man tent, meaning it was always swollen and my left shoulder sat higher than my right now as a consequence. So, to have bothies with chairs was a godsend. Boy, did I miss the simple luxury of a chair to sit on!

Rum was like no other island I had visited or would visit. It had one small road and one tiny shop, big enough for only two to stand in at a time. I got a real sense that if you really wanted to just get away from all the madness and were happy in your own skin, then this would be the place. From what I've been told, there was a school, but it only had one pupil. I spoke to a few locals, mainly the shopkeeper, but otherwise most just kept themselves to themselves when it came to tourists. I was fascinated by the insanely brilliant community spirit here. Each and every resident seemed to have a different skill, whether it be weaving, labouring, carpentry or shopkeeping – between them all, it just worked. I was so impressed.

I set off south around the rugged coastline to the first bothy. It was misty and raining but I didn't care. After what we'd been through, we were in for a treat. When we arrived, Jet was sniffing away as ever, now in her prime; so strong, muscular and fit, doing double the distance I was as she veered off to look for anything that moved for the chase. I've never seen such a healthy, happy dog. I knew I was giving her the perfect life – which is good, because the only reason I would have stopped the walk was if she'd been unhappy. I love her so much – what a dog I'd adopted!

High up on a coastal path, I turned the corner to find myself looking down at the most unbelievable mountain valley: 2,500-foot peaks and two rivers flowing either side of what was only a small dot – a bothy planted in the middle. The mist had cleared, as had the light rain. My heart beat faster with excitement at the thought of spending the night here. We swiftly descended, eager to make the most of our time in such a magical place.

Mist covered the surrounding mountain peaks and Jet and I were totally alone in the most idyllic spot. I took my boots off, having just had to wade through a mountain stream around fifteen feet wide, but shallow enough to cross relatively easily. I'd been warned about this often fast-flowing river when conditions were not good, but the weather looked okay for the next few days, so I decided to take a day off to rest up and just take in my surroundings. I had an extra day's rations and two days' worth for Jet, so we were set up nicely to take a break. All the best-laid plans, eh? I'd soon live to regret this bloody decision.

That evening, while Jet and I were sleeping, the heavens opened. It bucketed down and continued to do so all of the next day. I rushed outside that morning to witness the rivers now raging and swollen, impossible for us to cross on either side. We were stuck! I ventured higher up the mountains to locate a possible passing spot, but there was no chance. I rationed my food but ran out after two days. Foraging was impossible as the seafront was some thirty feet below a rockface and we were surrounded by boggy, long grass now swimming in rainwater. By the third morning, the rain had finally stopped and the river was better, with only one viable crossing point that would give us even the smallest of chances. My only problem was Jet. There was no way she could cross it, meaning I'd have to carry her over. But it was risky. Without anything to hold onto, one slip and we would be carried down the fast-flowing river swell and thrown into the sea.

Now very hungry, with Jet down to her last tin of Butcher's tripe, I made a plan. Two metal stakes about a metre long lay behind the bothy against the wall. I grabbed them, as well as a big rock, and took them over to the river. I hammered a stake into one side of the bank using the rock and slowly made my way precariously to the other side with the other stake and the rock, as well as my ever-useful length of rope. I drove the stake into the opposite bank until it was sturdy, tied the rope to it and made my way back over with the rest of the rope, tying it onto the first stake, creating something to hold onto as we crossed. It was taking a chance, but I knew if it rained heavily again we would be stranded for however many days with no food for myself or for Jet. Also, I had no phone signal, so was unable to check the weather. We had no choice but to move on, and this was our best shot.

Now *really* hungry and with a good stretch to do once we crossed over, Jet and I shared her last tin of food. As sick as I felt eating a tin of dog tripe, it was energy. I'd done it before and it had really helped. Luckily, we now had fresh water in abundance, so I slowly ate it, swigging water after every swallow. I must admit, as we started eating, I looked at the flow of the river nervously. *Only a fifteen-foot crossing and we'll be safe – in a few hours we'll be eating!* I tried to reassure myself.

We stood by the river, Jet looking nervously at me. With my bergen on and Jet in my arms, the added weight was actually a help, as it gave me more ballast and less chance of the river knocking me off my feet. I just had to be so careful not to trip on rocks underneath. I picked her up and wrapped my arm over and around the rope as a support and a safety net in case I slipped. Slowly, we waded through the fast-flowing water, at its deepest just above my knees. It was fucking scary! Using my toes, I'd feel around every single step to get a good footing, focusing intensely on a patch of grass on the other side to help my stability.

About two minutes later, we made it over. I put Jet down and started to take a minute. *Never* again. I hate taking chances with water, but I knew it well having spent so much of my life around it. I believed we could make it and I'd taken the right decision.

We made it back to the shop later that day, to stock up and complete the rest of the island. The second bothy is in a place called Kilmory – an equally stunning setting in another beautiful valley. This bothy had two floors with a huge whale vertebra outside the front door. Typically, as is the case with many bothies, there were deer skulls mounted on the walls inside with all sorts of interesting memorabilia left by other walkers. The morning of our last day on Rum, I opened the bothy door to see around thirty deer just lying on the floor outside relaxing. What a sight to wake up to!

Unfortunately I had to scare them off, as Jet would have had a field day chasing them. Despite my difficulties, I loved my time on Rum; it's a special place and I can't wait to return.

My next two islands, and my last of the Inner Hebrides, would be Eigg and Muck. After completing Muck, I experienced the worst boat journey ever trying to return to the mainland. A group who had been shooting birds for sport, a hobby that really doesn't sit well with me given my love for nature, happened to be on Muck at the same time. I was desperate to get back to the mainland as the weather was awful and there was still no sign of any ferries running anytime soon. Somehow this group had persuaded a fisherman to travel over to come and pick them up (for a lot of money no doubt).

I'd been on quite a few ferries, thirty times the size of the small boat we were about to catch over. Rough seas and small leisure boats are not my idea of fun, given how many disaster stories I'd been told of boats sinking, but I was desperate to get to a shop for food, so I picked up my gear and ran for the boat, Jet in tow.

I took one look at this thing and nearly ran back the way I came. 'Oh my God!' I said to one of the gaming crew. He too had a look of fear and said nothing as we both waited for the right time to get on the constantly swaying lollipop stick of a boat. It was open-top, so gave no protection from spray or wind, never mind a *huge* swell smashing the side of the boat, which was something I took no pleasure in being able to see for the whole one-and-a-half-hour journey back to the mainland. During this time, we all chatted, none of us letting on how much we were truly shitting ourselves!

At one point, one of the three-man boat crew hurried down the steps to a small hole leading to the engine room. 'If we break down here then we are fish food,' one of the fifteen passengers shouted. We laughed nervously as we rolled up and over waves, one minute able to see the horizon, the next sinking below the level of the next wave. When we eventually arrived on land, I shouted over to the skipper jokingly, 'Pal, if I were a gay man, I'd be making love to you right now!' He turned and stared at me blankly, clearly not finding it in the slightest bit funny, and nor did many of the others. Completely embarrassed but secretly laughing at the awkwardness of the situation, we said our goodbyes and went on our way. I know Jet got the joke.

While stranded on Muck for a few days, I started looking at the maps of Lewis and Harris (the Outer Hebrides), constantly unable to get the idea of going out of my head. I had a choice: carry on up the west coast of Scotland through winter (a less daunting task but still a brutal time of year to be in a tent), or finish my Hebridean adventure and head straight to Lewis, meaning that once it was done, then it was the west coast of Scotland to finish, then the north coast ready for the Northern Isles: Orkney and Shetland.

Around thirty-five miles to the west of mainland Scotland and completely exposed to the elements, the Outer Hebrides are renowned for harsh, relentless winter weather. It was going to be a serious challenge, unlike any I'd experienced before. Any other walker I've known of who was hiking the perimeter of mainland Britain, apart from Christian Knock, had avoided the north-west coast of Scotland during winter like the plague, and fair play – it's not for the faint-hearted, at least not in a tent!

I sat all day pondering the decision; to circumnavigate every inch of the coastline of the Outer Hebrides during winter would be genuinely dangerous. I had been warned not to do it and to wait it out until summer. I made coffee and put my maps away. *Chris*, I thought to myself, *stop second-guessing yourself and just bloody do it! If anything, it's going to be some experience.* Bar about a fortnight, I had camped every single night on this journey and had learned so much in the process.

'If anyone can do it, pal,' I said to Jet, 'it's us!' I stood up and made my decision. 'Jet, the Outer Hebrides it is! It's settled!' I posted that night on my page knowing that once I had made it official, then I was committed – there was no turning back.

After a few days' rest, we hitched up to Ullapool, ready to catch the next ferry to Lewis. We arrived very early and nothing was open. It was raining hard, so Jet and I hid in a disabled toilet to avoid getting soaked. Around four hours later, we finally boarded the ship ready to circumnavigate all of the Outer Hebrides for my second winter on the walk and our biggest challenge yet. By this stage, the fact that I had been walking for a year and a half had not really crossed my mind; it was fast becoming a lifestyle and so time had become immaterial. The only moment that mattered was the now, the present.

21

Fire and moonlight

Looking at the maps, it was clear that Harris had some far wilder mountain sections to cover. I decided I'd head north up to the Butt of Lewis (the most northerly point), then strike south towards Harris. This would mean for the first time on my walk the sea would be to my right as I walked, rather than to my left. It would give me a chance to suss out the terrain, get local knowledge, and experience just how nasty the winds can get, giving me a taste of what we would be up against before heading into the vaster parts of Harris. Once I'd posted on my page we'd arrived, the reception was incredible. Offers of help came flooding in. Again, news travels fast around the islands and I was getting good press as we started walking Lewis.

The actual coastline of Lewis and Harris (both joined together making one big island) is just shy of 600 miles long, whereas to walk through the middle is a little less than sixty miles – so a massive difference in distance! The coast of Lewis is relatively flat and easy-going, but as you head into Harris, the coastline breaks up, with sea lochs and much wider mountainous stretches covering the west, south and east; much harder-going but spectacular at the same time.

Jet and I made great progress up the east coast of Lewis from Stornoway, the capital, passing through Col, Gress, the beautiful Bay of New Tolsta and up and around the most northern tip, Buaile nan Caorach. Eager to get as much ground covered before January and February, when winter is at its coldest and most brutal, I spent very little time learning about the islanders and more about the terrain and the weather.

As we made our way down the west side of Lewis, I'd get my first real taste of the Outer Isles' weather. I knew it was coming, so bought the supplies we needed to wait it out. It was a westerly wind headed right at us. With little protection, I pitched the tent behind a boulder just big enough to keep us out of harm's way. I put huge rocks over my tent pegs (not your normal summer camping tent pegs, but proper winter pegs) to keep them from pulling out and watched the most incredible weather front roll in off the Atlantic.

By now, I had a good grasp on how long we had before it engulfed us. I'd got us ready in plenty of time. The weather had been windy but I knew this was different; gusts of eighty to 115 miles an hour were beyond the capabilities of my tent, but experience and good camping would, I hoped, keep us out of harm's way. When the weather rolled in, it hit us like a train. The noise was nothing like I'd heard before. The only thing protecting us from total disaster was the boulder slightly bigger than my one-man tent. We spent three days lying in that space, so small I couldn't sit up in it, my elbows and shoulders ruined by lying on my side all the time. Amazingly, Jet was calm as could be. So long as I was next to her, she was totally happy and had complete trust in me. Often, she would lie on her back playing around in hundred-mile-an-hour winds. That's my girl!

Eventually, it subsided enough to head outside. Stiff, incredibly bored and feeling like I'd crawled up and down a tennis court all day on my elbows, I walked the hundred feet to the seafront looking at the biggest waves I've ever seen in my life from the aftermath of the storm. As a surfer, I can appreciate a good wave, but this was world-class: forty-foot peaks crashing down so hard I could hear the noise a mile away. A spectacular sight but scary; a sobering demonstration of the power of Mother Nature.

Jet and I worked hard getting as much of the coast covered on the west side of Lewis. The further south we went, the more spectacular it became; so many beautiful coves and white sandy beaches. It was a real pleasure to walk, putting aside the weather and the dropping temperatures at night.

The day before Christmas Eve 2018, I arrived on an island just off the west coast of Lewis called Great Bernera, around five miles long and three miles at its widest. I aimed to get to the very west tip of the island, to a beautiful beach called Bosta, where I hoped to spend the rest of Christmas Eve and Christmas Day. It's so stunning and even has a bell to warn people of the incoming high tide.

Back in the 1990, a huge hurricane swept across the island. The sand dunes on Bosta beach were battered by the huge waves, revealing an old Iron Age settlement some 5,000 years old. I loved looking around it. As ever, I spent ages just imagining what life must have been like back then, often reminding myself how wonderful it was that in my spare time my mind was being consumed by interesting thoughts such as these rather than the negativity that had plagued my mind for so much of my life previously.

While I was camped up, a couple, Tim and Kath, and their teenage son Josh, who live next to Bosta beach, came to see me loaded with firewood and some cold meats and salad for the night, which was a very welcome break from tuna, beans and ready-made mashed potato, I can tell you! They asked me to pop over the next morning for a coffee when I woke. So, on Christmas Eve I made my way to their house. Tim was outside working on the house and stopped when he saw me.

'Chris!' he shouted excitedly. 'We have an idea if you're up for it?'

'I'm up for anything, mate,' I said. 'What's the plan?'

Tim pointed over to another island about 500 yards away. 'That's called Little Bernera – it's a stunning little island. If you like, you can borrow our dinghy to row you and Jet over and spend Christmas Day there.'

'Thank you! That sounds amazing. Let's do it!'

We loaded up the dinghy with my bag and Jet, and set off across the water. At the other side, I pulled the dinghy onto land and we made our way about half a mile to the eastern tip of the island, to a beach where we would settle down for the night. Immediately, I got to work putting up the tent, before heading off to find a water supply. The island is tiny, about a mile long and 500 yards wide. Next to where I pitched were the remains of an old chapel and a small graveyard. It must have been centuries old; the graves barely visible, old rocks sticking out of the grass. There was something about it; I felt completely at peace with nothing but the sound of a calm sea gently hitting the perfect white sands. The west side of the island is simply magical, with beaches so incredibly clean and white, the water a mixture of turquoise and an assortment of different-coloured blues. *This is what I signed up for*, I thought to myself. That evening, I got a fire on, settled Jet into the tent and fell asleep with my hands behind my head listening to the crackling fire and the gently lapping sea. It felt like heaven.

I woke up on Christmas morning and did some exercises on the beach, running around with Jet. After much of the day spent roaming the island, picking up shells, skimming stones and taking a naked, freezing Hebridean sea bath, I heard the sound of a boat engine getting louder and louder. We headed back to our secluded beach to see Tim, Kath and Josh hauling their boat onto the beach.

'There's no way we'd sit in our house knowing you're over here alone on Christmas Day, eating tuna and shitty mash!' Kath shouted. 'We'd be privileged if you would allow us to spend Christmas afternoon with you on the island.'

I gave them all a hug. 'It's my privilege, believe me!'

'Don't worry, Chris,' said Tim. 'We don't come empty-handed! Kath has been in the kitchen all morning cooking up a roast dinner: turkey, roast potatoes, honey-glazed vegetables, homemade gravy and endless Yorkshire puddings!'

I literally jumped with joy as Jet sniffed around happily picking up the scent of our dinner.

We rushed to unpack and get a fire on before the food got cold. As we sat down to eat what looked like a dream meal, Tim pulled out a bottle of top-class whisky along with some cups. We toasted each other, ate a delicious Christmas dinner and they sat back and drank whisky as I told them about my adventures. Their son, Josh, told me that he wanted to join the Paras and I gave him some training tips and advice.

By early evening, all of us in a heavy food coma and tanked up on whisky, it was time to say our goodbyes before it got too late for Tim to even attempt to drive a boat back. As they walked off, I couldn't stop smiling, so grateful for such a wonderful experience with such a lovely family on Christmas Day on Little Bernera. We pushed the boat back into the water and they set off. All I could hear was Kath telling Tim how all over the place he was! 'Straighten up, Tim!' she kept shouting as they disappeared out of sight. I ran up a hill to see they got back okay, silently thanking them for making Christmas 2018 one I'd never forget.

Left with half a bottle of single malt and a perfect fire, I decided to enjoy the rest of this calm, Christmas evening, nomad style. It was dark now, the moon reflecting off the sea in a straight path to our beach. But for my long johns, I took everything else off and out of nowhere started to sing, very badly, ACDC at the top of my lungs; a bottle in one hand, playing air guitar with the other, dancing around the fire, happy as a man can be. Pure freedom.

Eventually, I sat down, positioning myself so the moon's

reflection was perfectly in line with my fire. I drank a litre of water, lay back on the sand and looked up at the stars with only one thing on my mind: Caitlin.

When I'd arrived back in England from Belfast all those years ago, it was as a confused and lost man. I had no job, no money and no fixed address. I spent the next few years jumping from place to place seeking whatever work I could get. Sadly, the night I took a beating back in Northern Ireland, I'd lost my wallet and had no bank card or ID; the world was changing and job applications were being done online. I couldn't open an account without an address, and without an account I couldn't get paid, and without getting paid I couldn't hope to make enough rent to get a place to have an address.

I stayed in Reading for a few months sofa-surfing at friends' houses, while working as a sales rep for a credit card company earning enough to feed myself and help out with bills, but nowhere near enough to save. For about a year, I jumped from job to cash-in-hand job, still unable to get a bank account. I did my best to block out the fact that I'd had to leave Caitlin. I was a mess, and I couldn't see a way out. To make matters worse, as a consequence of having put everything in my name during my marriage, debts I had no idea existed began to come calling. One by one, my friends received county court judgements for me. I broke down. *What the fuck am I going to do now?* I thought.

I had no stability or the slightest clue how to get Caitlin back in my life, and finding out I was also in debt took a real toll on my mental health. I started getting down. I was tired of pretending every single night, wherever I stayed and whoever's sofa I slept on, that I was a happy guy. On the outside, I was always making jokes, but on the inside, I was being torn in every direction. I needed to get out of Reading and start again.

I read in a newspaper about a sales company in Cyprus who provided accommodation if you worked for them. Although I hated this kind of work, I was very good at it. Desperate to get away, maybe, just maybe, this could work and offer a much-needed break as well as a roof of my own over my head for once. I called my mother and stepdad to ask if they would lend me the flight money to get over. They agreed.

It was 2005. Armed with a passport, a borrowed suitcase and utterly penniless, I arrived in Cyprus. I worked my nuts off, but the company turned out to be dodgy and stiffed me on my commission. When I refused to work until they paid me what was owed, they fired me and evicted me from their accommodation. Once again, I had no money, no place to stay, no friends and was 2,228 miles from home. Again I returned to the UK feeling like a hopeless failure and no closer to bridging the gap with my daughter.

For the next few months I stayed in Clapham, London, with my brother and his girlfriend Angela, while I worked in Pimlico selling skin products. I hated being a burden on anyone and knew it would be a while before I saw any money coming in to pay rent or have the faintest hope of producing a deposit. I spent months sleeping on sofas, under Clapham Common bandstand and often on the floor of the office in my workplace.

What got to me the most was that instead of being able

to invest my time coming up with a plan to reunite with Caitlin, I felt like I was just trying to survive financially. The idea of getting back to her seemed such a far cry away. I had to live somewhere cheaper than London, so I made the decision to move to Wales, knowing I had some family there who might help me find work and put a roof over my head. It was now well over a year since I'd seen my daughter. The fact that I'd left so abruptly, without her knowing why, was eating me up inside. My life was crumbling around me and there was no light at the end of the tunnel.

In Wales, I stayed with the grandparents I'd lived with before joining the army. As ever, I was doing whatever work I could – gardening, labouring on building sites and working with my uncle Andy, as well as more sales work. I made some good friends and was lucky enough to be offered a place to stay with one of them, Mark Atreed, who lived in Llanelli where we worked together. The way I'd lived before joining the Paras and all that had happened after I'd left was having a real effect on me.

Constantly switching from place to place, scratching for work and being permanently stressed was my new normal. I'd constantly put on a happy, brave face, trying to hide how I really felt. I never talked or sought help, and it was like an anxiety balloon inside me slowly but surely inflating in size; inevitably, one day it was going to burst, and I knew it. Deep down, I felt real anger and frustration with myself. Often, I'd take a walk to the seafront and have a good old cry. I kept telling myself to not give up, that I'd see Caitlin again and when that day came, my spirits would be lifted. I'd be able to start thinking about my future, rather than being stuck in this rut; trying to conjure up the guts and funds to get back out to Northern Ireland to find her.

My family was getting worried about me, always offering advice, telling me to try and get a better, more stable job. I hated hearing it. I knew they were only doing what was best, but they didn't know how I felt inside nor anything about my plan to go and see Caitlin. They didn't know what had happened in Northern Ireland or why I'd left. To them, it must have seemed like I'd just given up on her, come back to the mainland and continuously fucked up anything I'd tried to do. As ever, I kept it all to myself, bottling up all my feelings. Every move I made, I'd just wait for it all to go wrong; it's all that ever seemed to happen. It was a vicious circle.

And then something changed . . . finally! I had a call from my mother telling me that Jo, my ex-wife, had been in contact. I experienced a numb feeling and held my breath out of shock. She'd asked if I could get in touch and if I wanted to speak to Caitlin. For a split second, all of my worries went away. It was the best feeling I'd had since the day she was born. Over the next few weeks, Caitlin and I chatted on the phone every day. God, how I loved it. Now five years old, Caitlin had a fast-paced Northern Irish accent. It was so sweet to listen to. I couldn't bear not seeing her any more; I just had to go. After a few discussions with Jo, who was very busy with work, we made a deal that I would come over and stay in her house while she worked away. It seemed odd, and I mean no disrespect in the slightest, but moving into your ex-wife's house did have its reservations for me. Jo had another partner now, so I had some comfort in knowing that there was no ulterior motive. The main thing was that I would see Caitlin, and if that's what I had to do to make it happen, then so be it. I would have done anything. I was also very excited to see Jo's three other children again, whom I had always adored.

For money, I decided to sell my only possession of any value: my car. I'd worked so hard to buy it, but its sale would give me a few grand in my bag to support myself. I handed in my notice and left work that same week, ready to head back over to Northern Ireland. I had some interest in the car from a few prospective buyers, so I decided to go and give it a good sort-out ready to sell. I had to park it miles away from my apartment above a pub on Llanelli High Street, as there was no parking allowed there. The car hadn't crossed my mind in weeks, nor had I seen it, what with work and the excitement of being back in touch with Caitlin. When I got to the street where the car was parked, my heart sank. All the wheels were gone, its windows had been smashed and the bodywork kicked in. Someone had even been kind enough to leave a shit on the driver's seat.

I was soul-destroyed. It was my ticket back over to Northern Ireland. Filled with rage, I kicked the car door repeatedly and walked away and left it, never to see it again. I told Jo my situation and that I now had no money to get over, but that I would find a way. I managed to scrape enough together for a ferry from Holyhead, Anglesey, to Dublin, Southern Ireland. It's all I had. The only way I could get to the ferry terminal was by train, and I had no option but to *jump* the train all the way there, hiding in the toilets whenever a conductor walked past. I knew fare-dodging was wrong, but in my head I kept telling myself, 'In two days' time, I'll be with Caitlin – and nothing is stopping me.'

I caught the ferry to Dublin that evening. The plan, once I got there, was to catch and jump the 10 p.m. train to Belfast and then walk the twenty miles to Jo's. Having successfully made it on to the train, on just my second stop, about nineteen miles north of Dublin, I got caught and turfed off. Now I really *was* in trouble. Belfast was another sixty miles north of Skerries, where I now found myself. Rather than sit around feeling sorry for myself, and knowing that the last train for the night had gone, I sneaked onto the railway track and made my way towards Belfast.

I figured if I walked all through the night, then that would mean less to travel the next day. *If I follow the train tracks, I can't go wrong*, I thought.

I marched as fast as I could for hours on end making it not too far from the border between the Republic of Ireland and Northern Ireland. I had no phone, but I did have Jo's number. Worried she might think I hadn't bothered coming, I walked off the track and made my way to Dundalk police station. A police officer asked what was wrong and I explained my case and asked for some water and if I could make a call. They were so kind and understanding. They made me coffee, gave me a banana and some water. I called Jo to explain my case and fortunately one of her friends offered to come and pick me up to take me to Bangor where they lived. It was such a relief.

Around midnight, I arrived in Bangor. Given what had happened the last time I was there, I was nervous so I decided I would only go out to go to a shop or the gym and just keep my head down. Jo had said that if I looked after Caitlin while she worked then I could lodge for free and get fed. It sounded like a good deal. I'd get to be with Caitlin and get some time to figure out a life-plan.

I was so nervous when I arrived that I said to Jo, 'Just let Caitlin sleep and I'll be there for her when she wakes up.' I said hello to the other kids and got my head down for the night, relieved that I'd made it there.

I got up early the next day to be ready and wide awake for when Caitlin woke. I sat outside the door to hear any sound coming from inside the room. My palms were sweating with nerves. I hadn't even seen a photo of her. *Does she look like me? Will she accept me? Will she be angry at me?* were the only thoughts going through my head.

Suddenly I heard footsteps in the room. With Jo standing just behind me to reassure Caitlin all was okay, I opened the door. Both Caitlin and I froze. All I could see was a fair-haired, mini female version of me. She immediately called me 'Dad' as she ran towards me with open arms and we had the biggest cuddle ever. To this day, I will never know how I held back my tears. I felt like the weight of the world had been lifted off my shoulders. Nothing mattered for that moment. I was back with Caitlin. I had dreamed of this moment for so long. Never again would I be away from her until the day she left home.

22

The *Iolaire*

Before I walked the south-west coast of Lewis, someone offered to take me back to Stornoway for the memorial of a ship and its crew: the *Iolaire* – the saddest post-war maritime disaster story I have ever heard.

The First World War was by all accounts a living hell, something we can never even begin to imagine; the awful conditions of the trenches, the sheer brutality experienced each and every day. For those who stayed at home, hearing of the horrors and loss of life over the radio must have been a war in itself – the people you loved: husbands, dads, brothers, sons, all falling in their thousands every day, never to return. There was scant information, just the occasional letter if it was lucky enough to get back to you. In my eyes, you don't need to be dead to go to hell; these men were already there.

Imagine receiving a letter from your loved one telling

you he's survived the war and will be back home on New Year's Day. What a way to celebrate New Year for the lucky survivors and their families who had for so long eagerly awaited their safe return. In the early hours of New Year's Day 1919, the people of Lewis and Harris gathered along the harbour of Stornoway, unimaginably excited to welcome home the men who had been gone for four long years. Onboard, around 280 men finally got to see the lights of their homes, almost in touching distance of their kin. But then, just a few minutes from docking, the *Iolaire* became engulfed in strong winds and rough waters and she ran aground on rocks near the small village of Holm. Families onshore watched in horror as most of the men drowned in front of their eyes, only yards from the shore. Only seventy-nine men managed to scramble to the rocks and were pulled up by ropes to safety. Thinking about the islanders' total excitement turning to shock, disbelief and then, finally, utter heartache, the story pulled on my heart-strings.

Lewis and Harris had a population of around 30,000 at the time, and villages and hamlets lost almost all their male population. Crofting (farming) the land they owned became impossible for the women and children who were left, and without any kind of wage coming in, many were forced to emigrate to mainland Scotland or even over to Canada. In all, the incident had a devastating effect on the Outer Hebrideans. From what I'd been told while in Lewis, the stoicism of the people of these islands meant that the tragedy was barely spoken about. Harsh winters and limited work meant that people just got on with things and rarely dwelled on the event. I'm sure the whole thing was just too much to keep reminding themselves of. It wasn't even until a hundred years later that a memorial would be held by Prince Charles for the very first time to commemorate the event. I just so happened to be on the island at the same time.

On New Year's Eve 2018, the men and women of Lewis and Harris came together in Stornoway to pay their respects. I was so impressed by the way they all gathered to watch a torch-lit procession through the streets of Stornoway. 201 torches were lit – one for every man that drowned that fateful night. At the front were a group of young men, eighteen years old and upwards – the same age as some of the soldiers who had died – all dressed in exact replica uniforms worn on the night of the disaster. I had become quite popular among the locals here, mainly out of respect for what I was doing, as they had never seen a man walk the entire circumference of Lewis and Harris during winter with a tent. Being told that you're a hardy man by the locals here is a huge compliment. They had accepted me as one of their own, and as I stood and watched the torches being lit, an officer called Malcolm, who had organized the event, ran over to me.

'Chris,' he shouted. 'You're ex-Forces and seem to have made an impact on the locals – we would all like you to carry a torch for one of the men through the procession.'

'Malcolm,' I said, 'I can't do that. I'm not from here. I would feel completely out of place – almost disrespectful.'

'Nonsense!' said Malcolm, putting a torch in my hands.

Never have I felt so honoured. I'd only been there a month, but I felt like I was a part of this community. As we passed, the crowds lining the streets clapped, locals shouting over to me while taking photos: 'Well done, Chris! Amazing effort what you're doing for our soldiers!'

The whole experience was incredibly special. I felt an immense sense of pride and privilege being part of something so few outsiders will ever get the chance to. Above all, it was a touching reminder to me as to why I was raising money for SSAFA and the Armed Forces, and just the boost I needed while pushing up the coast in bleak winter.

Malcolm, who had given me the torch, sat with me later that night chatting away. I'm not sure in my lifetime that I'd ever met a nicer gentleman. He worked so hard trying to help however he could. He made a few phone calls, determined to get me along with a select few down to the *Iolaire* monument on New Year's Day to lay a wreath after Prince Charles – and he succeeded.

The next day, crowds filed behind a barrier near the monument to pay their respects. Jet and I went along with around thirty others with our wreaths ready to lay. I noticed that every single person near me was dressed to perfection – shining boots, perfectly ironed military attire with medals and hair spotlessly groomed. And then there was me, filthy – having not had a bath or shower for as long as I could remember – wearing a stained bright yellow buff hat, ripped jumper and a kilt in Lewis tartan (my family name), with a pair of bright blue Rab slippers. Royalty or no royalty, if my boots could be off my feet, then they would be. I really got some looks!

After Prince Charles had laid his wreath, followed by Nicola Sturgeon, it was our turn. Nervous that Jet, attached to my waist, might have a piss – or even worse pop out a number two – I kept muttering, 'Good girl, Jet, good girl,' as we approached the memorial. I needn't have worried. While I stood and saluted the memorial, Jet adopted an incredibly respectful and majestic pose, looking straight at the wreaths. I could hear the cameras clicking away at such a great shot of a badly dressed veteran and his dog in perfect sync with each other. We'd nailed it! Again, I couldn't believe how privileged I was to be part of such a sacred occasion and wholly accepted by the Hebrideans. I will never forget it.

The next leg would take me through the beautiful bay near Carnish, Mangersta, and then an incredible wilder section eventually leading onto Hushinish; in all, around nineteen miles. The weather was getting colder and windier; temperatures now below freezing with constant forty-mile-an-hour-plus winds that now had a real bite to them. Parts of my beard would now freeze, and fire at night was an absolute must. In winter, depending on weather, you're lucky to see seven hours of daylight, leaving much shorter days to walk. We'd get up at first light and work hard while we covered the miles. Jet was in tremendous shape, as fit as they come, running around enjoying herself and sniffing away. By no means was it easy, though. The relentless routine of packing up the tent with frozen hands and putting it up again only a few hours later to allow enough time to forage firewood and make food before dark seemed never-ending.

From Mangersta, Jet and I started around a mountain called Griomabhal. The views here were something else. We were forging our own path, as there's no such thing as coast paths in these parts. In all, Scotland and its islands had been around 10 per cent coast paths and 90 per cent wild walking. We climbed for a while to get a better view and take photos, and as we scrambled over the top of a rocky section, there in front of me, oblivious I was there, was a white-tailed sea eagle in all its glory. I froze with excitement. Jet followed behind me but scared it away. As it took off, I marvelled at the sheer size of its wingspan, easily the length of my whole body.

Our last section for the day took us high enough to look down on an incredible sea loch stippled with seals. At the end of the six-mile sea loch, I could just see a bothy-shaped building. We pushed hard, excited by the prospect of not having to pitch the tent.

Eventually, we made it to Tarbert and had a few days' rest. Raring to get to the south from Tarbert, the plan was to swing up north on the east coast of Harris and then back to Stornoway. We set off in awful weather but it soon cleared, allowing us to scale Beinn Dhubh mountain. Just over 500 yards below was the most beautiful bay I've seen in my life. Imagine sugar-white beaches lapped by the most stunning palette; the freshwater river that runs underneath the sea water from the mountains gives a perfect dark green underlayer, covered by crystal-clear blue and light turquoise water. It was the stuff of dreams.

Just ahead of us and coming our way at a rate of knots was a menacing storm cloud, rolling in like a great wave swallowing everything in its path. I knew immediately that it was a hailstorm. As ever, these clouds bring ferocious winds with them. As fast as we could, we descended, passing the incredible Luskentyre Beach back onto the coast to find shelter. In no time we were engulfed by brutal winds and hail.

By now, we had walked solidly all day, using as much of the daylight as possible. Winter had been as brutal as anything I had ever experienced before, and the Outer Hebrides in our tent had proven beyond difficult. All of that day, Harris had bombarded us with constant hail and sixty-mile-an-hour winds. I had very little food left; only a roll, some butter and a packet of prawn cocktail crisps that had sat crushed in my bag for weeks. I knew this was going to be a bad night, that it would continue for days, and I had absolutely no escape from it. I was deflated but encouraged that I was not too far off conquering the Outer Hebrides; after Harris, the Uists would mark the last chapter of my Hebridean adventure.

In each break of the hail, we pressed on towards the sand dunes a few miles in the distance, Jet using my body as a shelter. I wanted to get her fed, warm and out of this. Sometimes, the hail hit so hard that I had to turn my back and lock my body around her to protect her eyes. My face had already been cut by the force of the hailstones. The cold had taken such a tight grip, each movement required every fibre of strength left in my body. We were not in a good place – mind or body. Suddenly, through the haze of hail, I noticed a blurry set of car lights to my right – I guessed around half a mile away, but inland. I couldn't check my maps as my hands had become unusable. I was in a constant battle, fighting both the cold and my frustration, but I knew the only option was to push on and find shelter.

I made the decision to veer off the coast, still heading towards the sand dunes, but in the direction of the road.

The current marshland was a mix of ice and water, a maze which seemed to be taking forever to navigate, hampered even further by the state of my boots, which were falling apart at the seams. Eventually, we made it to the road. It was such a comforting feeling! *Humans use this road*, I thought. If something was going to go tits up, at least here, a car would surely pass by at some point and see us.

The weather had kept people in their homes, bar just a few. One or two cars passed, but that was it. Before long, I caught sight of some house lights. I was so delighted! Immediately, my morale was boosted. 'Just knock on a bloody door,' I kept telling myself, but the adventurer within me said the opposite – I had done all of this so far living in a tent, refusing any kind offer of indoor accommodation in houses, and I wasn't going to back down now. From experience, I knew we were not in serious danger yet; it wasn't the first time I'd been this cold and pulled through. In my mind, it was a case of 'get the tent up, food on and we'd be okay'. So, we ploughed on past the houses on our left, towards the biggest sand dune I could find to my right on the coast, the plan being to set up camp on the south side and let it protect us from the cold northerly bashing we had taken all day.

About fifteen minutes later, as we walked past a hamlet of around eight houses, a small car pulled up next to us. A million thoughts stormed through my mind at once. Maybe an offer of a warm meal? Even better, a shed perhaps? On this occasion, it was simply a stranger who knew nothing of us, but the lady asked if we were okay. I just smiled and said, 'We're fine, thanks! Just looking for a place to camp.'

She looked at me, baffled. 'Are you serious?!'

I laughed. 'Afraid so.'

'Walk back on yourselves fifteen minutes or so; our house is the second on the right – come in and get warm.'

'Yep, I'll head there now!' I replied without hesitation, and we made our way back. With just an hour left of light now, I was sure I'd secured us a shed or a garage to sleep in. We arrived and the lights were on. I had such a smile on my face. *Warmth, finally! Yes!!* I thought. I slid the bag off my aching shoulders and, unable to feel my hands, used my elbow to knock on the door. No response. Jet and I walked around the outside of the house again and again.

We sat outside for forty-five minutes absolutely frozen, looking through the window, just a pane of glass away from being toasty. It was excruciating.

At that point, I had to face a harsh truth – it would soon be dark. Temperatures would plummet into the minuses and we'd be in trouble. I stood up, shouting 'FUUUUCK!' at the top of my voice. The effort to get my bag back on was immense. 'Get it into your head, Chris,' I told myself. 'It is what it is . . . the second we leave, she'll probably turn up!'

Hungry and extremely frustrated with myself, more so for letting Jet down, we reverted to our original plan and headed to camp up behind the sand dunes. The fact that I'd let my focus slip in the hope of some refuge in a warm house and then a night spent in a potential shed meant that our usual, efficient routine of ensuring we were camped up before dark had gone out the window. It was now already dark and I still had to find a place to pitch.

Even more of an issue, my head torch was nestled away

in a drybag inside my bergen. My hands were so numb, I spent twenty minutes trying to get the bag open. In the end, my teeth had to do the job, but I eventually located and pulled the torch onto my head. I was shattered and soul-destroyed after such a long and relentless battering from the Hebridean winter, as well as extremely thin and withdrawn from months of hard graft in freezing temperatures, that tonight's efforts seemed almost unbearable. I was so incredibly ready for spring! I knew I could take more – and I would – but at this point, I wasn't sure how much I wanted to. I knew I wasn't beaten yet, but I wasn't far off.

Sometimes, the most amazing things can happen in the most unexpected of places. As I walked around to the south side of the dune, still getting an absolute hammering from the hail, I saw a big shining object; to my disbelief, here, in the middle of the sand dunes, was a fucking bus. I couldn't believe it! I looked for a point of entry and noticed that the back window was smashed. I turned to Jet and smiled: 'Right – you ready, girl?'

Hobbling back to my bag, I hooked the strap onto my left arm and dragged the bugger to the bus. The window was too high to get inside, so I had to improvise with what I could find: a nearby wooden palette to make a platform, giving me enough height to throw the bag and Jet in. Squeezing my elbows together around my bag, I managed to grip it well enough to lift it and then used my head to push it up and inside. I got the bag in first to make sure it would protect both Jet and me from the broken glass and our inevitable fall to the bus floor. Then the weight of the bag on my head pushed my head torch off. 'Fuck!' I shouted.

I looked at Jet who, at this point, was shaking uncontrollably. I love her so much it was like watching my own child suffer. I grabbed her purposefully and lifted her as carefully as I could into the bus. As I did, I slipped and hit my chin off the broken windowsill and fell to the ground. Scrambling back to my feet, I used my elbows to pull me up and in through the broken window and fell on top of my bag with my legs landing on a pile of shattered glass. I just lay there for a minute, laughing. 'Jet,' I shouted. 'We've done it!'

I turned to look round at her and all I could see were her shining eyes reflected back at me through the beam of my head torch. 'We've done it, girl! Yes!' But work was still to be done. Given the fact we were now in an abandoned bus, a fire to keep us warm was out of the question. My sleeping bag was covering Jet to make sure she was warm. In no time, her shivers were gone and my pots were out to feed her. A tin of tripe and some water and Jet was sound asleep. The pressure I felt to make sure she was okay immediately dissipated. My girl was happy and so was I to see it.

Now I was finally out of the force of the wind, my body began to warm – the part where the real pain sets in. Cold creeps into your body and it begins to shut down, with the fingers, nose and toes first. Next, it penetrates your very core and vital organs with the first stage of hypothermia. Once you've reached this stage but then begin to warm up again, the pain is terrible. I'd had chilblains many times before, but this was different; my fingers and toes burned so strongly, I was in tears of pain. I felt like I was being dipped into a fire on a piece of rope. As a child, I'd loved reading stories of mountaineering adventures like *The White Spider*, and often wondered what the experience of severe cold on the body described in such stories actually felt like. Now I had a good idea.

My thoughts returned to my hunger. I knew how much more energy the human body needs in winter. Even in my sleep, being in a tent in such conditions night after night, I was burning as much energy as I had been working hard during the day just to keep my core body temperature up. A decent meal was not an option and I just had to accept it was going to be a long, hungry night. The hardest part of all was knowing that we had it all to come again tomorrow, and the next day and the day after that. The thought of putting on my frozen, wet clothes again in the morning was something I dreaded; instead, I had to remain focused and consistently remind myself why I was doing this. Was it for myself or was it for charity? If I'm honest, it was mostly about the process of rebuilding myself.

I started to breathe in deeply and think back to the beginning of my journey, as I often did when times were really hard. I always came back to that same question: would I rather be here, facing this ordeal, or be back in Swansea battling the demons that had plagued me before I left? The answer was obvious, but it's always good to look and reflect how far you've come, and the hardships you've faced that have led you to where you are.

The next day, we made great progress down to the south of Harris and up the east side once again, heading north in the direction of Stornoway. We arrived on the beautiful island of Scalpay, joined to the mainland of Harris by a bridge. Both Jet and I, in much need of a rest, were kindly given a place to stay for a few days by a wonderful woman, Joan. This gave me a chance to wash clothes, clean out all my gear and do some essential admin. Sadly, my boots, now riddled with holes around the seams, were causing me real problems. 'It is what it is,' I told myself.

Soon after Scalpay, another incredible privilege came my way; I was invited to a Burns Night – a celebration of the famous Scottish poet Robert Burns – on 25 January for a traditional meal of haggis, neeps (turnip) and tatties (potatoes) rounded off with a dram of whisky. Traditionally, a bagpiper, dressed in a kilt, leads the way playing the pipes as a respected member of the community walks behind carrying the haggis. Once the haggis is on the table, the carrier is given a whisky, everyone toasts and the meal and festivities then begin. Well, I had been asked to carry the haggis. You can imagine the honour I felt; a room of old and young Hebrideans and then me – not to mention the fact I'd been asked to undertake such a respected role in the festivities. I felt a bit the same as I did at the memorial; unworthy of such an honour but taken in as one of their own. As I carried the haggis, the locals all came to chat with me to congratulate me for, well, essentially not dying! It was a beautiful evening and yet another special moment in my life.

I'd stayed in touch with Malcolm, whom I'd met on New Year's Eve. I had a massive section coming up that would take me around the completely wild and mountainous Eishken Estate. It was a big ambition of his to walk this stretch, and he had asked if he could join me. I agreed. The estate was run by the most wonderful man, Chris McCrea, and his wife, Donna. This section was no joke –

the estate is used for gaming, but to Chris's knowledge nobody had ever attempted to walk its coastline. It was essentially uncharted territory for walkers. Malcolm knew Chris and got in touch to tell him about our plans and ask any advice he may have. Chris knows the land here better than anyone and we knew it was a good idea to pick his brains. His main concern was how we would be able to carry enough supplies for myself and, of course, Jet, given it was total wilderness and going to take us around five days to complete, but he had a plan.

Malcolm came to pick me up to go and meet Chris and Donna, loaded with army rations: quick and easy food. He had arranged with Chris to use their boats to drop supplies off in advance along our route. We sat together and pinpointed realistic, achievable places to reach each night on our OS maps. Loaded with water and our food rations, we set off on the boat that had one rib (a smaller engine-powered boat that gets launched off a bigger boat) attached to the back. It was absolutely freezing; all of us were shivering as we edged around the coastline, using the rib to drop our supplies off at various locations ready for when we arrived as we walked. The boat ride gave us a chance to look at the scale of what we would be walking from the sea – probably not the best idea. It was going to be seriously hard graft and in bitter cold temperatures.

Our supply drop plan made life so much easier for us. Once Malcolm, Jet and I had finished on the boat, we went back to the Eishken Estate where Chris and Donna promised us a hot plate of their finest venison stew upon our completion. I couldn't have thought of anything better – what an incentive! Malcolm and I then headed back to

Stornoway to give ourselves two days to prepare for what we were about to undertake. I must say I was never a huge fan of walking with other people – it was my journey and I was really enjoying the peace and solitude of the daily walking. I found that anybody who wanted to walk with me always seemed to want to talk, and often I was already exhausted from telling my story time after time. However, I found that Malcolm was very relaxed and easy to get along with because he respected my personal space and was comfortable with silence.

The coastguard had been in touch asking us to go and see them. They kindly let us sign out two radios to use in case of an emergency and asked us to keep them in the loop. They also said they would do a fly-by to check on us and our location. They were simply amazing. I know they were wary of our mission and concerned for us, but I also think they admired our determination and resolve for what we were about to do and wanted to support us.

Carrying the haggis for Burns Night! A real honour to have been asked. I felt so welcomed by the islanders, almost like I was one of their own.

Malcolm about to take the smaller boat to shore to drop off supplies, which we would collect as we passed through the wilderness of the Eishken Estate.

An early-morning start, ready to get cracking at first light to make the most of short winter days. Jet sensibly hiding in the back of the tent in my sleeping bag!

After five days of walking in these conditions, the holes around the seams of my boots let the snow in, causing my feet the most horrific pain each night. I would lay in the tent in agony as they began to warm up again.

Above and right: The dilapidated
hermit's house where we spent
one night. The walls inside were
covered in old newspapers.

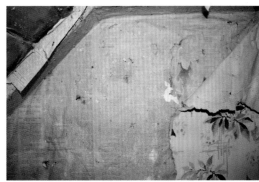

Looking over to a gnarly snow
cloud heading our way. It's
time to get moving, my friend.

Left: Malcolm looking proud to have found the ideal seat to keep him off the cold ground. The perfect pose, if I say so myself!

Jet in the best shape of her life. So nimble and unbelievably powerful for her breed.

Our kit packed up and ready to set off for the next stretch, starting with a big climb. Packing away with frozen feet and hands was not fun but it's the price one pays to see such beautiful landscapes in the Hebridean winter.

Knoydart on the west coast of Scotland. Many had warned me of walking this section along the coast and advised me to take the pathed mountain routes instead. I ignored the advice. Jet and I camped on a small ledge halfway up this mountain, and once again had the time of our lives.

Hildasay. The plane from Fair Isle coming in to land on Shetland did a fly-past for me and someone on board took this picture. I was stood outside waving to the plane as it dipped its wings to say hello.

Dragging the water barrels from the shore to the
house on Hildasay for my water supply.

Some of the sheep I counted daily as part of my routine during lockdown.

Foraging was starting to become second nature. I put a lot of time and effort into mastering such a primitive and lost art.

An oven I built on the south side of Hildasay, ready to cook up my catch of the day along with some leftover leeks. There's something about catching your own food and building your own fire that makes a meal that much more satisfying.

The beautiful Scandinavian-style house I lived in on Hildasay. It had no running water, electricity or heating but the thick stone walls provided the perfect shelter from the relentless Shetland winds.

Right and below: After finding a washed-up football I took inspiration from the Tom Hanks film *Castaway* and got to work making my very own Wilson. I named her Hilda and would place her on different sides of the island every week, making sure to say hello when I crossed her path.

Our very last night on Hildasay. It was all-round mixed emotions!

23

Walking in a winter wonderland

All packed and ready to go the next morning, I took Jet outside for a wee only to see the ground covered in thick snow – not a common thing on the islands. I couldn't believe it! This would make life much harder for us as we walked, but we agreed we would go regardless. Overnight, the temperature had plummeted, freezing the snow solid. My main concern was the holes in my boots, as well as Jet's paws, but by now I knew her so well; she would tell me if it was too much. Jet's paws were as tough as they came after all the walking; not even thorns would get through them!

Our first day of walking gave us spectacular scenery, the small freshwater lochs and landscape frozen solid, muffled by the snow in a silent Narnia. Once again, there was no such thing as a coast path; it was down to us to forge our own way through this white wilderness. Once in a while, all three of us would take shelter from the hail inside Malcolm's storm shelter, sipping on hot tea waiting for the worst of it to pass.

As the first evening drew in, we were at the top of a peak with only an hour and a half to get down to make our first rendezvous point. In between snow clouds, the sun started to give off an incredible red reflection of the frozen landscape. It was a sight to behold – and made even more special given we were miles from civilization. We made it to our camp spot forty minutes before dark, the air incredibly cold, and pitched up at the end of a sea loch in a huge valley surrounded by ice and snow-covered mountains. It was total freedom!

I fed Jet and nestled her away in my sleeping bag, cosy and warm. Soon enough, the snow fell again, covering our tents. This was good, as snow is a great insulator. As the night drew in, the temperature dropped way into the minuses, to around minus fifteen degrees. The snow covering luckily stopped the tents from freezing over, keeping us out of harm's way. We all slept like babies that night, exhausted from the day's excursions.

The following day, we packed up sharpish ready to leave. Malcolm took a photo of Jet and it is one of my favourites from the entire walk. It really shows how blisteringly cold it was. It could have been Alaska! Our first stretch was an immediate ascent of 1,352 feet. By this point, my boots were really becoming a problem. The first day we'd been shin-high in snow all day, completely covering my boots, and the insides were soaked with melted snow, which then froze overnight. When I woke, I'd had to slide my feet into my boots, now completely iced over inside. Within minutes it was unbearable. The only option was to keep moving. We worked hard, covering as much ground of this incredible landscape as possible, spotting our first grouse – it flew off with great speed covering the same ground in ten seconds that had taken us hours. I thought to myself, *You and I are no longer friends, pal!*

No matter how hard we walked, my feet were at breaking point, utterly frozen. I was desperate to get my boots and wet socks off and slide into my Rab slippers with dry socks as soon as possible. We arrived in a valley called Mul Thagaraidh, which once again had some out-of-this-world scenery, and walked through the centre following a frozen stream to be confronted with a beautiful east-facing bay. In the middle was an old croft house, abandoned and now uninhabitable. We dropped our gear and took a look inside to see if it was safe enough to sleep in. It was like walking into a time capsule.

By all accounts, a hardy Hebridean had once lived alone in the house, who had his supplies delivered to him by boat from Stornoway. Come summer or winter, he would walk into the sea and help drag the supply boat to shore and pull out all the supplies: food, wood, coal and whisky, then push the boat back into the water, sending the crew on their way. One day, back in the 1930s, a boat turned up with his supplies, but there was no sign of him. Worried, the crew jumped out to see where he was, as this was out of character. After a good look around while calling his name, they ventured inside to investigate. They made their way up the steep (then wooden) staircase leading to his bedroom and a spare room to find that he had passed away in his sleep. The men pulled back the woollen bed covers and carried him back to the boat to be buried. We didn't know how he died or where he was buried, but the inside of the house had been left completely untouched. Apart from a few fallen rafters, it was in incredible condition. I contemplated the location of his house – completely sheltered from westerly, southerly and northerly winds by the surrounding hills and mountains, all of which are the most brutal out there, especially the westerlies. In my eyes, it was the perfect spot.

Malcolm found a room upstairs for us to bivvy up for the night. We got sorted and I changed into my Rab slippers. My feet were a very funny colour, unlike I'd seen before. I put on my socks so I couldn't see them and sat for half an hour with the most intense burning pain in my feet. After some food and once I was able to walk, I went to explore while Jet stayed with Malcolm. As I walked through the door again like it was my first time, I felt like an archaeologist who had just discovered an Iron Age tomb! I was astonished by what I saw.

Remember, nobody ever comes here – it's not on the tourist map at all and it's a total ball-ache to get to on foot. In the living room was a small chair and table near the fire. On top of the table was a steel mug. The way the seat was positioned next to the table, I could just imagine this man with his feet up sipping away on a mug of whisky before bed the night he died. All around, the walls were covered in pinned-up old newspaper articles, almost like wallpaper – evidently, his way of keeping a grasp on the outside world. I read articles about submarines spotted off the coast of Lewis in the First World War, as well as games segments with crosswords dating back to 1917. It was just fascinating. The cupboards were in pieces, with the occasional completely rusted tin can still unopened and a knife and fork still sat in the sink.

I walked up the stairs into the bedroom where he would have slept and my jaw dropped. 'Malcolm,' I said. 'Come and see this!'

Moth-eaten bed sheets had been pulled over to one side, left in the exact same position, I have no doubt, as the day that he was found and carried out to be put on the boat and buried. We both stood silent, as a mark of respect more than anything. We were in a very sacred and special place.

Due to the intensity of our walking, always checking maps and out of breath scaling up and down hills all day for days on end, for once Malcolm and I got a real chance to just relax and talk. We soon realized we shared a love for relaxing music, and had similar life ambitions. We sat in complete darkness with just our head torches and listened to music on my phone; Pink Floyd, Bon Iver and a song called, 'Down to the River to Pray' from the film *O Brother, Where Art Thou?* It was perfect. Just what we needed after days of hard slog. I really felt like I'd made a friend for life in Malcolm.

Tomorrow was our fourth and last day. With no way to check the weather and completely out of signal, all we could do was hope that our passage through would see us back safely. Just before going to sleep, I told Malcolm I was popping outside to go to the toilet and asked if he was okay keeping an eye on Jet, as I didn't want her descending down the steep, narrow staircase. Outside, I noticed the clouds had cleared. It was bitterly cold still, but the sky looked like something out of a Star Trek episode; stars dominated the night and through the centre was the most incredible display of nature – the Milky Way in all her glory. All of the struggles to get to this point over the years suddenly seemed worthwhile. I could not comprehend how beautiful it was. I sat down on a rock facing the house and turned off my head torch.

After half a minute's attuning my eyes, the stars burned brighter. After years of not being exposed to fake lighting, my eyes had become far more alert and focused. Similarly, no longer listening to the constant distracting noise of busy cities: cars, buses, people, ambulances, television and so on, also meant that my ears were sharper than they had ever been before. The slightest sound, even the smallest stone breaking away from a rock, immediately caught my attention and had my head turning to see what it was. I would often just close my eyes and pinpoint exactly where that noise had come from, even able to identify if it was a bird half a mile away. I really had become in sync with my surroundings. For me, it was a reminder of how most of us living in the busy western world, including myself, have really forgotten how to just switch off and be in the moment enough to really appreciate our surroundings.

I looked over at the house and started thinking about how the last tenant must have lived and how my life was before the walk. I thought about his pared-down existence. Now that I had lived outside for quite a while, I felt like I understood him; collecting water and wood for a fire to keep warm every day, no doubt hunting deer, fishing, making lobster pots and crabbing, all of which kept him so busy. Storing up for winter in itself would take a whole summer and autumn. By no means would it have been an easy way to survive here, but it was no doubt a satisfying, if simplistic, life.

He did his own thing and was no bother to anyone. It takes a certain kind of person to break away from everything, and I respected him for it. Undisturbed by the clutter and business of the modern world, without pressures from other people, and away from the rat race or our societal demands and expectations of how we should be, he was free. This mundane hamster wheel of life: going to school, then college or university, striving to get a good job, saving for a mortgage, buying a house, paying your bills on time, getting a pet, building a family, buying nice things, making sure you save enough for a pension and to pass on to your kids and grandkids . . . This was always a concept that I struggled with. I felt like we are brought up to just be cogs in a societal machine; fodder to fuel the economy. In my eyes, building a future for our kids and grandkids is showing them how important it is to enjoy and really love what you do, and learning the discipline and what it takes to sustain that kind of lifestyle. Happiness is measured in many different ways, and for me, learning from people like the man who'd lived here, and just doing whatever makes you happy, is truly the ultimate success.

That night I wished I was him. I had no idea what his name was, but I respected his resilience and how comfortable he must have been in his own skin. I sat there and contemplated how I wanted this kind of life; the only thing that would have been missing for me would be Caitlin, or a woman to share the same kind of existence with, but in my head that seemed an impossibility.

Our last day walking did not disappoint. We woke up early knowing our first stretch once again was a massive climb over another frozen peak. I'd hardly slept that night, my feet constantly waking me. At one point, I actually woke in a panic, having dreamed they were getting sawn off. Getting my kit together had, over the years, become a very slick operation and took me no time. Only when I was with someone else would I realize just how well-oiled my routine had become.

Knowing we had a behemoth to climb as soon as we started, and that my feet were already refreezing, I told Malcolm I was going to get moving, push up the mountain and would wait for him near the top. I just needed to try and get some warmth into my feet. Jet and I slowly started our ascent. As we got higher, the bitter winds became stronger and more cutting, and then I noticed a shiny object in the snow about a hundred feet from the top. Prior to leaving, I had been told about a military plane that had crashed into the side of the mountain here during the war, ironically while testing a navigation system. This was definitely it. The whole area was scattered with parts of the plane, and the wings were still intact. I know that at least one of the passengers survived the initial crash, and having seen the house below, badly injured, began to make his way down the mountain. Sadly, he died of his injuries and exposure.

Malcolm joined me half an hour later. We stood in silence taking it all in. How awful it must have been to have survived the crash only to then look around, helpless, half freezing to death in such a desolate, intimidating landscape. We both saluted the wreckage and paid our respects before heading off for our fourth and final day.

As we reached the summit, we became exposed to the crushing February winds of the Outer Hebrides. A strong south-easterly wind was pushing some hefty snow clouds our way. We moved as swiftly and carefully as possible so as not to lose our footing and stumble, Malcolm on the radio to the coastguard giving them our position in case a rescue was needed. It was intense but incredibly exciting, my body fuelled with adrenalin and nerves at the same time. With a sense of urgency, we soon made it safe and sound down to the bottom, leaving us only around seven miles before we would be sitting in a house eating a bowl of freshly made venison stew cooked by a couple who knew how to make it to perfection. We were so excited, I can't tell you! Our supply drops around the coast had worked a treat, but we couldn't wait to devour a stew rather than another packet of army rations.

Six hours later, when we were exhausted and, quite frankly, ready to eat and just go to bed, Chris and Donna welcomed us with open arms and immediately got the stew on. My ideas of relaxing came to an abrupt end forty minutes later, however, when a taxi rocked up with Steve behind the wheel. 'Chris, we have to go,' he said. 'They're waiting for you!'

I had completely forgotten I'd agreed to visit the locals of Scalpay and be part of a ceilidh that evening. Lovely as it was to be invited, at that moment, I actually couldn't think of anything worse. Nevertheless, I shovelled my stew down, quickly said goodbye to Malcolm, Chris and Donna and, before I knew it, I was on my way to a party! Steve, the taxi driver, has to be the nicest taxi man in the UK. He wouldn't take any money and said that any time I needed a lift anywhere, even to a shop to get supplies, he was at my disposal.

I arrived at a hall with my Rab slippers on. It was full of locals already tanked up on whisky welcoming me like one of their own. As I was greeted, I smiled, shaking hands with them all, putting on a brave face, but my feet were in agony. The intensity of the prickling was like putting them in hot tar. I asked someone to hold Jet while I went to the toilet, and when I took my slippers off to have a look at them, I found that they were swollen, the skin totally discoloured, and looked like wax. I knew this was the first stage of frostbite. I sat for ten minutes groaning and rubbing them with my hands. I couldn't stay in the toilet for ever, as I knew Jet would be getting anxious by now, so I went back into the hall and necked the whisky to help the pain.

I sat people-watching, and was slightly baffled by such an extreme and sudden contrast of experience. One minute we were in the middle of nowhere scaling mountains and calling the coastguard because of an imminent snowstorm in the wilderness, the next I was drinking whisky at a ceilidh party with all the locals; it was surreal! I took three days off to bring my feet back to some kind of life and to give Jet and me a well-deserved rest after what we had just achieved. With not too far left to go, on 23 February, Jet and I finally completed our 585-mile walk around the coastline of Harris and Lewis. What an adventure it had been! I felt that now we had done this, the rest of the walk would be well within our grasp. The prospect of actually completing our journey now felt like it was achievable.

24

Norway bound,
a friendly hound

The last of the Outer Hebrides were the Uists and the small island of Eriskay. Now, I'd say most tourists who visit this region usually either go to Lewis then Harris, catch a ferry to the Uists, drive through the centre and catch a ferry to Barra, where they then return to the mainland; or the other way round – essentially missing out the Uists. Even I had dismissed it, as all anyone really talked about was Harris, Lewis and Barra, but, boy, was I in for a treat.

When you look at a map of the Uists, you will see endless small lochs scattered all the way down North and South Uist. The south-east side has the only mountains on the island, the biggest being 2,034 feet. Now, if you drive the main road that cuts through the middle, what you won't see is that the entire west side is essentially one long continuous perfect white sand beach, again with unspoilt, barely visited, crystal-clear waters.

As I circumnavigated the islands, I had a real sense that the Uists, being further out, were still mainly populated by indigenous people, compared with the much more cosmopolitan islands just a stone's throw away from the mainland. I was excited to be here and really wanted to get a feel of how people lived in what can be a brutal place during winter. It's one of the many reasons I love the Outer Hebrides so much – it had taught me so much about survival and a different way of life.

While walking in the Uists, I bumped into an elderly lady who was putting her washing out in forty-mile-an-hour winds and offered to help. I'd never seen this done before. We chatted a while outside in the winds, and before I knew it, I was sitting in the home of a ninety-year-old indigenous Hebridean lady, eating dinner with her and sipping whisky together – she was sure that her key to long life was down to a dram each night before bed!

We sat up and talked together for hours as she got the family albums out and showed me photos of her ancestors crafting the land and digging for peat. The slightly mottled black-and-white photos of her family in their traditional dress left a big impression on me. The deep lines on the faces of the elderly back in the early 1900s told a story of how tied these people had been to their land; it was their subsistence, and they dedicated their lives to harnessing it for their survival. Knowing something now of what this took, I felt a deep respect for them and was honoured to be given such an intimate insight into this lovely lady's present and past.

I made a great connection with the locals and loved their community spirit and how kindly they treated each other. Everyone says hello as you walk past. In fact, I can honestly say I said hello to more people in the Outer Hebrides than I ever had in London or in any big city. Youngsters, including teenagers, would often knock on the doors of the elderly to ask if anything was needed. People simply looked out for each other. It really made me feel like there was a place I might just fit in. I'd never felt that anywhere I'd lived before; it was all too busy, fast-paced and money-oriented. These people have very little in the way of money, but their quality of life totally exceeds that. I felt this more so in the Uists than any other island. It's as if they are still living in the late eighteenth century.

Still bitterly cold, Jet and I made great progress down the west side, walking beautiful never-ending white beaches. We even passed a washed-up sperm whale! I couldn't believe the size; he must have been sixty feet long. I was sad to see such a mesmerizing creature stranded on earth, decaying, when he was regent of the deep and belonged in his watery realm.

At the very south tip of this beach, enjoined by a bridge, is the lovely quaint island of Eriskay, around thirty-five miles long with a population of around 1,250 people; a considerable difference from Lewis and Harris, given it's only twenty-five miles shorter. White ponies roam free and a small town on the north side called Balla offers a shop and a friendly pub where we rested up a few days before hitting our last section of all the Hebridean islands – the east coast of the Uists.

I spent my last day walking the Hebrides edging around beautiful wild mountains, and my last night camped up smack bang in the middle of them on the coast. I pitched up early so we could climb the 1,995-foot peak of Beinn Corradail. Already tired but determined to see the Uists from a height, we pushed on up, eventually making it to the summit. I stood at the top in total disbelief at what I was seeing. Myriad lochs scattered the island like nature's swimming pools. I could see Harris to my right, the Isle of Skye behind me and even Rum. To my left was Barra. A perfectly clear and crisp winter's day made for unbeatable visibility.

I sat down with Jet huddled between my legs just looking around at what she and I had walked. Taking things one day at a time, one *step* at a time, was the only way to do something like this. You simply cannot plan ahead. If I'd had the faintest idea before I started of what lay in store, I would have had my reservations. Out on this walk, my 'cross that bridge when I come to it' attitude was working. I felt a sense of vindication; that I wasn't always wrong and totally useless. Here I was, living unbounded by monotonous schedules and endless prior planning – and succeeding! More than just succeeding; I was thriving. Heading back down, I wrapped my arms around Jet and gave her the biggest kiss on her head. 'Jet, my friend, we've done it! We've bloody done it!'

That night, with the fire crackling and Jet snoring away in the tent, I sat deep in thought, picking up stones, throwing them into the water and just staring into space. At this point, I was still unable to really put my finger on exactly what walking these islands had done for me, but one thing was clear: I *was* getting better, my mind clearing from the cluttered fog of the life I led before I started. I still had no idea what I wanted to do with my life, but at least I was giving myself the headspace to think about it, rather than constantly worrying. It had been a very long time since I'd felt such calm; in fact, it was probably the first time in my entire adult life I'd had this feeling. For the first time I could remember, I was free of worry and stress; I had no bills, no debts, no pressures and, most importantly, I had a purpose again. People even admired me!

Walking the Hebrides was no easy task, but as a consequence my mind had been consumed by it. It had forced me to live completely in the moment day after day, which in turn had given me a sense of peace, belonging and an incredible respect for its inhabitants, its weather and a slower pace of life. There is not a single material thing in the world that could have given me the same feeling as I had sitting up on that mountain that day. For the first time in however long, I felt a real sense of pride and self-worth again, and I had a little cry knowing it was my last night. It had been such an experience!

My Hebridean adventure had now come to an end, but my coastline adventure was still firmly in full swing. Now full of confidence as an adventurer, the next day we set sail to finish the west coast of Scotland, the north coast and then up to the Northern Isles: Orkney and its islands followed by Shetland and its islands.

We arrived back on the mainland on 20 April 2019. It had taken four months to complete all of the Outer Hebrides. The one thing that I was genuinely excited about returning to was an abundance of trees. I can't tell you how hard I'd had to work to keep Jet and me warm through our most brutal winter yet. After a tiring day's work, it's so nice just to stop and put your feet up, but for me the work really started once I'd pitched the tent. It would then take hours to find kindling and wood sizeable enough to keep a fire going, source fresh water to drink and to cook with, and then cook. Having trees again for fallen wood would make a big difference, that I did know.

Equally exciting was that I was about to tackle the famous Knoydart peninsula. This whole section would take me from Mallaig into the wilderness, around three sea lochs, two of which are around twelve miles each side. It has one tiny hamlet called Inverie that's only accessible by either boat, a hike through the mountains or, in my case, walking a twenty-two-mile stretch of coast. There are no roads at all to get there. After that, along the coast it would be another thirty-five miles before I reached my next shop in Glenelg; in all, around sixty miles of pure wilderness and epic landscape surrounded by mountains.

The twenty-two-mile stretch to Inverie, working our way down one side of the thirty-mile loch, then up the other side, was spectacular. I worked hard for it, but God, it didn't disappoint! Peaks 2,500 to 3,000 feet high towered above us as if they never wanted us to escape. My camp spots were incredible: eagles soaring above us and total peace and tranquillity. Unlike my thirty-eighth, birthday, which was spent playing music in a bar in Oban, I was in a far more natural setting this year, pitched on the side of a mountain, out of signal, swimming in a cold mountain burn as naked as can be, swigging on my hip flask of whisky and looking at incredible views. It was the best birthday I've ever had. I couldn't have asked for a better setting as I watched the sun set to the west of me. I felt like nature was giving me a thumbs up for all my hard work.

Just before Inverie, I spent the night camped up next to a bothy at the end of Loch Nevis. The bothy was full of walkers, so I camped a hundred yards away to get some peace. I did introduce myself and said hello to the others and we all sat and chatted for a good while listening to each other's stories. It was amazing. The next morning, we said our goodbyes and signed the bothy book. One entry in the book read:

5/5/19 – fabulous evening in Sowlie, with Chris Lewis walking the UK coastline, also Tom from Bristol – an Arctic explorer with his dad, other occupations – a priest, a lawyer, a lava scientist, a carpenter, a philosopher, a finance manager, a GP, a criminal officer and another lawyer. What a random bunch!

I arrived in Inverie the next day, ready to rest for a day before heading around the next section. Inverie has one pub called the Old Forge. I sat down at the bar and was offered a pint by the owner. As I looked around, I noticed the people sitting at the tables were constantly staring in my direction. I thought to myself, *Shit, I'm in the most isolated pub in the UK and people know who we are! That's insane!*

The next minute, I felt a tap on the shoulder from behind. I turned around and immediately recognized the guy – it was Rory McCann. I was a massive fan of the hit series *Game of Thrones*, and I particularly liked the character Sandor, 'The Hound' – the part Rory plays in the show.

'Chris,' Rory said, 'you met a friend of mine back on Jura – Badger! He told me about you. Fair play, lad, that takes some doing! I don't do social media, so haven't been able to follow you, but do you fancy a pint?'

'That would be great!' I said, now realizing that the whole bar was of course not looking at me but at the much more famous Rory!

We went outside with a few of the locals who had known Rory from previous visits. The man was a really nice guy and a gent; he was constantly heading back inside to get us another whisky. He showed me his boat and told me that he was on his way to Norway in it with a lovely Scandinavian friend. I loved how humble he was, totally down to earth and not at all wrapped up in the fact that the final episode of *Game of Thrones* was being aired the following night. The fame had not at all gone to his head. I really liked him.

The next day we carried on scaling around Knoydart. I took a bad tumble and used my right foot to stop me sliding further down, wedging it between two rocks. I immediately knew I'd cracked a small metatarsal bone underneath. My foot was badly swollen, but I'd had worse, and I needed to carry on in order to get supplies for Jet and me. It slowed us down a lot, but I found it okay. If I'm honest, it was the least of my worries. I knew any day now that my enemies the midges and the cleggs would be making an unwelcome appearance, and I felt more afraid of those critters than of any section I had walked to date. They are not a showstopper – rather a freedom stopper!

Jet and I spent the next two months edging in and around the Scottish Highlands' sea lochs, passing Kyle of Lochalsh,

Ullapool and Loch Inver, eventually getting us to our final section, Cape Wrath. It was an incredibly difficult few months. As before, water was scarce and the constant evening threat of the midges plagued my thoughts all day. I'd get so worked up knowing that after a hard day's graft edging around the mountains through forests and valleys, sweating all the time and being incredibly uncomfortable, we would then be confined to the tent for hours, sweltering in our pitched-up oven, just to avoid these beasts! It was unbearable. All I wanted it to do was rain or be windy.

Kinlochbervie is the last village before you get to Cape Wrath. From here it's about twelve miles to reach the north-west lighthouse before hitting the north coast of Scotland. Then it's another fifteen miles to Durness, our next town to resupply. Again, I had been warned multiple times about Cape Wrath, and to be very careful, but, if I'm honest, I found it a pleasure to walk. The first part would take us down to the beautiful Sandwood Bay, a one-and-a-half-mile beach with stunning sea stacks to the left of it and a rather sizeable mountain burn to cross. There was no choice but to get wet crossing it, so Jet and I just ploughed through. I knew a further two miles on we would end up at Kearvaig bothy for the night. I couldn't wait!

Kearvaig bothy is said to be one of the most isolated bothies in Britain, although I actually disagree, having been to so many now. Even so, it was a wonderful place to rest up for the night. Years ago, a woman was found dead inside from hypothermia. It's such a sad and horrible way to go, but a constant reminder of the need to be prepared. Nature simply doesn't give second chances.

When I arrived, it had just started raining heavily. Inside the bedroom, there were paintings of African women all over the walls. It was fascinating. A man called James McCrory Smith (Sandy) lived inside this bothy as a hermit until 1996, when he fell ill, eventually passing away in 1999. Sandy just wanted to cut himself off from the world and live a simple life away from the hustle and bustle. After asking locals about him, I was told that every two weeks he would walk into Kinlochbervie to cash in his dole money, stock up with food and whisky and not return until the next payment came in. Walkers had reported going to the bothy and being chased out by a drunken man holding an axe. He clearly just wanted to be left alone!

Looking at the paintings gave an insight into his mindset. I'd love to have known what his connection was with all this artwork – it was such a random selection! But I can speak for him when I say that so much time spent on your own can play funny games with your mind.

I collected as much driftwood as I could for the bothy. Inside was a pile of slightly damp peat – a nightmare to light, but it can be done. I set up camp in what would have been Sandy's bedroom. A fella then walked in, soaked to the bone. He was a German guy who spoke very little English. Obviously cold, he got to work trying to get the fire started. It was painful to watch, as I knew how desperate he was to warm up. For around an hour he tried as we managed a few minutes of conversation at a time.

'Hanz, mate, I'm quite good with fire. Let me get it going for you,' I said, trying my hardest not to sound arrogant.

'It's okay!' he said. 'I've been lighting fires for a long time.'

'It's not going to light,' I said, now getting impatient, as

I was also desperate to get food on and knew that within an hour we could have a blazing campfire to dry out with. I told him to move over. He sat and watched as I stripped down his attempt and got to work doing what I do best, explaining to him what I was doing and why his didn't light. Soon enough, the man's pride barrier dropped and the heat from the fire was enough for us to cook and to stop both of us from shaking with the cold.

Over food, we got chatting. He was on a two-week trip camping and walking some of Scotland. I told him what I was up to. After a slightly rocky start, we relaxed and had a lovely evening together, warm with our clothes hanging over the fire. I already knew we were in for a big problem the following day, but I didn't say anything so as not to worry Hanz. It had rained hard all night and was still raining hard by the morning. The river we had come over at Sandwood Bay would be raging and impossible to cross. Right next to the bothy was a smaller burn about ten feet wide, equally raging and fast-flowing. That night, I'd checked my maps closely and noticed that a few miles up into the mountains was a network of much smaller streams all heading into the same burn – the one next to our bothy. I figured that if we followed the river upstream, passing as many of the smaller streams that flowed into the one next to our bothy, then we might just have a chance of crossing.

I told Hanz my plan and he asked if it was okay if he followed Jet and me, or he would be stuck there. I happily agreed. We set off out into the heavy rainfall in the hope that my plan would work. It took hours of backtracking and climbing higher, constantly jumping over little burns that helped the flow of the bigger one. Eventually, I found a spot possible to cross. I took off my bag and, with all the strength I had, threw it over to the other side. 'Well, Hanz, we haven't got a choice now!' We both laughed but were equally nervous not to trip and get washed downstream!

I took a huge run-up and made it over. Jet, as nimble as could be, made a laughing stock of my attempt, making it look so easy. Hanz followed after. We had made it across safe and sound, thank goodness. What would have only been half a mile to the lighthouse from our bothy had now been eight miles. Once we had gotten out of the danger zone, I asked Hanz if he didn't mind going ahead. I wanted to walk the last few miles of the west coast of Scotland on my own. This was a monumental moment for me: the completion of the west coast of Scotland and its islands. I needed to process this alone. We said our goodbyes and would keep in touch every once in a while after this.

Soon enough, Jet and I would take our final few steps on the west coast of Scotland, making it to Cape Wrath lighthouse. I sat down with Jet and hugged her. I couldn't believe we had actually done it! I walked into the west coast of Scotland in December 2017. We completed it on 13 July 2019 – not too far off two years later. What a journey it had been! We'd pushed so hard and for so long to reach this point, and I was immensely proud. We had proven all the naysayers wrong and I now believed that anything was possible. There was only one show-stopper left to tackle. I knew by the time we completed the north coast of Scotland, followed by Orkney and its islands, that our biggest challenge yet awaited us, and it was to be in winter in the most brutal place the UK has to offer: Shetland.

That night the lovely couple who ran the lighthouse, who knew about what I was doing, allowed me to stay inside. They handed me a load of beers as a celebration for completing the west coast. Very soon, I was joined by an American called Josh, who was on his own adventure, and we spent the night sipping beer outside, toasting the great outdoors and the closing chapter of this part of my journey. It was an incredibly special night.

Once we'd turned the corner heading east for the first time along the north coast, we pushed ahead hard. I was keen to get the ferry over to Orkney as soon as we could. To get there, we'd walk around eighty miles, edging around a few sea lochs on our way to end up in Scrabster, Thurso, where we could cross the pond to the first of our Northern Isles. I was eager to get Orkney and its islands in the bag as soon as possible in the hope that we could get to Shetland before midwinter. I wanted to make sure we had some time to acclimatize and suss out the weather and terrain up there before arriving slap bang in the middle of its harshest months.

On the way, we spent a night camped up in Smoo Cave. About three miles south is a huge freshwater loch. In the right conditions, with rain and a strong southerly wind, the loch bursts its banks, pushing water into a vast hole in the cave roof, creating a massive waterfall inside. At around 1 a.m., I jumped out of my sleeping bag and clambered out of the tent to marvel at the gushing waterfall.

It took Jet and me a month to eventually get to Thurso. It was the height of summer, making life difficult for us both. Always aware of Jet walking in heat, it meant resorting to walking in the early mornings and later in the evenings, making progress slow at times. However, this wasn't a race, and it gave me a lot of time to PR the charity and make connections as we went.

At times, getting constantly bitten, sweltering from the heat as well as the constant search for water could become incredibly frustrating. I'd worked hard on the media side of things and on this particularly hot day, the BBC was putting out a feature on Jet, me and the walk. I pushed hard to get to a campsite so we could watch it. When I arrived, I went into the bar – the TV was already on the exact channel and it was perfect timing, as it had just started. The bar only had one person inside. I turned to the boss and asked if he wouldn't mind turning it up. 'Me and my dog are on it as we speak!' I said.

'Sorry. We don't turn up the volume in the bar; it disturbs the customers,' he said.

The gentleman sat at the bar turned and said, 'I don't mind – it won't bother me for a few minutes.'

The owner rudely refused and walked off. I asked the bar lady if I could possibly plug my headphones into the TV or we'd miss it and I'd never get to see it. I never had enough battery or signal on my phone to watch any TV in the tent at night, not to mention any money to pay for anything like a monthly subscription to Netflix or a TV licence. The boss walked back over. 'I already fucking told you – we don't allow noise. Now, please leave!' as he looked me up and down.

Both the barmaids and the customer looked at me, obviously feeling awkward. Tired and frustrated, I walked outside and sat on a bench. A group of cyclists pulled up and immediately recognized me. They all came over, offering me some food and a drink. Someone obviously said something in the bar to the staff and the owner came outside offering his apologies.

'Too late now, fella, I've missed it. You were so rude. I know I don't look the cleanest, but there was no need for it. Never judge a book by its cover.'

I left the campsite and carried on.

25

Tombs day

On 11 August 2019, Jet and I set sail to complete Orkney and its islands. Orkney's coastline is approximately 570 miles, more than half of which is taken up by the mainland; the rest is a group of twenty islands that surround it, all of which are inhabited. Orkney has a population of around 22,000, who mostly live in the two main towns: Stromness, located on the south-west tip, and Kirkwall, over on the east side of the island. By the time Jet and I arrived, it was clear that we would definitely be spending the winter up in Shetland. We would make the most of the last of summer while in Orkney.

We arrived in Stromness late afternoon. I was blown away by the quaint town with its network of thin cobbled roads running in and around it. It was like going back in time. I could just imagine the horses and carts ferrying everything from fish to timber around the small streets barely big enough for a car nowadays. Houses once occupied by famous Orkadians had plaques on the walls, such as Rae's Close – 'Ray' being one of the island's most successful nineteenth-century Arctic explorers. His success was largely due to his willingness to learn from the Inuit and First Nations people. One plaque read, 'Mrs Humphrey House, temporary hospital 1835–1836', which had been erected to care for a scurvy-ridden whaling men who had been trapped on the ice for months on end. I loved these small historic touches.

Orkney was a much easier and flatter coastline to walk compared to what we had been used to. It's much greener and less marshy and peaty than on previous islands. Its biggest hill is called Ward Hill at 1,578 feet and belongs to a neighbouring island called Hoy just over the water from Stromness. Hoy looked beautiful and I immediately made the decision to make it our first walk of Orkney.

Hoy has a population of around 400, although it was much larger when originally inhabited by the Picts and then the Vikings. It's a stunning island and was the perfect choice for us to tackle first. Eager to see Orkney from above and blessed with a good day, we headed up the hill. We'd only been walking a few hours before I stumbled upon yet another plane wreckage, the remnants scattered all over just near the very top. On 19 March 1941, a twin engine, *Lockheed Hudson*, crashed into the moorland on Hoy and exploded. It had strayed off course due to low dense clouds. All three men on board tragically died. The man who was sent up to guard the wreckage also sadly died from exposure. Another tragic loss of life and the reminder of it still scattered all around me. Here was another testament to the huge sacrifices made in the world wars. Whenever in the presence of such a stark reminder, I sat and thought about the hardships those men must have faced and the courage that must have been needed. It always made me feel proud to be doing this walk for SSAFA, in support of our veterans.

I sat down for a rest looking over at mainland Orkney. I could see the entire island from here. It was spectacular to say the least. One of the reasons I was so looking forward to Orkney was its history. The island is scattered with Iron Age tombs all with their own names: 'Tomb of the Eagles', 'Tomb of the Dogs', 'Tomb of the Otters' and so on. It is also home to the famous Ring of Brodgar, a Neolithic stone circle around 5,000 years old, predating Stonehenge (built around 2,500 BC). From where I sat, I could see its location ahead of me in the distance. I would put my bottom dollar on the fact that whoever chose its location had done so sat in the same spot I was. It provided a perfect viewpoint over the island and during late summer and autumn, the purple heather completely surrounds the stone circle. It is so beautiful and colourful when in bloom, almost like a painting.

We made our way around, passing the huge sea stack, 'The Old Man of Hoy', and continued south around the island until arriving back at the small harbour to get the ferry. Not long before getting the ferry, I noticed a white grave sitting alone in a peaty moorland and went to investigate. I did my research and I was astonished and deeply saddened by what I discovered.

In the late 1770s, in a place called Greengairs Cottage, a young woman had lived by the name of Betty Corrigall.

At the age of just twenty-seven, Betty had fallen pregnant by a man who deserted her after finding out. Back then, this was not a good situation to be in at all due to religious beliefs. The castigation of the local people simply became too much for Betty. She was eventually driven to attempt suicide. She tried once, throwing herself into the sea, but was rescued by a nearby boat. She then made a second attempt, this time hanging herself with her child in her belly – and succeeded. Suicide was a big no-no in the Christian church, meaning a Christian burial for Betty in the kirkyard was not permitted. Even the lairds of Melsetter and Hoy refused to have her body laid to rest on their land, so it was placed in an unmarked grave abandoned in the peaty moorland near the Water O' Hoy, on the east of the island, and was totally forgotten.

A few hundred years later, in 1933, two men were cutting peat for fuel when they stumbled upon a wooden box. They opened the coffin only to find a perfectly preserved body of a young woman with long dark hair and the noose she had used to hang herself placed beside her. Her skin was still perfect apart from a small tinge of brown because of the peat. Peat bogs are renowned for churning up mummified bodies from hundreds of thousands of years ago. Because of the density of its mud, it admits no oxygen, which is what makes a body decompose. The body was put back into the peat and returned to the earth. Now, Orkney had a huge presence of soldiers after the outbreak of the Second World War. Another group of soldiers digging up peat once again found an unmarked grave; it was Betty. She was given the name 'The Lady of Hoy' and her grave was moved fifty yards from its original spot to a final resting place and her coffin was covered in concrete. Then, in 1976, Mr Harry Barry finally fashioned a gravestone for Betty and erected a fence around her grave. It still stands proud today.

As I left her grave, I felt a real deep sadness for her – she must have been so scared, rejected and alone. I couldn't help but think how different life would have been for her if she had been born now – at a time when mental health issues are coming much more to the forefront of everyday conversation, and the stigma of unmarried women getting pregnant is far less. Sad as it was, I was also pleased that these stories were still being told – gems that tell us so much about local history and culture.

Jet and I headed back to mainland Orkney, leaving Stromness and making our way towards Kirkwall, following the coast towards another two islands this time joined by a causeway: Burray and South Ronaldsay. The walking itself was incredibly easy. God, a winter here would be much easier, kinder and safer than Shetland! We were pretty much always near a road, with villages or the odd house at least dotted all around the coast – a huge safety net if we were to run into trouble. It was pretty much flat all the way around. Shetland would be a different ball game altogether. I'd seen the maps and I knew it.

True to ourselves, we stuck religiously to the coast, even if a road was only one farmer's field away. We would be scaling fences or even keeping to the tiny, narrow gaps on the other side of the fences just to stick to the coast. Keeping safe from cows was without a doubt our biggest problem on Orkney, as were the electric fences, keeping the cows out of harm's way. Jet and I would spend hours in a day running through fields of cows, narrowly escaping the stampede hurtling towards us, and getting zapped by electric fences.

During the Second World War, Orkney housed the bulk of Britain's ship fleet at one time at Scapa Flow. On 14 October 1939, a British warship called the *Royal Oak* was torpedoed by a German submarine – U-47. 835 men were killed. It was an incredibly brave thing to do by the Germans so close to Britain's main naval fleet and they did some real damage. As a result of the sinking of the *Royal Oak*, the prime minister Winston Churchill commissioned the construction of four causeways to block future intrusions and attacks from U-boats, linking the mainland of Orkney to the islands of Lamb Holm, Glimps Holm, Burray and south Ronaldsay. The one-and-a-half-mile-long causeways were built by Italian prisoners of war. The construction of the barriers was a complete success and walking over them really gave a good insight into the unbelievable wartime effort. Made of thousands of huge concrete blocks with a road directly through the middle, the Churchill barriers remain completely intact today and are used by the locals as a link to mainland Orkney.

Once Jet and I reached Kirkwall, it was time to start banging out the Orkney Islands. From Westray, we caught our first flight together – the shortest commercial flight in the world, lasting a whole ninety seconds, taking us to Papa Westray. I loved the islands around Orkney, Sanday in particular. Like the Hebrides, each island has its own character. Sanday, given its name because of its beautiful white beaches, reminded me very much of the Outer Hebrides.

Vast expanses of white sands and dunes made for easy and relaxing walking; a welcome break from the outrage of cow chases we'd just had to endure, and the people were so kind, always offering help wherever we went. There was not a single shop Jet and I walked into where we were given anything less than the biggest welcome and sent on our way with supplies after refusing to take money from us.

One at a time, we knocked off the islands as the weather started to take a turn from summer into autumn. In Orkney, everywhere I went people came up to say hello. I had around 20,000 followers now and £40,000 in donations for SSAFA. I was forever being interviewed on radio stations and for walking magazines, women's magazines and newspapers. We also by this point had visited hundreds of schools giving talks to children about our adventures. Really they only wanted to see Jet, but as always I loved interacting and talking about my adventures with them.

Adults predominantly ask questions like, 'How many pairs of boots have you gone through?' and 'How do you wash?' Or the most frequent and annoying of them all, 'How many miles do you walk a day?' Kids, on the other hand, ask far more creative and insightful questions, like, 'What do you do if you break a leg and there's no hospital?' right through to 'What would you do if a bear attacked you?' I loved it! Having walked all these miles on all of these islands for all of these years, 'How do you wash?' would be the last thing I'd ask someone who had done all that! I had a great time in the schools, encouraging kids to get outdoors and believe in themselves. It's been one of my biggest pleasures on this walk.

As we skirted around mainland Orkney, having now finished its islands, I couldn't get enough of its history. The tombs were incredible! The Tomb of the Eagles was given its name because eagle bones were found inside, similarly the case with the Tomb of the Otters and the Tomb of the Dogs. Our ancestors cleverly devised a way to teach these animals to fish for them, though sadly in a somewhat brutal fashion. They would tie a noose around their neck and send them on their way to go and catch fish. Unable to swallow, they would return to the humans with their catch, bringing them an easy meal, and were often rewarded for their efforts in return. As a mark of respect and loyalty to the animals who had served them, they would be buried alongside humans in these tombs. Deceased humans were placed for months out in the open air away from the tombs, left so that other animals would feed on the remains until the bodies became mere skeletons. The bones were then taken to the tombs and laid to rest.

When I arrived near the Tomb of the Dogs, I pitched up a few hundred yards from it on a patch of grass. One by one, the locals came down to say hello. As lovely as this was, it was getting late and I really needed to get some shut-eye, so I packed up my gear and headed up to the tomb. Now dark, I had a good look around inside and decided that if I was going to get some peace, then this would be the spot. I paid my respects out loud, asking if they didn't mind me staying. I'm not sure why; it just seemed right. I had a great night's sleep and it was my first experience sleeping inside a 4,000-year-old tomb!

As we worked our way around the north and north-west

coast, we got to marvel at the Neolithic settlement of Skara Brae, a perfectly preserved Neolithic settlement. I'd always been fascinated by how our ancestors lived and believe we should celebrate our earlier ancestors much more. They lived through an ice age under the most brutal of circumstances to allow us to be here, after all. I have a deep respect for their resilience and fortitude to survive such conditions. Having spent so long living outside foraging food and wood, I had the smallest understanding of how it must have been. It's relentless; physically and mentally demanding. Even a simple toothache must have been excruciating. Orkney offers a wonderful insight into these bygone ages; it has such a strong, fascinating historical presence.

On 20 October, Jet and I finally arrived back at Stromness, completing the beautiful green island of mainland Orkney along with its islands. It had been some experience! The people and kindness I had been met with once again reminded me how wonderful the islands are. It was a wonderful part of our adventure, and my mind had been constantly consumed with its history, beautiful landscape and yet more proof that humans are kind and wonderful when we work together.

The next day, we set sail for Shetland. It was blowing a gale and, to my horror, the boat decided to cross the 110 miles of open sea to Lerwick, the capital of Shetland. Jet and I nestled inside a cabin skirting from side to side like something out of a cartoon. It was an awful crossing.

We had left Orkney with £73,000 in the kitty for SSAFA, around 40,000 followers and a whole bag of nerves knowing we would be spending winter in an incredibly inhospitable place. This was it. If we made it through Shetland during winter then, in my mind, this walk was in the bag! The rest would just be a case of moving forward day by day. Nothing on this walk would test our minerals as much as this. It was go-time.

26

The land of the Norsemen

Shetland is 136 miles north of mainland Scotland and sits between the Atlantic Ocean and the North Sea. If you were to sail directly east, you would land about sixty miles north of Bergen in Norway, and if you head directly north, there is nothing between Shetland and the North Pole. Its location and the fact that it's an island mean its 1,000-mile coastline is subjected to some of the most brutal winter winds going. Its coastline is shaped by these winds as well as a constant battering from the sea, leaving a unique and stunning landscape. It has around a hundred islands surrounding the east and west coasts, of which sixteen are inhabited. To drive from the south directly through the centre of mainland Shetland is only sixty miles, but the coastline, like so much of Scotland, veers in and out with sea lochs scattered all over (particularly in the north).

Running through the centre all the way up Shetland are

peaty, moor-covered hills. It's said that there is so much peat on Shetland that it would last 23,000 inhabitants around 3,000 years. Again, Shetland has no trees, just vast expanses of exposed moorland, beautiful weathered coastline and white sandy beaches. It was the last of our major Scottish islands, and I knew once it was completed that it would then be a case of finishing the north coast of Scotland and heading down the east coast back into the more built-up areas and busy cities. Unbelievably, the last city I had seen was Glasgow, and that had been years ago. Little did I know it would be more than a year before I saw one again!

We arrived in Lerwick in the early hours of the morning on 22 October 2019. My body was tired. For over two years now, I'd been lugging my home on my back day after day. As a result, my posture was starting to change. The constant weight on my shoulders over time meant they had started to roll forward, and any chest muscle I had left had tightened to a point that was uncomfortable. My neck and back were so tight that when I turned to look at anything, my whole torso would follow. During winter, the cold affected this even more. Mornings were just not fun at all! So stiff, it was a real ordeal to wake up and get out the tent, constantly psyching myself up mentally to get the bag back on. It was hard, hard work but this was my last push before heading back to mainland Scotland. I believed we could do it and that belief was all I needed.

My first night in Shetland alerted me to what we were in for. I hadn't yet posted on my page to say I'd arrived, as I just wanted a day or two without constant questions to get a feel for the place and acquire some local knowledge. I only had £1.40 to my name, so stocked up on tins of cheap rice pudding. I already had food for Jet, so she was okay. I set off to find a camp spot on the outskirts of Lerwick, eventually finding a patch of grass. It was calm and lovely, and the weather looked okay for the night: at most thirty-mile-an-hour winds – not a problem for me and Jet; we'd had much worse before. After a tin of rice pudding, Jet and I hit the sack.

Around two hours into our sleep, my tent got hit like we had camped up behind a fighter plane's engines on full power! In only a few minutes, my poles snapped, piercing the outer skin of my tent. The wind ripped open a hole, allowing the rain to soak the inside of the tent and everything within. I have never in my life felt gusts so powerful and frightening. How happy I was that we were in Lerwick – an immediate bail was totally necessary. We had to ditch the tent and make a run for it. With only my sleeping bag to pack, I threw my bag on and stood up outside, at which point the wind caught the back of the bag, slamming me to the floor.

'FUCK!' I screamed at the top of my voice.

Knowing these winds would be too powerful for Jet, I dropped the bag and made my way up a small hill holding her tightly in my arms. I managed to get us behind a disused building out of the wind for a minute. There I used Jet's lead to tie her up, so she didn't attempt to follow me, while I ran back for the bag. I grabbed our stuff – everything except my tent, now a blistery pancake on the floor – and made a run for it.

It was around midnight, and Lerwick was asleep. We searched the streets for a refuge, even trying my luck with a disabled toilet. Sadly, it had a steel gate over it. Next, we headed to the shore, using buildings as a cover from the insanely strong winds. My best and only option was a bus stop opposite the pub.

As I started taking my gear out to get Jet warm, I noticed to my right a pub sign switched on and a light on at the bar. I packed up and ran over, banging at the door in the hope we could go in. The barman unlocked the door and, seeing what a state we were in, said, 'Get yourself inside, you're soaked!'

'Thank you so much. We're desperate!' I replied.

He locked the door behind us and we walked into the bar. Three people were sat down finishing their drinks and asked what on earth we were doing out in this! In no time, a couple offered Jet and me a roof for the night so we could dry off. It was a brutal few hours.

The next morning the winds had dropped. I stood and looked at the sorry remains of the tent before me. *Mate,* I thought to myself, *This is only the first night!* It was a sobering realization of what we were up against.

Soon enough, with help from my incredible followers, I had a new tent and was back on the coast ready to nail Shetland. We headed north-west, passing through Mangaster, Gunnister, then through Hillswick and eventually up to the most northern point of mainland Shetland – Fethaland Lighthouse. This whole section of coast was incredible: high cliffs towered above the sea most of the way around, with abundances of seals and seal pups. As we walked into November, we were blessed with the constant spectacle of the most incredible winter clouds often filling the skies with rainbows you could only dream of.

By the time we'd made our way around Shetland's biggest hill (Ronas Hill), winter had truly set in. Huge clouds bringing ferocious winds carrying hail along with them would be a constant battle for us. I'd become very good at reading weather, and time after time, we would take cover for hours in the frozen peat bog trenches to avoid the oncoming slaughter, Jet and I both hiding under our storm shelter just thinking, *This is just crazy! What on earth have we let ourselves in for?!* I kept thinking about how isolated we were, so far from help if we'd needed it, but experience and mistakes I'd made years prior had taught me well. It was simply a case of edging forward every time we had a break in the clouds. It was a race against the weather all of the time.

As we headed north around the corner from Ronas Hill, we saw huge scars in the land, the extent to which I'd never seen before – tears in the earth caused by the now not so active Great Glen fault line which had left huge openings in the ground. Like rocky ice crevasses, they are not something you would want to fall into – a scary dark place but equally absolutely fascinating.

Shetland and the Outer Hebrides lay claim to some of the oldest rock in the world, dating back some 700 million years. To put that into perspective, that's around fifty times the age of Mount Everest. The once-Arctic landscape was cracked and torn by millions of years of constant freezing and repeated Ice Ages. I found it hard to process what I was walking on and what these rocks had seen in their time. I would think about things like this all day, as well as passing old Viking settlements still in plain sight. It was a good way to occupy my mind and keep the brain from tiring through seemingly endless days of bitter wind, cold and the monotony of walking. It worked a treat. Also, I'd always point things out to Jet and tell her what I thought, as if I was talking to someone who could reply. I wasn't losing my mind; I just knew how important it was to focus on other things rather than simply how cold it was.

After a gruelling few days and camping up among the frozen peat, barely able to get my tent pegs in, we made it past the northern tip and started heading south through Ollaberry and then back down to Brea.

As I walked Shetland, I worked hard on bettering my survival skills. Being so far north and now in winter, days were very short and the nights very long. To keep myself occupied, I would find anything I could along the coastline with which to learn and improvise. I'd experiment with making all sorts of different ovens, often creating makeshift cooking stoves from rocks and chains I'd found lying around. I'd cut my own peat and sit working out the texture to see how long it would take to dry next to a fire when it was damp so I could use it the next day. I'd also find washed up broken lobster creels and study how they worked and how to maintain and fix them up, so if ever the day came when I needed one, I knew what I was doing.

We put in serious effort getting to Mossbank. If the winds were forty miles an hour, then I'd consider it a good day. It truly was non-stop. It just so happened that Jet and I came into Shetland on the most wind-struck winter for over thirty years! There are no words to describe how much it took to get out of the tent each morning and just keep going. As a result of our efforts, the Shetlanders really started to warm to Jet and me. They respected our resilience and our integrity as we worked our way around, sticking rigidly to the coastline and sleeping in a tent in the brutal winter weather night after night. We turned down kind offers of accommodation again and again and they really admired us for it. I would become the first person to circumnavigate Shetland and its islands.

My next island would be Yell, which, with a population of just under 1,000, was the largest of all the surrounding islands of mainland Shetland and a peach to say the least! For Jet and me, it was one big slog, the peaty moorland like nothing I'd seen before. We would hop from one peat bog over to the other, often finding ourselves at a dead end, unable to jump any further. One of the perks of walking through this kind of terrain in winter was the abundance of white mountain hares, and I loved to watch them jumping elegantly from peat bog to peat bog. During summer, hares are a grey colour, much like a rabbit, but during the winter, their coats change to a stunning, clean white as a disguise from predators. Sadly, the forever-warming climate means that very little snow now settles in these parts and salty sea winds make it even more difficult, which in turn makes the hares very easy to spot. Fortunately for them, eagles no longer dominate the skies of Shetland, giving them a much greater chance of survival.

The coast of Yell was beautiful, particularly the west and north; towering sea cliffs and lovely beaches would bless my eyes until I eventually made it to a place called Gutcher, where we'd get the ferry to the UK's most northern isle, Unst. It was yet to sink in that, very soon, as I reached its northern tip, for the first time on my journey, in over two and a half years, I would now be heading south. This was it, my last push north – a monumental personal achievement!

Unst has a population of around 650 people and is one of the richest Viking heritage sites in Europe. Over sixty Viking long houses were uncovered by archaeologists and it's believed that being on the trading route between Scandinavia and Greenland made Unst the perfect resting point for Norse travellers, which makes perfect sense. Even the names of the places in Unst are amazing: Skaw, Haroldswick, Burrafirth, Clivocast, Belmont and Baliasta. It has around sixty miles of coastline, three sizeable sea lochs and Shetland's biggest freshwater loch. My plan was to get up to the very northern tip: Muckle Flugga, to spend Christmas Eve camped up as far north in the UK as you can be. We made good progress using the cold as an incentive to keep us moving fast; pushing through Muness, Uyeasound and Clivocast and into Haroldswick. There we could stop and marvel at a perfect replica of a Viking long boat, sitting next to which is a Viking longhouse that has been rebuilt on the same spot as the original. It's fascinating to see and even better that you're allowed to go inside and see how they once lived. With separate rooms inside for cattle during the winter months, a main room for everyday work with a firepit in the middle for heat and cooking, I decided there and then this was where I was going to see the new year in.

Finally, on 23 December 2019, we made it to the very north of Unst. It has a beautiful sea loch surrounded by high sea cliffs on either side, crystal-clear water and I was trigger happy, snapping away with my camera getting photos. It had taken me two and a half years to get to this point, but I'd done it!

'Jet,' I shouted. 'It's all south from here now, pal!'

That night, sipping out of my hip flask as a celebration, I stared out to sea directly north, mesmerized by the idea that, from the point where I sat, there was absolutely nothing in front of me until you reached the Arctic. My last Christmas had been spent on an uninhabited island off the west coast of the Outer Hebrides, and this Christmas I was looking out to sea in the direction of the North Pole, having completed both the west and the north. That night I was quite emotional. I couldn't compute that after all that time pushing hard, be it looking through bins for food, pulling my teeth out, suffering the harsh winter winds or summers midges, here I finally was. They say that it's not the destination, but the journey that counts. In this case, it was definitely both.

I spent New Year with a fire on, sitting in the freezing Viking longhouse imagining what it would have been like living in a place like this some thousand years ago. As I peered out of the window, my view was exactly the same as they'd enjoyed back then – untamed, untampered by masses of people. It was a lovely reminder that some places still exist in the world that feel unspoilt by humans.

That evening, after I did a post telling people where I was staying, slowly but surely, one by one, locals and their families came down to the house armed with a couple of glasses and a bottle of whisky. I spent hours chatting away with them, but none stayed long, having just come from the warmth of their homes, and I really don't blame them. I met an amazing couple, Andrew and Caron Reeves, who throughout the rest of my time in Unst helped me no end. They fed me, and after a night of playing guitar and having a dram, gave me what is called a 'nip' glass (a beautiful, thimble-sized blue glass for drinking a 'nip' of whisky out of on special occasions). Unst was a turning point on my walk; I would now be walking *into* the sun rather than it being constantly behind me. It was such an incredibly special, unique place in which to spend Christmas and New Year and an experience I shall never forget.

My next island was Fetlar, otherwise known as the Garden of Shetland. It gets its name because of the unique green terrain, which was a stark contrast to the peaty moorland I'd seen throughout the centre of Shetland. I loved walking it. Although constantly smashed by January winds, its coastline was thirty-one miles of beautiful sea cliffs and spectacular wildlife. By this point, I'd become pretty popular in Shetland; the locals had really started to take me seriously, knowing the conditions that we had ploughed through since arriving back in November. I slept in a small ferry terminal for a few nights and another couple of nights in an old house. In all, my time on Fetlar was amazing.

One of the things that I loved was getting told stories by the locals. Each island had its very own. One story in particular I remember was about a baby that got snatched by a sea eagle when eagles once inhabited Shetland. This powerful bird of prey carried the baby in its claws from Unst over to the cliffs of Fetlar, where it nested. Fortunately, a young lad on Fetlar saw the eagle with the small baby in its grasp and followed it. As the eagle left the baby with the chicks and flew off, the boy scrambled down the cliffs to save the baby from being eaten alive and miraculously succeeded. Many years later, the baby, now a young woman, and the boy who saved her, now a man, ended up getting married. I could just imagine the man saying to the woman: 'I climbed up a cliff and saved you from getting eaten alive by a sea eagle! Fancy a pint?' I'm not sure any pick-up line can beat that!

Before heading to my next island, Skerries, we had to continue south down the east coast of the mainland from Mossbank, taking us around two weeks before arriving at Vidlin ferry terminal, where you get the boat to Skerries. Through the grapevine, I had heard about a flu-like virus spreading across the world – Covid-19. At this point, it seemed irrelevant to Jet and me; we were outside in remote areas and I dismissed it, as I did the rest of the news. Not having a TV or radio was a blessing in my eyes, and we were too focused on the task ahead all the time to worry about tabloids or politics. I was a much happier man without it. Waking up to a barrage of bad news every morning is not my idea of a good start to the day; as much as it's always helpful to be kept informed, I just ignored it all while I was walking.

We made it to Vidlin ferry terminal a few weeks later and headed over to Skerries, the most easterly inhabited island in Shetland. With only thirty-five inhabitants, Skerries is quite unique. It's only 164 nautical miles from the nearest lighthouse in Norway. We had the most horrendous crossing, and since Jet and I were the only passengers onboard, we had nobody to ask if it was normal for the boat to rock around this much. On arrival, we pitched the tent up near the small harbour with a plan to walk the island the next day. That evening, we were awoken by a massive storm; the winds reached around seventy-five miles an hour, and once again, my tent gave me that all too familiar sound of poles snapping and ripping through the material. Having learned my lesson on that memorable first day in Shetland, I pitched up near a small toilet at the harbour. Although impossible for one to lie down in the toilet, as it was too small, it would at least provide some kind of shelter. Once again, I grabbed our gear and abandoned the tent, making our way to the toilet. The onshore winds and the close proximity of the toilet to the sea meant the waves crashing violently against the rocks spat up huge amounts of water right over us. Unable to move with so little room, I just sat on the toilet for the entire night, listening to the waves constantly crashing against our tiny refuge. It was scary. Jet, as ever, was fine; as long as she was by my side, she could sleep through a volcanic eruption! For me, however, it was a long night. We managed to walk the small island the next day, only seeing two of the locals. At this time of year, I didn't blame them for staying inside.

Arriving back at Vidlin ferry terminal the next afternoon, it was more of the same. On the opposite side of the sea loch from the terminal, a couple, James and Kathleen, could see from my tent that it was unusable. James immediately jumped into his car and drove down to see us, begging me to come to the house and stay over. I declined, sticking true to my word, adamant that we would continue wild camping, but the thought of a hot meal and not having to lie down on my side in the tent for more hours than absolutely necessary was very appealing. We left the tent where it was and jumped into the car. That night, I made two more friends for life.

Kathleen knocked up a hearty meal along with a few beers to wash it down. She also knits the most incredible Shetland woollen hats for pleasure and immediately got to work making one for me. I was elated, as I loved these kinds of sentimental gifts. Over the next few weeks, James and Kathleen would help me endlessly, even taking my bag for the day so I could walk weight-free; what a huge difference it made! In no time, Kathleen had knitted me my first ever Shetland wool hat – I loved it and wore it every day. Although it was a different hat, I was still sticking to my promise to Michael by keeping one on at all times.

We pushed on with only a two-day walk around Whalsay, before heading south on the mainland and eventually reaching Lerwick, Shetland's capital. It was 25 January and we were deep into our Shetland winter. No part of my walk so far had been so challenging or relentless in its quest to try and stop us from moving forward every day. It was Groundhog Day: getting up freezing until I'd packed our gear, then camping up again only a few hours later because of the limited light during the day, hoping another tent wouldn't bite the dust. It was evident from my photo posts that my tent was not in good shape. I was contacted by a fella from the British Special Forces who, at the time, was watching my slog through Shetland while serving abroad. He was absolutely adamant he wanted to buy me a new one, a £500 Terra Nova tent – and he refused to take no for an answer. I was so, so grateful!

Only six days after receiving my first Terra Nova, we were camping up on our next island, Bressay, opposite

Lerwick, and once again, the poles were annihilated by the unnerving Shetland winds.

While in Bressay, however, I got to be part of something very special indeed: the Up Helly Aa, Europe's biggest fire festival.

27

The torch bearer

In late January every year, thousands of people line the streets in Lerwick to watch the torch procession of 1,000 Shetlanders divided into groups known as 'squads'. The front squad is led by the head of the entire procession, called the 'Jarl', dressed head to toe in the most incredible Viking attire. I was incredibly privileged that one of the men in one of the squads had dressed up as me. I knew I'd made a good rapport with the locals but seeing how sacred this event was to the Shetlanders, someone dressed up in a kilt with a fake beard and a buff hat was an incredible honour. I'd even been invited to be part of the procession in one of the squads. This in itself was a serious honour. I was blown away and would have absolutely loved to have been part of it but, sadly, I had to decline, as it would have meant leaving Jet for too long.

I'd always thought the Up Helly Aa was a festival paying

homage to the Vikings but I was wrong. It's far more simple and logical than that. During winter, Shetland sees very little light. On the shortest day of the year, the sun rises at roughly nine o'clock and sets at around half past two in the afternoon. It's a lot of time to spend in darkness, especially with the weather to contend with as well. As a result, the festival was born out of the islanders' need for another focus during winter. They would get together, organize and build a galley – a replica of a Viking boat. I can tell you that the work that goes into building these replicas is mind-blowing! While the festival's origins date back to the early 1800s when groups of dressed-up young men would light barrels of tar on sledges and drag them through the streets, this 'tar-barrelling' was banned in 1871, as too much damage was caused by the burning tar that was accidentally spilled as the men navigated the sledges through the narrow streets. It evolved into a torchlit parade, the first of which took place in 1881.

Jet and I stood on the balcony of a house and watched in awe as 1,000 lit torches paraded through the streets of Lerwick in the direction of the community-erected galley ready to set fire to it. All the street lights are turned off to give the light from the burning torches greater effect. Watching the Viking-dressed men circle the galley really was a sight to behold; I felt like I was at the ceremonious burial of the Greek legend Achilles. One by one, the torches are thrown onto the Viking ship as it explodes in flame. I've never seen anything like it and I'm not sure I will again.

Much smaller Up Helly Aas are held in different parts of Shetland on different dates, one of which I just happened to be walking past that same day on the island of Bressay. These are much more intimate, and I loved that I could be up so close to it all. The locals once again had been incredible to me; they were all so friendly and kind. I was invited to be part of their procession once again and this time, I was able to. Standing next to all the Viking-dressed men, I held a burning torch while Jet walked right by my side. We made our way to the galley as everybody sang songs, and despite the fact that they were in a language I would never understand, I just moved my lips like I knew what I was doing to feel as much a part of it all as possible. From what I'd been told, it was unheard of to let outsiders be part of such a unique, intimate and heartfelt demonstration of their heritage.

As I looked around at all of the men and women singing and drinking, having put so much effort into all of this, I felt a real sense of pride among the Shetlanders. The whole experience was magical. Like in Lewis, carrying the torch for one of the men whose life had been taken by the *Iolaire* disaster, I felt like I'd earned the love and respect of its people.

As we made our way towards the south of Shetland, there were lots more small villages and hamlets. Still with a broken tent, I bumped into a man called John James who had been following my journey for a good while now, along with his wife, Alexis. He simply couldn't do enough for me. They allowed me to stay in their polytunnel for a while to keep me safe from the winds. Each day, John would drop me off, I'd then walk for the day weight-free and wherever I'd got to that day, he would come and pick me up and bring me back to the polytunnel and feed us.

I loved the guy – and I really needed a good feeding up!

Through a family member, Alexis had managed to get me a plane ticket to head south to another island called Fair Isle. I knew I had no tent, but this was an opportunity that needed to be seized. With just my bag and Jet, clueless as to what the hell I was going to do, we hopped onto the tiny plane and made our way to the beautiful island of Fair Isle. Always the optimist, I just believed that I would find a way, took the plunge and went for it!

We landed on Fair Isle on 6 March 2020. The island has around sixty inhabitants and is mainly famous for its Fair Isle woollen jumpers. There are twenty-six miles of stunning coastline and the north side has incredibly high cliffs teeming with birds and other wildlife. The name Fair Isle comes from the Norse name, 'Friðarey', literally meaning 'calm, peaceful isle'. It's situated between Orkney and Shetland and reported in the Orkneyinga Saga to have had a huge beacon (fire) to warn Orkney of any attacks from Shetland. Eventually, after the Vikings had settled there, they became farmers on this peaceful island.

When we arrived, the locals came to greet us. I told them that I had no accommodation, and a lady called Rachel, an ex-officer in the Armed Forces, who lived there told me about an old, disused fish house on the east side of the island at the end of a small, beautiful sea loch. Always wearing wellies and tending to her sheep, it was as if she belonged outdoors. The island itself was only a two-day walk, heading past both the north and west lighthouses. The sea below the cliffs was scattered with amazing sea stacks teeming with gulls using the wind to swoop up and down the rock faces. It was some sight and, as always, a constant reminder of how much I loved being on the coast. I could see it a million times over and never tire of it. I knew that I'd never be able to live inland again after this.

One evening, while I was nestled inside the fish house that was built from stone, it started to rain incredibly hard. This was actually a great sign, as it meant that the weather was finally starting to warm – a nice break from the constant freezing temperatures that we'd had and being battered with hail. However, the roof of my temporary home was riddled with holes and loose tiles. With no tent to cover us, we started to get a real soaking. I got up and rushed around to find whatever I could in the hope of sorting some kind of cover. To my delight, I found a huge sheet of ply. Using my bag and whatever else I could find to rest it on, I covered the sleeping spot to stop the rain dripping all over us. Only twenty minutes later, after getting back into my sleeping bag, I heard a bang on the door. It was Rachel.

'Chris, I'm part of a Fair Isle band. I know you love to play music, and we wondered if you would like to come jam with us? And we have wine!'

In seconds, Jet and I were both in the car on our way to band practice with a great chance to have a few hours away from our fish house digs for the night, now fast becoming a swimming pool! As we drove, I smiled to myself, enjoying such a random, off-the-cuff, sporadic lifestyle. I loved the fact that I never knew what was coming next!

We pulled up at Rachel's, where I met the band. In no time, we were drinking wine and playing our instruments: guitars, a saxophone and the piano. It was such a fun evening and all the while we played, I sat there thinking just how surreal it was that I was here, on the tiny island of Fair Isle, playing music with the locals over drinks – such a far cry from my previous life in Swansea. We played a slow version of 'Dakota' by Stereophonics; I sang and played the guitar and the others just went along with it, improvising. I decided to post it on my page the next day, and once it was up, I received a video message from Richard Jones, the bassist, pianist and backing vocalist from Stereophonics! In the message, he told me how much he loved our version of the song and congratulated me on my efforts to date. I was chuffed to receive it and really appreciated the thoughtfulness of it.

I was soon slapped back to reality, however, when off I returned to my soaking wet fish shed for the night. The water, by now all over the floor, had absolutely saturated our stuff. *Fuck!* I thought to myself. I nestled Jet inside my now very damp sleeping bag, got her warm and just sat up the whole night, hoping that we would get a dry day come morning to be able to air out our gear.

The next day was our last day on Fair Isle and we completed it in good time. Now back at the fish shed for our second night, I noticed an injured sheep. I phoned Rachel, who came down right away with medicine, and we spent the afternoon herding the sheep to get our hands on the one limping. It took a long time but we got him in the end. We bandaged him up and gave him an injection and he was good as gold! The next morning, I said goodbye to Fair Isle and its amazing people before taking to the skies to return to mainland Shetland.

Our next section would take a month or so walking to

the very south of Shetland to Sumburgh and then back up the west side, eventually leading us back to Brea where we'd started. John James had been an absolute star throughout this part of the walk, again letting us stay in his polytunnel each night, picking us up and dropping us off each morning back to our starting point. I could never leave my bergen for the day as I couldn't afford to get caught out weather-wise, but it was such a huge help as we made our way around this section. As we progressed up the west coast, we passed the insanely beautiful St Ninian's Isle, a small island connected to the land by a stunning white beach acting as a causeway, again world-class – so peaceful and another treat for the eyes. Eventually, we made it up to a bridge that connects two islands: Trondra and Burra.

Throughout my time being helped by John and Alexis, he had kept me up to date with the news surrounding Covid-19 and the ever-increasing chance of the UK being put into a strict lockdown, with people unable to leave their homes. He had some good friends on the island of Burra who were only too happy to help me while I walked around the two islands. A hostel on Burra also offered me a few nights to relax, wash my clothes and sleep with a roof over our heads. I jumped at the chance.

The next morning, I got a knock on the door from a man called Victor Lawrenson. He introduced himself and we got chatting. I asked if he would mind getting me to a shop for food and supplies for Jet. We jumped into his truck and made our way.

'Chris,' said Victor. 'It's been confirmed that the country is going into a national lockdown on 23 March, in two days' time. What are you going to do?'

'I have no idea! I suppose I'll just have to camp up and wait it out.'

Because I hadn't been subjected to constant alarming news, I had no great worries about the imminent pandemic; it was just another hurdle that Jet and I had to tackle.

'Listen,' said Victor. 'There's an uninhabited island about a mile off the coast. It's called Hildasay. If you like, I can take you over on my boat and drop you off. We can work out a plan to help you once you're there, but at least you'll be in your own space without any worries of catching this illness.'

Without a single hesitation, and no thought of how it would even be possible, I agreed.

'Victor, that would be amazing!' I said. 'What an incredible adventure – my own island! How long is lockdown going to last?' I asked.

'It could be for weeks; it could be months. Who knows?'

'Okay, well, I'll spend lockdown on Hildasay. God knows how I'm going to do it.' We both laughed. 'But I'll find a way!'

The next morning, I packed up my gear and we loaded the boat with barrels of fresh water as well as some food for me and Jet. Little did I know at the time, I would spend three months on Hildasay, just off the west coast of Shetland.

28

As low as you can go

After being reunited with Caitlin and living with her for a short time under Jo's roof in Northern Ireland, having not seen my daughter for over two years before I was able to return, my dream came true. In 2008, it was decided that Caitlin would come and live with me. After all it had taken to get to this point, this was a truly triumphant day for me. I felt euphoric to have her properly in my life again after six years.

It wasn't long after joining the Paras that I rekindled my relationship with my dad and his now wife, Jane. I knew Jane had a soft spot for me, having always been the cheeky adventurous one. In fact, Jane was the first person I told that I was going to do my walk. Desperate for help, before winning custody of Caitlin, I contacted my dad and Jane to tell them of my plans. They invited both Caitlin and me to go and stay with them and my half-sister, Molly, while we figured out a plan.

To win the court case, I'd needed to be in full-time work and have my own place. I managed to bag myself a job as a personal trainer at the Whittlebury Hall Hotel. My dad and Jane had bought a second house just outside of Whittlebury and kindly offered Caitlin and me their original house to rent while I fought the court case. Luckily, it was also only a stone's throw from my new job. To help give us a good start, Jane had offered to look after Caitlin in the hours that she wasn't in school while I had to work. We established a simple, effective routine where Jane would pick Caitlin up from school if I was unable to and look after her until I could go and pick her up in the evening after finishing work. They developed an incredibly close relationship and Jane's help was invaluable. After about a year of the same routine – work, picking up Caitlin, feeding and putting her to bed and then spending the rest of the evening always on my own just thinking – it was still not something I got particularly used to. Life had always been so fast-paced, but now, with a fixed abode, one by one, small debts started catching up with me from years before.

There was no chance I could afford my rent, food and all the other day-to-day bits one needs as a single parent on the wage that I was earning. My rent alone left me with only a few hundred quid to last the month. The pressure was starting to build. I started to take on an incredible sense of guilt: Jane looking after Caitlin so much made me feel indebted. This was supposed to be the most amazing time, now having custody of my beautiful girl, but instead, at night I would sit alone with my head in my hands just wondering what the hell I was going to do. This was not like any of my previous sticky situations when I'd just had me to look after. Having Caitlin only exacerbated the pressure, but I was determined to give her the best life.

Whittlebury is a lovely area, but the expense of my rent and now growing pressures to keep up with the bills and pay back debts meant that my only option would be to find somewhere cheaper. I couldn't pay for babysitting costs, so I decided the best thing I could do to alleviate some of the pressure and make life easier would be to look after her myself. Just over a year after moving in and doing my very best to pay my debts off with the little income I had, financially it started to cripple me.

Sadly, I actually owned none of the things that I was in debt for. My financial situation had never been particularly brilliant, but at least it was only me that would suffer for it. I can remember telling myself, 'Just bloody tell somebody. Ask for help,' but my deeply insular and private nature wouldn't allow me to do it. As ever, I just kept everything inside. I had to get out of this situation, and the only way I knew to do that was to start fresh.

In 2009, I decided to up sticks and move to Wales. My situation by this point had very quickly spiralled. Already, I was in financial ruin. Caitlin, who was now seven, and I left for Wales in the crappiest, oldest white Vauxhall you can imagine; it had no tax, no insurance, no MOT and the driver's side window was completely smashed after someone had broken into and stolen my passport. Despite all this, Caitlin and I still made the four-hour journey up to Wales. At points it rained and we would both laugh our heads off at the ridiculousness of our situation as rain poured in on us through the driver's window.

Through a friend that he'd met at university, my brother found us a cheap place to rent a few miles out of Swansea in a place called Killay. Over the next few years, I worked as hard as I could bringing in just enough to keep us afloat. Any job I did was only about paying the bills in order to keep a roof over our heads, regardless if I hated it. My inability to pay off any of my debts was still a constant worry. I had absolutely no help whatsoever with babysitting or anybody to look after Caitlin, so my days would consist of getting Caitlin to school, working as hard and fast as I could, sneaking off early from work to pick her up, constantly feeling the pressure of getting there on time for her and panicking if I was late, and then having to bring her back to work with me until my day ended. At this point, I was working as a labourer on building sites and would have to hide Caitlin in the car until I finished. I was forever under pressure, made worse by the fact that all I wanted for Caitlin was for us to be spending quality time together, or for her to be playing with her mates; just enjoying herself.

After a few years of this, I had become run-down and extremely tired – and then I started to get letters and knocks at the door from debt collectors. One day, I was sitting at home on a rare day off when I heard a bang at the door while Caitlin was at school. It was Excel Debt Collectors in Swansea. Fraught with fear, I burst into tears and tried to explain my situation, hoping they would have some kind of heart. We had so little for them to take but they didn't care. They went through my house like a hitman looking for information. Even Caitlin's room was ransacked. I later found out this was illegal as she was a minor. They took everything, pulled the sofa apart, throwing all the cushions onto the floor and walking over them in their boots like they were trash.

I told them I'd been in the Paras and that I might just be able to seek help from one of the Forces' charities. One of them laughed at me and called me a Walter Mitty (someone who lies about being in the Forces) – accusing me of stolen valour. My tears at this point had started to turn to rage. One of them took Caitlin's laptop from her room and I shouted, 'Take whatever you like, but that's my daughter's and she needs it for school!'

He smiled, knowing by the look on my face it could possibly set me off, almost egging me on to do something irrational. I went to grab her laptop back and before I knew it, I was pinned against the wall hard enough to put a dent in the plasterboard. As they left and got into their car, I sat on my doorstep, devastated and feeling thoroughly undeserving of such harsh treatment. 'I won't forget this!' I shouted. 'And I *was* a soldier!'

They drove off in the car looking incredibly pleased with themselves, knowing how much they'd riled me up. That night, I had to tell Caitlin that we'd been robbed. I saw no other way out of it as I felt so completely and utterly ashamed of myself.

Slowly but surely, I became depressed. Always determined to maintain a brave face, never once did it cross my mind that this was an unhealthy way to bring up a child. All through my adult life, I had just simply kept at it. I actually saw this as a strength at the time, but looking back, the truth is that my ability to just keep going would start to become my biggest weakness, even more so because

I kept it all so private. No matter how strong you are, every person has a breaking point. With all the pressures weighing down on me for so long, I had started to sink into self-meltdown. I stopped socializing or wanting to be around people. Instead, I would hide away, consumed by worry. Each day, I became more and more annoyed with myself, as all I wanted to do was be a better dad. My faith in humanity was slipping away, as was my ability to respond effectively to everyday struggles.

My now deepening depression and inability to deal with anything resulted in Caitlin and me getting evicted. I couldn't find it in myself to even walk into the Civic Centre in Swansea to be around a load of people to fill out forms and answer personal questions; it made me incredibly anxious. The house we'd lived in in Killay was now no longer ours. The eviction resulted in us having to sleep in a car. We were homeless. I'd been homeless before, but this was different. It wasn't just me; I had a daughter who depended on me and I knew I wasn't being the role model that I needed to be for her sake. Completely desperate, I finally reached out for some help and called my friend Chris Carree. Chris told us to come and live with him for a while so that we'd have a roof over our heads, rent-free, until we got ourselves back on our feet.

Over the next few years, my depression took on a whole different form. Honestly, at that point I had no idea that I was depressed. It's only looking back on it now that I can see it. What was worse was the anxiety side of it. At night, I would wake up in fits of sweat, fists clenched in a panic. It felt like I was unable to breathe and that I was going to die. When I had my first ever panic attack, I had no idea what it was and just thought that my whole body had given up. Through all this, I'd managed to bag myself a council flat in Three Crosses, Swansea.

I was still working on building sites and, for extra cash over Christmases, I would wash dishes for the local golf club. I was also working at my friend Rob's farm, who owns Gower Fresh Christmas Trees. I was doing anything to get the money in, though found I was drawn to more physical work, as it really helped me. On days when I felt like I just wanted the ground to swallow me up, I'd go to work and take out all my frustrations by hauling breeze blocks around, mixing concrete and cement, spending weeks carrying Christmas trees over my shoulders just to release the tension.

The banter on building sites and being around general working men was the closest I'd got to the feeling of being in the Forces. One thing about leaving the Paras that really hit home as soon as I left was just how few people got my sense of humour. You could say whatever you liked when you were in and nobody got offended. Coming out onto civvy street is almost like having your sense of humour stripped away. Never in my life had I felt so isolated.

Each night, if I had a chance to get a surf in, I would. If I didn't, I'd simply be sitting in my flat, a prisoner in my own mind. In my eyes, the strange thing about depression and anxiety is how I would blow the smallest of things completely out of proportion. A simple knock at the door and I'd act like a Russian spy was there to get me! Quite ridiculous really, but it's just how it was. I felt like I was stuck inside a wooden box that was closing in on me and I was unable to fight my way out. My inability to speak up and share how I felt inside only made it worse. Evidently, I was on a slippery slope to self-destruction.

Sadly, I believed it was just life. As far as I was concerned, I was living two different lives; one as the outgoing, laughing, jokey person that everybody saw, and the other, the polar opposite of this. After many years of this, I finally reached breaking point. My mind could no longer take any more of the incessant worry and feeling like such a failure. I just needed a break. I would normally run, cycle or skateboard everywhere. Even picking Caitlin up from school, I would tie a rope around my waist, Caitlin would hop onto the skateboard and hold onto the piece of rope and I'd run the three and a half miles home, up some very sizeable hills I might add, with Caitlin in tow.

I thought she really loved it but, looking back, it definitely wasn't the coolest mode of transport for a thirteen-year-old girl! I can't tell you how many drivers passed us with their jaws dropped in disbelief. I had few friends by this point, only two of whom I really saw: Alan Pugh and Chris Carree. Unfortunately, I would see them as an escape from my problems rather than people to talk to about them. My problems at home had become my only focus. I was even finding it hard to hold down jobs where I'd have to put on this false persona, pretending all the time that things were fine and dandy. I had distanced myself from my family completely.

The strain on mine and Caitlin's relationship was becoming evident. I hated it and it hurt me so much that she would see me in this way. As Caitlin was older now and nearing the end of secondary school, I found it better for her not to be around me. After school and on the weekends, Caitlin would go straight to her friends' houses for the evening and often stay the night. I was giving her far too much freedom, but I couldn't see it at the time; I'd rather she be at her friends' having fun than being around an anxiety-stricken dad. I think she had started to lose her respect for me, which was understandable, as I wasn't the best role model.

I selfishly gave very little time to listening to any of her problems, unable to think past my own. It had come to a point where my idea of being a good dad was putting a plate of food in front of her and maintaining a roof over her head, but I gave her very little emotional support. Now that she was a fully fledged teenager, I even took it personally when she had her little moments, instead of seeing through it; we argued a lot. My failure as a parent eventually broke me. I knew that I wasn't a bad guy; I had simply lost my way. In my head, I was absolutely no use to anybody, not even my pride and joy, Caitlin; I had failed at every aspect of life and let down everybody that I'd ever held dear to me.

I know how much she loved me, sticking by my side for as long as she did. At sixteen years old, Caitlin told me she had decided to leave home and she was going to move down to Bournemouth. Enough was enough. Obviously, it broke me to hear it, but I was and still am so proud of her resilience and strength to make such a huge decision. What she didn't know at the time was that we were only a few weeks away from losing our flat. David Singletree, the head of SSAFA South Wales, had helped Caitlin and me so many times. Without him, I would have lost it all a long time ago. He had pulled us through so many scrapes.

Both Caitlin and I loved him, but this time, I would not accept his help again. I knew the best thing was to just let Caitlin do what she felt was best for her; it was no longer my decision to make.

The morning she left, Caitlin and I caught the bus to the train station, hardly even talking. It was just too sad. We said our goodbyes, and with Caitlin now on the train to her new life, I walked home, numb, a shell of a man.

29

Purpose

As the rest of the world locked itself up country by country, I prepared to hunker down on the uninhabited island of Hildasay. I picked out points on the island on the north, east, south and west sides where I could build some ovens to cook depending on different wind directions. Saving gas for my burners was also imperative; if we were caught out in big storms, I would need to conserve it for emergency cooking. It was all about being prepared for any situation.

Although the house had a bundle of wood outside, I was conscious not to rip the arse out of it. The tide on the south side would bring in the majority if not all of the driftwood that the island had to offer. I was going to be here a while totally alone (aside from Jet), and I knew how important it would be to keep my mind occupied so as not to go insane. A daily routine would be vital. Jet and I retired early to the tent that night, having been blessed with a good day of weather. I got Jet settled inside the tent about an hour before the sun went down, got a fire on to make food and sat in total silence.

There was one thing that had been on my mind since pretty much the second I'd said yes to coming to Hildasay. In terms of human interaction, I'd spent 90 per cent of the walk so far on my own; walking alone during the day and being alone in the tent at night. I'd always been okay with this, as I'm very comfortable in my own company. But this level of isolation was different. Each and every day for over two and a half years, I'd had a very clear goal: to keep moving forward, to just keep going. It had taken a while, but my problems had gradually dispersed as I had so much to focus on each day to achieve that goal. I thought back and realized that the last time that I'd been in one place for a decent amount of time was before starting the walk, when I'd been in pretty bad mental shape. I was worried that being so isolated on this island for a long period of time may not bode well for me.

Would this level of isolation bring back my anxiety and depression? *Please don't let me sink back into that headspace,* I thought to myself. I knew it was a risk, but had enough faith in myself by now that I felt it was one worth taking.

I looked up at the clear, starry night sky as I lay down by the fire with my hands behind my head, thinking about how lost I'd been before starting this walk and how I had sought to see if I could find myself again; who I might be without the crushing pressures of modern-day life that had caused me to crumble. It would be so easy to just say that my goal was to return a happy man. But, for that to happen, a combination of things would have to take place. First and foremost, I needed to forgive myself for not being the dad I had hoped to be. That was so important if I was ever going to be able to move on. I needed to declutter my head and strip away any anxieties linked to things that I was simply helpless to do anything about. I couldn't change the past; I could only learn from it. I also needed to believe that I would be able to reintegrate myself into society without the feeling that everyone wanted my blood. Thirdly, the walk wouldn't last for ever; I knew I needed to figure out what it was I wanted to do with my life once it was all over; that was equally important. Finishing the walk only to suddenly find myself homeless, jobless and back to square one again was not an option. Now that I had stopped, it was make or break. Hildasay would be my test. 'I'll either leave this island realizing the walk was just a temporary plaster,' I told myself, 'or I'll leave it having found what I had been searching for all this time: acceptance, forgiveness and, ultimately, happiness.'

Victor and I, along with his family, had planned that when our food stocks were running low, at the first possible opportunity, one of them would come over on the boat with a resupply. This wasn't always possible due to the weather, however: even as the weeks passed and we moved into spring, the weather was still as unpredictable as ever, with storms and fiercely strong winds. This dictated when the boat could come over. Water was my biggest issue, as now the lambs had been born, often a lamb would fall into the fresh water and perish, in turn contaminating the water and making it undrinkable. Falling seriously sick here could be fatal, so I had to be on my toes at all times for both Jet and myself. Victor and his family were our lifeline.

About a week and a half into our stay, Victor and his family got the boat over with fresh water and supplies. His wife, Pauline, had been in touch with Morgan, who owned the island and the house on it. To my sheer delight, Morgan and his family had kindly given Pauline the keys to the house so that Jet and I could stay inside it. I was absolutely thrilled! I will forever be grateful to him for such a gesture. The house inside was beautiful; decked out with wooden flooring, it had a kitchen area, bedroom and a living room. It was perfection; I couldn't believe I had been given access to it. More so, the excitement of now having a sofa to sit on. The Scandinavian-style home was the perfect respite from the winds and the ever torturous lying down on my side back in our tiny, still broken tent.

Having been out of use for years, the house had no running water, electricity or heating. Essentially, it was four very pretty walls and a roof covered in peat and heather, but I really didn't care. If anything, knowing I still had a long way to go on the walk, I was concerned that having such luxuries for a time would only make us soft. In fact, I felt far healthier having had no central heating for years than I ever had while living in a house. Not once had I had a flu, cold or even a sniffle on my entire walk. My immune system was definitely the strongest it had ever been.

Each night, I would sit and write down a list of things I could do the next day. With no running water, just going to the toilet meant work. I'd get up and head to the fresh-water loch to fill up buckets to flush it down. After, I'd make breakfast and then go and collect a bag of coal to bring back to the house. I'd then take my empty ten-litre water barrel and head down to the harbour, fill it up out of the twenty-litre barrels still down there, and carry it back. I'd then have lunch, after which I would do an hour's running around the house and then get busy in my outdoor gym, which consisted of rocks, filled-up buckets of water and a tennis ball. I'd use the rocks as weights, the filled-up buckets with a broom handle through the middle for squats, and I'd throw the tennis ball hard against the wall until I dropped it. Every time I dropped it, it would be either a hundred press-ups or a hundred sit-ups as a punishment. I loved training and I gave myself a goal to double what I'd been able to do on my first effort by the time I left the island. After that, I would then go back down to the harbour and drag up a second bag of coal. Every day, I would run around on the island playing with Jet. My final tasks of the day were getting a fire on, cooking dinner and washing up before cuddling up in my sleeping bag with Jet for the night.

Having no running water meant dragging twenty-litre barrels of it when it arrived over 600 yards from the small harbour back to the house. I didn't mind; it was great fitness and something to do. For heat, Victor and his family came over armed with bags of coal for me to light fires, which also needed lifting from the harbour. I felt I had no choice but to see the positives in everything, and that kind of mindset was really working for me.

On 6 May (my birthday), Victor and his family – my Covid 'support bubble' – came over as a surprise, bringing with them a birthday cake, wine and a barbecue. It was my fortieth birthday – something of a milestone. I couldn't have had better people around me to share it with.

What really amazed me was the amount of gifts I received. They arrived on the island from people all over the world, from all corners of the British Isles as well as a load of other European countries, even Canada and America. As soon as the postman at the sorting office in Lerwick saw they were for 'Chris Walks the UK', they were then taken over to Burra, and from there, Victor and Pauline would collect them and bring them all over by boat to Hildasay. Never in my life had I received so many presents, and it was just amazing given my isolated location.

I had the best time on my birthday. After they had left on their boat to go back home, Victor messaged me to say he had hidden a small bottle of the good stuff for me to find. I loved the idea. It would keep me busy from morning to evening looking for it.

Every other day, I would walk the island twice, keeping count of the sheep and the new lambs. I'd had a visit from the crofter who owned the sheep and he had given me medicine so that I could treat them in case any of them fell ill. I loved that job. After a while, I became very attached to them, giving each of them names. Once in a while, I'd be devastated after finding a dead lamb lying in the water. Even worse, upon the arrival of the great skuas – or bonxies as they call them in Shetland (a type of predatory bird) – I would run to scare them off, as they were known to peck at the eyes of the small lambs. Often I succeeded, but sometimes I would find one half eaten by the skuas.

One day as I was doing my sheep rounds, I spotted an old football floating in the water, so I jumped in (rather stupidly, as the water was ice cold after winter) and retrieved it. Immediately, the thought of the film *Castaway* starring Tom Hanks came to mind. *How ironic to find a football now I too am essentially stranded on my own uninhabited island!* I thought. I got to work making a face on the football. With the help of Pauline and her and Victor's daughter, Marie, my next shipment of supplies came with makeup, marker pens and a Viking hat with horns. I decided my football was to become a woman; I gave her big black eyes, a nose and bright red lips. I then used driftwood to make her a body, complete with arms and legs, with old wetsuit gloves for hands.

I had to give her a bit of modesty, so I made her a bra out of clam shells. Unintentionally (I promise), her face looked like a seedy blow-up doll, but I didn't care. I stood my creation up outside the house, walked away and turned to look. At the top of my voice, I shouted proudly, 'I shall call you Hilda, goddess of war!'

From that day on, every time I went outside to go about my daily chores, I'd stop next to her. 'Hilda,' I'd say, 'Jet and I are off to count the sheep. Hold the fort until we return!' And that she did. Every now and then, I'd move her to a different location to freak out anyone who came over by boat to visit. It was great fun and I became very attached to her. I had my very own Wilson!

My plan of making stone ovens around the island worked a treat. We still had huge hail storms and snow clouds rolled over us from time to time, but the temperature was slowly rising, without a doubt. On the odd occasion, depending on the wind direction, it even climbed up to around twelve or thirteen degrees. It was by no means down south temperatures for the time of year, but when you've just spent the winter out here in a tent, twelve degrees seemed almost tropical. I'd even walk around in a pair of shorts I'd been lent. They were so small they felt like spandex, but it was the first time I'd had my legs out since before I started the walk. Even in the height of summer, I'd always wear long johns to protect my legs from midges, ferns and ticks. For the first time in two and a half years, I would strip off completely and feel the breeze on my naked body. I'd had naked baths in streams, but they were always freezing. My clothes would be back on in minutes. To sit for hours in what I can only describe as budgie smugglers, after wearing pretty much just one change of clothes all day and all night for years, made this moment very special.

After about a month and a half of being on the island, I started to feel that my daily routine was getting monotonous. I knew I had to change it. Now the weather had started giving us at least three good days of sun in a week, it meant I could become more productive. As well as switching up my routine, I began jotting down things that I wanted to get better at. Unlike most of you, I didn't have the luxury of electricity, computers or enough battery power to sit and research things online. For me, learning new skills and knowledge would be a case of physical trial and error. I loved foraging and I wanted to up the ante. Every few weeks, a fisherman named John would come over on his boat with fish, crab and the occasional lobster for me as a treat. I loved the guy. We would sit and I would pick his brains on how to catch lobster. He was so helpful. I was determined to give it a go. I'd borrowed a wetsuit from Victor and Pauline's son, James, and every day, with a rope tied to my waist to hunt with, I would jump into the water and look for lobster holes.

I tried for weeks with no success. I'd even fixed up a washed-up creel I'd found on the other side of the island. Mackerel season was now in full swing, and lobsters love a bit of mackerel. I'd been given some by another fisherman, so I baited up my creel, tied a boulder onto my length of rope, which I then attached to the creel, and swam around thirty yards out. God, it was heavy to swim with, but I managed to get it down to the seabed. Day after day, I dived down hoping to spot the long orange tentacle, but nothing. Then one day, about three weeks later, I hovered over the rocks and there, at the bottom, I saw one! The excitement really took hold of me – it was a jump-for-joy feeling.

It was about a metre below me, and I knew the tide was on its way out so decided to let the creel drop until I could stand in order to give my feet some kind of pressure on the ground. Eventually, it dropped enough for me to make my move. There's a very specific way to pick up a lobster, which John had taught me. If you get a finger inside its claws, inevitably you will run around like a wounded cartoon character with its arse on fire. With my snorkel, I grabbed a heavy rock to help sink me to the sea floor. Nervously, I counted to ten and made my move. On my first attempt, I managed to grab it behind the claws. Success!

I released the rock and floated to the top. Immediately double-checking the lobster wasn't able to nip me, I rushed over to my phone that I'd set up in the hope of recording my monumental first lobster catch. In documentary presenter style, I started to describe the lobster. As I turned it over, I immediately noticed hundreds of black bubbly coated eggs all over its underneath.

'For fuck's sake!' I shouted out loud, as my food supplies at this point were at an all-time low and it would be another two days before Victor would be able to make it over again. This lobster would have gone down perfectly with the few vegetables I had left, but I couldn't do it. Only if it was already on death's door would I make such a sacrifice of its babies. I dropped her back into the water after a quick selfie and let her go. In one respect, I was gutted, but I also felt good knowing I'd done the right thing by her. I started making my way back to the house, and as I neared, I could hear the roaring sound of a helicopter.

I looked around to see the search and rescue helicopter heading our way. I didn't think much of it until it started to circle around our island. It did one or two laps and then started to back off. For a second, I thought they were going to do a flyby for us. As I turned to call Jet into the house, I saw orange smoke about 200 yards away from us. It was a smoke flare. I ran over excitedly, thinking they had perhaps dropped a package for me. Soon enough, the helicopter came back around and started its descent.

Jet, petrified of the noise, ran to the top of the hill, keeping her eyes on me. The noise was insane, and the wind from the rotas got more and more powerful as it neared the ground. I could not believe it had landed here. One of the crew jumped out and ran towards me. I sprinted over to him. He spoke as loud as he could, but I only just about made out his words: 'Chris, this is for your efforts! Well done!' he said, and handed me a Shetland Search and Rescue badge. We shook hands and he ran off back to the helicopter and they flew away. Jet ran back to me as I sat looking at my new uniform patch. I felt so privileged, and my lobster loss was now a thing of the past. What a boost! Shetland Search and Rescue, thank you for making my day!

My presence on Hildasay and consistent upbeat attitude despite the challenges ahead of me had really started to get noticed. I even spent an afternoon dragging twenty litres of water around the island on a rope tied around my waist to get more donations for SSAFA. Despite us being on hold, I figured I could still do my best to keep raising money. Throughout the first lockdown, even from afar on my little island, it was clear to me how badly it was affecting people, especially in terms of mental health.

Personally, whenever I was finding isolation difficult, I would think back to people who served in the great wars. Years of fighting in trenches wondering every day if that day would be their last. I used it as a reminder that this situation wasn't really so bad. God, what they would have given to have been told they had to stay at home for three months. It would have been a dream come true! But times have changed, as have people. With mental health issues now becoming such a prominent part of our modern-day society, I wanted to model positive and upbeat behaviour to try and inspire others. Being in a place like this with no power to charge my phone meant I had little or no chance to Zoom, Skype or WhatsApp any of my friends or family in order to keep in touch. And as difficult as lockdown was, that was a luxury that nearly everybody did have. It wasn't easy, but I knew I had no choice so I just got on with it.

In mid-April, I got a call from a woman called Clare who worked for the Press Association, which writes stories and then filters them out to various different newspapers and magazines. I remember doing the interview huddled in a corner of the house with Jet, a sleeping bag over us as the weather was doing its normal thing. I didn't think about it too much after I'd done the interview, but once it was released, it suddenly became massive. I was getting calls from newspapers and news channels from around the world, including CNN in America, as well as walking magazines and about fifteen different radio stations: BBC Radio 2, 5Live, Heart FM and so on.

Somebody staying on an uninhabited island off the west coast of Shetland, alone, seemed to have really caught the media's attention, and I worked so hard while I was there to talk to the press (saving enough battery for them was a job in itself) on top of all my other daily chores. In between interviews, I'd be shovelling food down me as fast as I could to get ready for the next one. My phone was constantly being charged by a solar panel to be able to do this – once there was finally enough sun, as sun is not in abundance out in Shetland! It doesn't sound like a lot, but for about two weeks, it felt like all I did.

My favourite of all the coverage – and please don't think this is me being big-headed because, if anything, I found it hilarious – was mine and Jet's mugshot centre page on the front of the paper, between the North Korean dictator Kim Jong-un and Donald Trump! And that same shot of us was also used as a Google homepage image!

As I've said before, I really wasn't in it for this kind of attention, but as a result of the hard work we had put in, things really started to pay off. After only three days or so of this media attention, my donations shot up from around

£74,000 to £99,100. One evening, I sat watching the amount rise just short of my target goal for completing the walk. I'd never asked for anything on my page, including any support with donations. I always believed that continuously asking people for money was very cheeky and that people would tire of it. In my mind, I firmly believed that if I just showed the hard work and tenacity that it takes even when the chips are down, people would donate if they wanted to. I also knew how important the press was. But on this one occasion, I couldn't help it. With only £900 to go to reach my original target, I thought it over and decided to put out a post to try to bump it up to the nice round figure of £100,000.

It was a beautiful sunset and I sat and looked at it, plucking up the courage to ask. Eventually, I did. That night, I sat with my hands behind my head as I watched my donations go from £99,100 to £145,000 in a matter of hours. I really believe that I got this huge response precisely because I'd never asked for donations before. I'd been saving a hip flask of whisky for the day that I reached £100,000, and that night I went outside, slightly numb, continuously looking at my phone to see if there had been some kind of error on my JustGiving page. I built a fire, sat down next to it, sipped away on my whisky, with Jet as ever by my side, and out of utter joy, sat and cried tears of pure elation, knowing that all of our efforts to get here had been rewarded. £145,000 was a huge sum of money that I knew could genuinely make a difference to the lives of those people I'd set out to help: our veterans and their families.

As rumours that lockdown would soon be over circulated,

I started to feel a real sense of sadness, as it would mean an end to my time on Hildasay. I thought a lot about all the things that had made me fall in love with this island. I'd say what I loved most of all was probably just the pure peace of it.

Hildasay's location and its two freshwater lochs make it the perfect nesting ground for birds. I would often think of it as one giant bird's nest. Every single morning that the weather held out for us, I would lie outside with a cup of coffee, staring up at the sky, mesmerized by the sheer number of different species it boasted. Arctic terns migrate from Antarctica to these parts to lay their eggs once a year, which is around a 25,000-mile-long trip, making it the longest bird migration in the world, and as much as they are aggressive and continually dive-bomb you, they are beautiful to watch. Common snipes sing their incredible mating songs, while lapwings, oystercatchers and gulls also litter the sky in an incredible fashion. I would lie and close my eyes, just listening to what you could say is the most incredibly loud yet utterly peaceful sound you will ever hear. To this day, I can close my eyes and still hear it.

Each day, I would slowly walk around the island that I now knew like the back of my hand and just take in what had been my home for nearly three months now. Coming here to spend the lockdown had been the best decision I could have made. I really felt a part of the island – it's no exaggeration to say the soil of Hildasay holds my blood, sweat and tears.

As I walked around, I often thought of Victor and his wonderful family, who had been instrumental in helping me survive this. There are no words or amount of thanks that I could give to show my appreciation. I had fallen in love with them just as I had with the people and islands of Shetland. I also thought of my new friend, John, who would often come over to see me on his small boat armed with fish and his incredible knowledge of how to harness the sea. All of the people, all of the press and all of the donations were incredible, but I realized that I had found something else here, too – something truly priceless: a purpose.

30

Finding Hildasay

My last night on the island of Hildasay was incredibly special. I had a fire blazing next to me, Jet lying by my side, a belly full of food, a sky overhead absolutely littered with birds, and the occasional sheep scurrying past with its lambs. I was really excited about getting back on the walk, but I could have stayed in what had been my home for the last three months a lot longer. It had been an incredibly powerful and fulfilling experience, and I had learned so much.

As Jet cuddled up next to me, snoozing away, I sat and looked at her and thought about what she had achieved. No dog had ever walked as much of the UK coast as she had. She is a legend in her own right. It was her sheer devotion to me that had always shone through the most. Through all of those bitterly cold nights, blistery winter days, hot insect-filled summers and endlessly tough, mountainous, unpathed coastlines, her following me so loyally was, in my eyes, a testament to the word love. I lay with a happy tear in my eye, so glad and genuinely honoured to call her my best friend. Jet had helped me in so many ways: she was someone I could always talk to and the only one who truly shared both the rough and the smooth with me throughout our journey, not from behind a screen but every single step of the way.

Of all the incredible places that I had seen and the thousands of amazing people that I had met on my journey, it would be safe to say that Jet was the real light of it all. Perhaps giving her the best life a dog could have in some way counteracted my feelings of failure as a father. She was someone who depended on me completely, and this time I wanted to do it right; I had learned from my mistakes. Deep down, I saw a lot of Caitlin in Jet: determined, beautiful, loyal and never leaving my side, regardless of how difficult things with me could be at times.

No doctor, psychiatrist or mental health professional could have come close to helping me like Jet did. So thank you, Jet. The best thing about you is that you really have no idea just how special you are. I love you and will until my last breath, my ever-faithful friend.

Warmed by the fire, I turned my attention to the stars, and it wasn't long before I was deep in thought; of the people I had met along the way that had helped me, of how proud I was for finally opening up about my mental health and how the burden had finally been lifted. I thought a lot about the people over the years who had been in touch and opened up to me about their mental health problems. I realized that, with me being open about it, others were taking their first steps to do the same. What a wonderful gift and an incredible feeling. Nothing gives me greater pleasure than to inspire someone who needs it.

I'd often been asked, 'What are you going to do when this walk is over? How will you get back into the real world?'

Well, I now knew that this *was* my world.

Living a life of adventure while raising money for charities – and in turn inspiring others to keep going and realize that anything is possible with the right mindset – is a job that I would do for life. It took me forty years, but I had finally found my purpose. How I was going to continue and make a living from doing something like this, I had no idea, but getting so far on this journey had taught me a great lesson in life: the importance of doing something that you truly love. Waking up each day excited, because you have a passion for what you do, in my eyes, is the epitome of success, however you measure it. In my eyes, it's better to spend your days failing at something you love than succeeding at something you hate.

I had realized by this point how little I needed in the way of material possessions or home comforts to wake up each day and feel really happy to be alive. Never in my life had I felt stronger, both physically and mentally. It was like the world was now mine to conquer. The walk had shown me that if you just keep going, one step at a time, and never give up on your dream, one day you will get there. Having accepted that you simply cannot change the past – only learn from it and harness its lessons – I was also now more at peace with myself than ever.

As I lay back with my hands behind my head looking up at the stars, I thought that, on a personal level, Hildasay had been the most important part of my journey. My time here had shown me that I had truly found happiness and a direction in life. It was exactly what I'd come to search for. I looked over at Jet and chuckled, 'Jet, pal, if ever I write a book, I'm going to call it "Finding Happiness". In fact, make that "Finding Hildasay".'

Although I had finally found peace within myself, our adventure was far from over. We still had a long way to go, and it was not going to be easy. There would be many more challenges ahead, but little did I know that, only a month after completing Shetland, once again, my life would change for ever.

In a few years' time, I would be crossing the line where I started in Swansea with a fiancée and a baby boy.

The adventure continues . . .

Acknowledgements

I'd like to thank my dog, Jet, for being my constant; my best friend, loyal companion, and for showing me the true meaning of unconditional love.

To my fiancée, Kate, for being a real light in my life and my rock, always. I could not have written this book without your help, especially since I started writing it only three days after the birth of our son, Magnus. I love you.

Richard Walters, my editor – working with you felt so natural and easy. I wrote this entire book the old-fashioned way with a pen and paper. You gave me complete freedom and autonomy and allowed my creative juices to flow. It was a real pleasure and I hope to do many more books with you in future. Thanks for being real, pal.

I would like to also say a huge and heartfelt thank you to all of the people around the UK coast who I've been unable to mention in this book, for all your love and support over the past half a decade. You helped me to rebuild a sense of pride in myself and faith in others and were pivotal in my journey to self-discovery. For that, I want to thank you all from the bottom of my heart. The smallest of gestures can have the biggest of impacts.

Last but not least, I would like to thank my daughter, Caitlin. I started this walk because I wanted to change my life for you. When times got tough, you were all that was on my mind. Without you even knowing, you drove me forward every single day. I am now a better person because of you. You were my inspiration and my drive from the very start. I love you.